Published by VisitBritain Publishing
Thames Tower, Blacks Road, London W6 9EL

First published 2006

© British Tourist Authority (trading as VisitBritain) 2006

Maps reproduced by kind permission of Ordnance Survey on behalf of HMSO.
© Crown copyright 2006. All rights reserved. Ordnance Survey Licence number 100040235.

ISBN 0 7095 8282 X
Product code: TOURG03

A CIP catalogue record for this book is available from the British Library.

The information contained in this publication has been published in good faith on the basis of
information submitted to VisitBritain and is believed to be correct at time of going to press. Nevertheless,
VisitBritain regrets that it cannot guarantee complete accuracy and all liability for loss, disappointment,
negligence or other damages caused by reliance on the information contained
in this publication, is hereby excluded.

As changes also often occur after press date, it is advisable to confirm information and any special
requirements before your visit. We would be grateful if you would advise us of any
inaccuracies you identify.

Produced for VisitBritain Publishing by Departure Lounge Limited
Contributing authors: Lindsay Hunt, Terry Marsh
Cartography: Cosmographics (pages 8–9); Draughtsman Maps
Reprographics by Blaze Creative
Printed and bound in the UK by Butler and Tanner

**Jacket**: Winding road, Cumbria

**Title page:** Beeston Castle with view of Cheshire Plain, Cheshire; **pages 6–7**: Near Pooley Bridge, Ullswater; **pages 10–11**: Alnwick Castle and the River Aln, Northumberland; **pages 32–33**: Sailing boats on Derwent Water, Cumbria; **pages 64–65**: Bramhall Hall, Cheshire; **pages 96–97**: Robin Hood's Bay, North Yorkshire

# TOURING
## Northern England

TWENTY SPECIALLY CREATED DRIVING ITINERARIES

Published by VisitBritain

# Contents

## Northumbria

## Cumbria and Lancashire

## Cheshire, Staffordshire and Derbyshire

## Yorkshire

# Northern England

From the lonely beauty of the wild moors and dales to the steep cliffs and deserted beaches of the rugged coast, our tours lead you through the stunning landscape and historic towns of England's North. A region of marked contrast, the North's industrial heritage is matched by cathedrals, castles and quaint villages, the wild hills and romantic lakes of some of England's most loved national parks and the resolute character that makes this area so special. From Hadrian's Wall to York, Chatsworth and The Potteries, this region is steeped in living history.

Specialist travel writers have crafted the 20 guided driving tours in this book to cover circular routes of two to four days, which include famous and lesser-known sights alike. The itineraries can be joined at any point along the way or easily linked to shape a longer journey, and where appropriate, each itinerary also suggests ways to extend your trip with scenic walks, tours on heritage railways and boat trips.

## A PROMISE OF QUALITY

We have not included specific details in this guide of places to stay on your short break in England, but you will find a wide choice of places to stay across the region. Choosing somewhere displaying the Enjoy England Quality Rose ensures you know what to expect and can book with confidence.

The following tourist board websites will provide you with detailed information on where you can stay and eat in the areas covered by this guide, as well as other useful travel advice.

www.enjoyengland.com
www.visitbritain.com
www.visitenglandsnorthwest.com
www.visitnortheastengland.com
www.yorkshirevisitor.com

# The Tours

The book comprises four colour-coded chapters divided by county, each of which contains between four and six tours. Each tour follows the route plotted on the map, giving short descriptions of places of interest along the way. Feature boxes highlight additional information such as literary links and walks. A final box suggests places off the tour route that, with a little more time, are worth a detour. Remember, in larger towns and cities and at popular attractions, it's a good idea to use park-and-ride schemes where they are provided.

**Introduction**
Each tour has a short introduction that gives a flavour of the area covered by the tour route.

**Tour map**
Each route is plotted on the tour map in blue. Blue numbered bullets correspond to the number of each entry and the name is labelled in blue. Places mentioned in the 'with more time' box are also labelled in blue – and where located off the map, are arrowed off.

**Approximate length of tour** in distance and duration.

**Selected Tourist Information Centres** in the area.

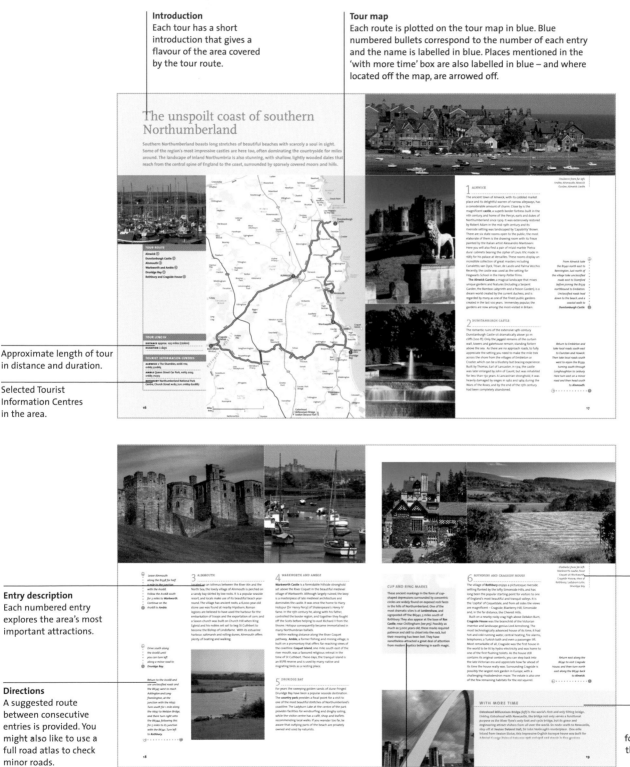

**Entry description**
Each numbered entry explores the area's most important attractions.

**Directions**
A suggested route between consecutive entries is provided. You might also like to use a full road atlas to check minor roads.

**Picture captions**
Each image has a caption; boxed images are explained in the relevant box.

**With more time box**
This offers suggestions for places and attractions that are off the route but worth exploring if you have more time.

**Feature boxes**
The story behind selected places; literary and historical links; local legends and heroes; or suggested walks and cycle rides.

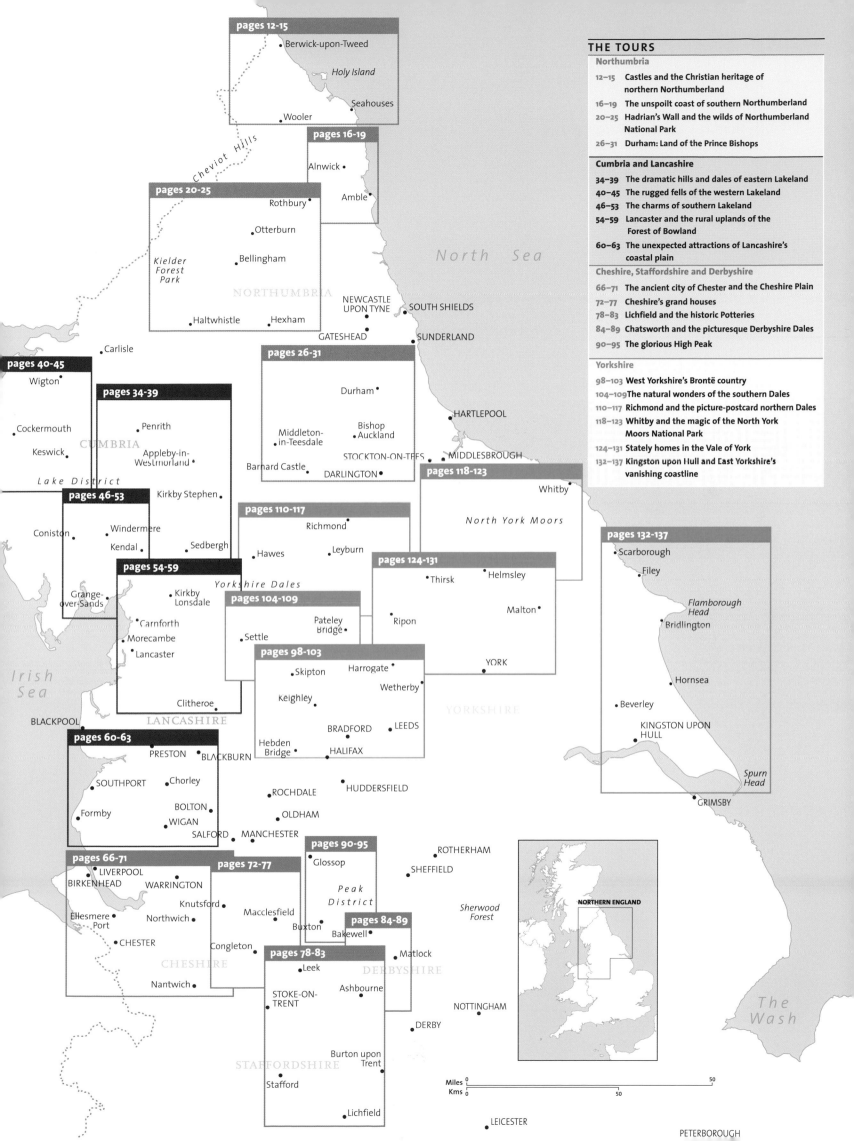

## THE TOURS

# Northumbria

# Castles and the Christian heritage of northern Northumberland

This north eastern extremity of England is a place rich in history, the location of ancient kingdoms, castles, legends, border warfare, and murder and mayhem. Today, the coast is an area of great natural beauty, lined with golden beaches and rocky shorelines. Off the coast, the Farne Islands draw birdwatchers just as the Holy Island of Lindisfarne attracts those interested in early Christian history.

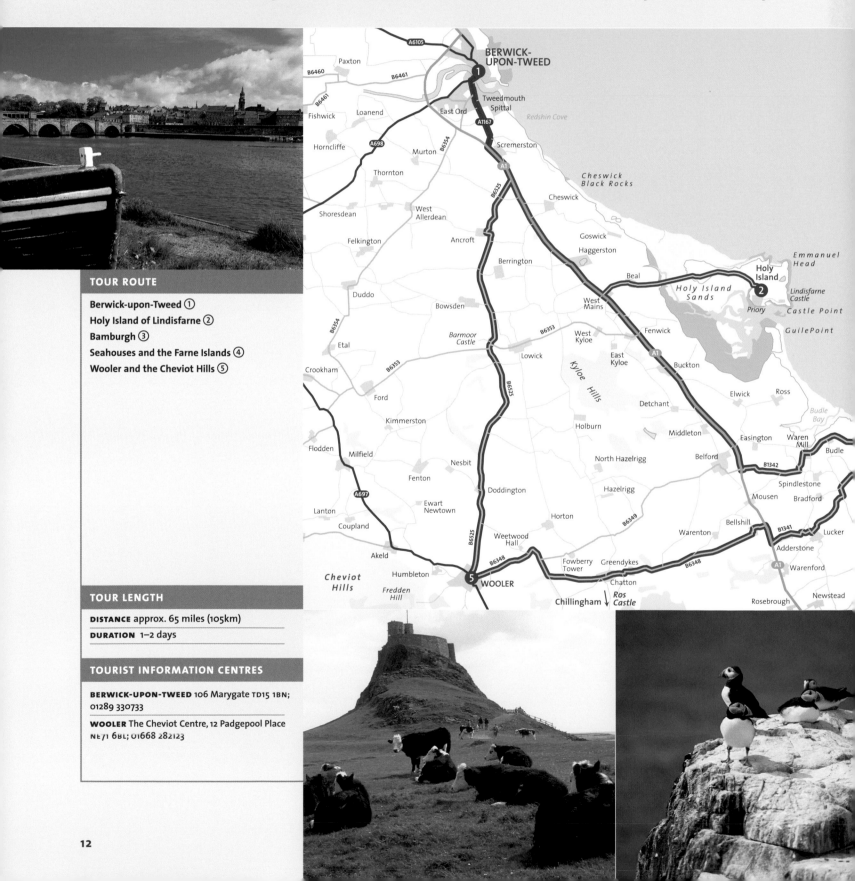

## TOUR ROUTE

Berwick-upon-Tweed ①
Holy Island of Lindisfarne ②
Bamburgh ③
Seahouses and the Farne Islands ④
Wooler and the Cheviot Hills ⑤

## TOUR LENGTH

**DISTANCE** approx. 65 miles (105km)

**DURATION** 1–2 days

## TOURIST INFORMATION CENTRES

**BERWICK-UPON-TWEED** 106 Marygate TD15 1BN; 01289 330733

**WOOLER** The Cheviot Centre, 12 Padgepool Place NE71 6BL; 01668 282123

*Clockwise from far left:*
View of Berwick-
upon-Tweed; Bamburgh
Castle; statue of
St Aidan, Holy Island;
puffins, Farne Islands;
Lindisfarne Castle

**Miles** 0 |———————————————| 5
**Kms** 0 |———————————————| 5

*N o r t h*

*S e a*

Farne
Islands

*Staple Sound*

Bamburgh
**3**

*Inner Sound*

Burton

Elford

Seahouses
**4**

North
Sunderland

Newham
Hall

Beadnell

Swinhoe

Newham

West
Fleetham

*Beadnell
Bay*

Chathill

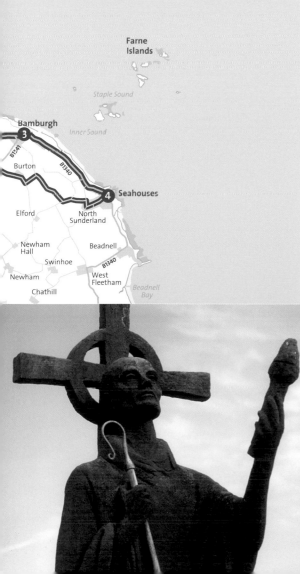

## 1 BERWICK-UPON-TWEED

This historic border town changed hands no fewer
than 14 times between the time of its capture by the
Scots in around 1018 and its final recovery by the
English in 1482. Despite its turbulent past, Berwick
became a bustling market town – and only swans now
patrol the River Tweed beneath its famous border
bridges. The Tudor **walls and ramparts** offer excellent
views of the town as well as the surrounding countryside. Though on the south side of the border, Berwick is
more than just a little Scottish: it is the only English
town with a team in the Scottish Football League; and
its river, the Tweed, is officially classified as Scottish and
consequently may not be fished on a Sunday.

## 2 HOLY ISLAND OF LINDISFARNE

Once a major centre of pilgrimage, the Holy Island of
Lindisfarne is only accessible at low tide, and even
today the journey over the causeway invokes a sense of
trepidation, awe and reverence. The sand dunes on the
north of the island are a conservation area, but to the
south lie the historic priory and the harbour, which
used to be home to one of the largest herring fleets on
the east coast. The **priory** was founded by St Aidan and
his missionary monks in AD635, and they established
the first known school in the area. The island became a
centre for Christianity and learning, and this early period
is often referred to as the 'golden age' of Lindisfarne.
Viking raids eventually drove the monks off the island by
875. A smaller monastery was re-established in the 11th
century, but all that remains now are its handsome ruins.

Half a mile from the village, the brooding **castle**, perched
on a rocky island crag, cuts a dramatic outline. It was
built as an artillery fort in 1548, though it was attacked
only once, and was abandoned in the 19th century. Then,
in 1902, Edward Hudson, the founder of *Country Life*
magazine, bought the castle and promptly engaged
the youthful Edwin Lutyens to restore it as a private
residence. The small rooms, with Norman pillars and huge
fireplaces, are full of intimate details, and the deeply
recessed mullioned windows overlook the charming
walled garden planned by Gertrude Jekyll.

*Leave Berwick, heading
south onto the A1167 to its
junction with the A1. Follow
the A1 for almost 6 miles,
and then turn east to Beal,
crossing to **Holy Island** at
low tide. Don't forget to
check the tide times for the
return journey.* **2**

*Return through Beal and
continue south on the A1,
then turn east onto the
B1342, following this
into **Bamburgh**.*
**3**

⊕ *Continue south east along the B1340 coast road to **Seahouses**, from where trips out to the **Farne** ④ **Islands** can be arranged.*

## 3 BAMBURGH

Once the capital of the 7th-century kingdom of Northumbria, Bamburgh is now a peaceful seaside village dominated by its magnificent 11th-century **castle**. Sir Thomas Mallory, the author of *Le Morte d'Arthur*, believed that Bamburgh was the site of Lancelot's castle. During the Wars of the Roses, the castle fell to the artillery of Edward IV, and following a period of decline was restored in the late 19th century by Lord Armstrong *(see p19)*. It now houses an excellent collection of arms and artwork. With a fine view of the Farne Islands, the sand dunes below Bamburgh are an ideal place for a bracing stroll. If you have an interest in heroics, you'll find the **Grace Darling Museum** worth visiting; it commemorates the lifeboat heroine who is buried in the village church.

## 4 SEAHOUSES AND THE FARNE ISLANDS

Seahouses is a colourful and lively seaside resort and fishing harbour, but little remains of its 19th-century maritime heritage. Initially its harbour was used for the shipment of corn, then of limestone transported to Scotland for fertiliser. The closing of the draw kilns in 1860 coincided with the upsurge of the fishing industry, but today most of the activity off the coast is from boat trips to see the bird and seal colonies on the Farne Islands (available throughout the summer). Comprising between 15 and 28 islands – depending on the tide – the low-lying Farnes lie midway between Seahouses and Bamburgh. The islands are one of the finest seabird breeding colonies in Europe, and the nature reserve is home to more than 100,000 puffins. The islands remain a fascinating venue for birdwatchers – don't forget to take binoculars.

*Use unclassified roads west to Glororum, and turn south west along the B1341 until it meets the A1. Head north for half-a-mile, and then branch left along the B6348 to **Wooler** and the **Cheviot Hills**.*

→ • • • • • • • • • ⑤

## LINDISFARNE GOSPELS

The *Lindisfarne Gospels* is one of the world's greatest books. It was probably created between AD680 and 720 by Eadfrith, Bishop of Lindisfarne, a gifted artist who merged words and images to create a beautiful, enduring symbol of faith. The Gospels is certainly a book of its time, a fusion of the beliefs, politics and challenges of the day. The original is in the British Library, London, but some pages are on view electronically in the Lindisfarne Heritage Centre.

*Clockwise from top right:*
*view of the Cheviots; bird*
*colonies on the Farne*
*Islands; Bamburgh Castle*

## 5 WOOLER AND THE CHEVIOT HILLS

The pleasant stone-built town of Wooler sits at the foot of the Cheviot Hills. Its previous prosperity was based on the wool from the local Cheviot sheep, which are farmed on the surrounding hills, though nothing of the wool industry now remains. The town still acts as the main shopping centre for the area, and the busy main street is lined with specialist shops, a working pottery and grocery stores. Located in an Area of Outstanding Natural Beauty, Wooler serves as a gateway to the Cheviot Hills and the Northumberland National Park. There are many fine walks from Wooler: Kettle's Camp, Humbleton Hill and Pin, a local wishing well, are within a short distance from town, while Happy Valley is a longer stretch of 6 miles. The area around Wooler is known locally as Glendale, and it was the inspiration for the children's story about Postman Pat and his fictional village of Greendale. Author John Cuncliffe ran the Wooler mobile library service for a year in the early 1950s.

Straddling the border with Scotland, and carrying the Pennine Way to its final destination, the Cheviot Hills are wild and windswept, dominated by open moorland horizons and almost totally devoid of settlement. Steep-sided valleys with fast-flowing streams radiate from the hills, characterised by broadleaved woodland, gorse scrub and meadow grassland, which provide sheltered sites for dispersed farmsteads and small hamlets. The Cheviot Hills are networked by quiet backroads and bridleways that are perfect for those who enjoy walking, cycling and riding.

*Head north on the B6525.*
*Join the A1 south of*
*Berwick, and turn north to*
*the junction with the A1167*
*following this back*
*into Berwick.*

← • • • • • • • • • • • ❶

## WITH MORE TIME

Britain's most haunted castle, 14th-century **Chillingham** *(left),* dares you to visit. At least two of the ghosts, the Radiant Boy and the Grey Lady, are thought to be based on historical figures, and a visit to the torture chamber, with its display of gruesome implements of punishment, is not for the faint-hearted. In complete contrast, all the state rooms, lined with patterned silk screens, are brilliantly furnished with antique and modern furniture and hung with paintings and enamels. The drawing room is particularly renowned for its Elizabethan ceiling. Nearby, the sandstone conical hill named **Ros Castle** was never the site of a real castle, but it is one of the best viewpoints around.

# The unspoilt coast of southern Northumberland

Southern Northumberland boasts long stretches of beautiful beaches with scarcely a soul in sight. Some of the region's most impressive castles are here too, often dominating the countryside for miles around. The landscape of inland Northumbria is also stunning, with shallow, lightly wooded dales that reach from the central spine of England to the coast, surrounded by sparsely covered moors and hills.

## TOUR ROUTE

Alnwick ①
Dunstanburgh Castle ②
Alnmouth ③
Warkworth and Amble ④
Druridge Bay ⑤
Rothbury and Cragside House ⑥

## TOUR LENGTH

**DISTANCE** approx. 105 miles (170km)

**DURATION** 2 days

## TOURIST INFORMATION CENTRES

**ALNWICK** 2 The Shambles, NE66 1TN;
01665 510665

**AMBLE** Queen Street Car Park, NE65 0DQ;
01665 712313

**ROTHBURY** Northumberland National Park
Centre, Church Street NE65 7UP; 01669 620887

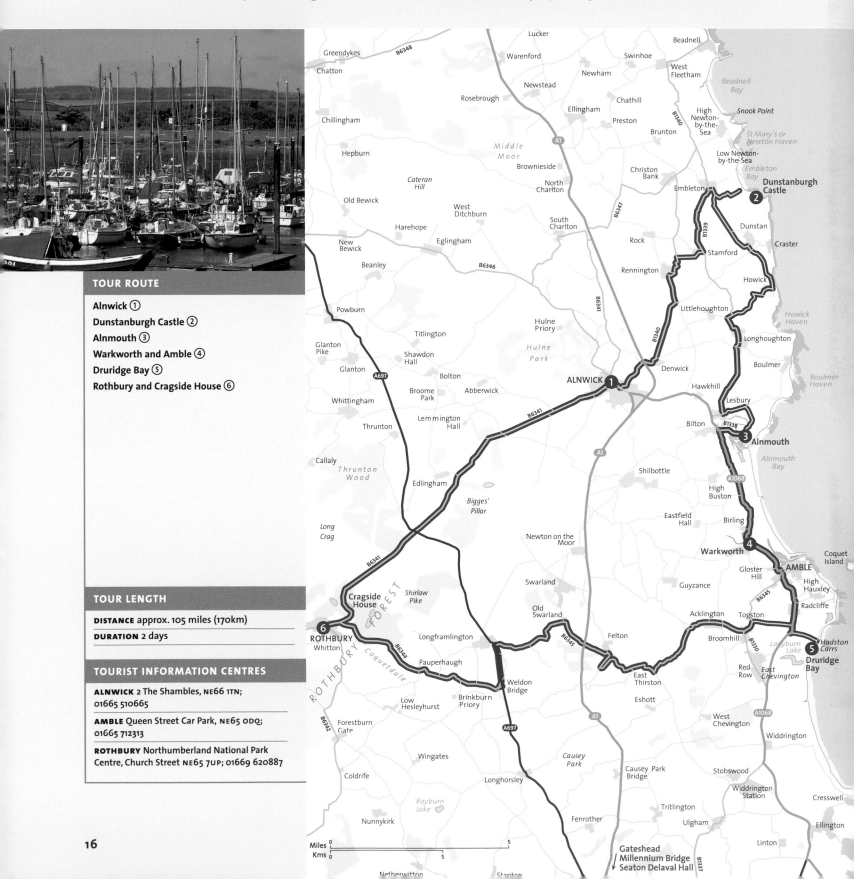

16

Clockwise from far left:
Amble; Alnmouth; Alnwick
Garden; Alnwick Castle

# 1 ALNWICK

The ancient town of Alnwick, with its cobbled market place and its delightful warren of narrow alleyways, has a considerable amount of charm. Close by is the magnificent **castle**, a superb border fortress built in the 11th century, and home of the Percys, earls and dukes of Northumberland since 1309. It was extensively restored by Robert Adam in the mid 19th century and its riverside setting was landscaped by 'Capability' Brown. There are six state rooms open to the public; the most elaborate of them is the drawing room with its frieze painted by the Italian artist Alessandro Mantovani. Here you will also find a pair of inlaid marble 'Pietra-dura' cabinets bearing the cipher of Louis XIV, made in 1683 for his palace at Versailles. These rooms display an incredible collection of great masters including Canaletto, van Dyck, Titian, de Laszlo and Palma Vecchio. Recently, the castle was used as the setting for Hogwarts School in the *Harry Potter* films.

   **The Alnwick Garden**, a magical landscape that mixes unique gardens and features (including a Serpent Garden, the Bamboo Labyrinth and a Poison Garden), is a dream world created by the current duchess, and is regarded by many as one of the finest public gardens created in the last 100 years. Immensley popular, the gardens are now among the most-visited in Britain.

*From Alnwick take
the B1340 north east to
Rennington. Just north of
the village take unclassified
roads east to Stamford
before joining the B1339
northbound to Embleton.
Unclassified roads lead
down to the beach, and a
coastal walk to
Dunstanburgh Castle.* 2

# 2 DUNSTANBURGH CASTLE

The romantic ruins of the extensive 14th-century Dunstanburgh Castle sit dramatically above 30-m cliffs (100-ft). Only the jagged remains of the curtain wall, towers and gatehouse remain, standing forlorn above the sea. As there are no approach roads, to fully appreciate the setting you need to make the mile trek across the shore from the villages of Embleton or Craster, which can be a blustery but bracing experience. Built by Thomas, Earl of Lancaster, in 1314, the castle was later enlarged by John of Gaunt, but was inhabited for less than 150 years. A Lancastrian stronghold, it was heavily damaged by sieges in 1462 and 1464 during the Wars of the Roses, and by the end of the 15th century had been completely abandoned.

*Return to Embleton and
take local roads south east
to Dunstan and Howick.
Then take local roads south
west to rejoin the B1339,
turning south through
Longhoughton to Lesbury.
Here turn east on a minor
road and then head south
to Alnmouth.*

→ • • • • • • • • • • • 3

⊕ *Leave Alnmouth along the B1338 for half a mile to the junction with the A1068. Follow the A1068 south for 3 miles to* **Warkworth**. *Continue on the* **④** *A1068 to* **Amble**.

## 3 ALNMOUTH

Located on an isthmus between the River Aln and the North Sea, the lovely village of Alnmouth is perched on a sandy bay skirted by low rocks. It is a popular seaside resort, and locals make use of its beautiful beach year-round. The village has ancient roots: a 6,000-year-old stone axe was found at nearby Hipsburn; Roman legions are believed to have used the harbour for the embarkation of troops and the exportation of corn; and a Saxon church was built on Church Hill when King Egbrid and his nobles set sail to beg St Cuthbert to become the Bishop of Lindisfarne. With its estuarine harbour, saltmarsh and rolling dunes, Alnmouth offers plenty of boating and walking.

## 4 WARKWORTH AND AMBLE

**Warkworth Castle** is a formidable hillside stronghold set above the River Coquet in the beautiful medieval village of Warkworth. Although largely ruined, the keep is a masterpiece of late medieval architecture and dominates the castle. It was once the home to Harry Hotspur (Sir Henry Percy) of Shakespeare's *Henry IV* fame. In the 15th century he, along with his father, controlled the border region, and together they fought off the Scots before helping to oust Richard II from the throne. Hotspur consequently became immortalised in many Northumbrian ballads.

Within walking distance along the River Coquet pathway, **Amble**, a former fishing and mining village, is built on a promontory that offers far-reaching views of the coastline. **Coquet Island**, one mile south east of the river mouth, was a favoured religious retreat in the time of St Cuthbert. These days, the tranquil island is an RSPB reserve and is used by many native and migrating birds as a nesting place.

⊕ *Drive south along the A1068 until you can turn left along a minor road to* **⑤** **Druridge Bay**.

*Return to the A1068 and use unclassified roads and the B6345 west to reach Acklington and Long-framlington, at the junction with the A697. Turn south for 1 mile along the A697 to Weldon Bridge, and there turn right onto the B6344, following this for 5 miles to its junction with the B6341. Turn left to* **Rothbury**.

→ • • • • • • • • • • ⑥

## 5 DRURIDGE BAY

For years the sweeping golden sands of dune-fringed Druridge Bay have been a popular seaside destination. The **country park** provides a focal point for a visit to one of the most beautiful stretches of Northumberland's coastline. The Ladyburn Lake at the centre of the park provides facilities for windsurfing and dinghy sailing, while the visitor centre has a café, shop and leaflets recommending local walks. If you wander too far, be aware that outlying parts of the beach are privately owned and used by naturists.

*Clockwise from far left: Warkworth Castle; River Coquet at Warkworth; Cragside House; view of Rothbury; Ladyburn Lake, Druridge Bay*

## 6 ROTHBURY AND CRAGSIDE HOUSE

The village of **Rothbury** enjoys a picturesque riverside setting flanked by the lofty Simonside Hills, and has long been the popular starting point for visitors to one of England's most beautiful and tranquil valleys. It is the 'capital' of Coquetdale, and from all sides the views are magnificent – Cragside, Blaeberry Hill, Simonside and, in the far distance, the Cheviot Hills.

Built on a nearby rocky crag high above Debdon Burn, **Cragside House** was the brainchild of the Victorian inventor and landscape genius Lord Armstrong. The most technologically advanced house of its time, it had hot and cold running water, central heating, fire alarms, telephones, a Turkish bath and even a passenger lift. Most remarkable of all, Cragside was the first house in the world to be lit by hydro-electricity and was home to one of the first flushing toilets. As the house still contains its original contents, you can step back into the late Victorian era and appreciate how far ahead of its time the house really was. Surrounding Cragside is possibly the largest rock garden in Europe, with a challenging rhododendron maze. The estate is also one of the few remaining habitats for the red squirrel.

### CUP AND RING MARKS

These ancient markings in the form of cup-shaped depressions surrounded by concentric circles are widely found on exposed rock faces in the hills of Northumberland. One of the most dramatic sites is at **Lordenshaw**, and signposted off the B6342, 3 miles south of Rothbury. They also appear at the base of **Ros Castle**, near Chillingham *(see p15)*. Possibly as much as 5,000 years old, these marks required patience and skill to chisel into the rock, but their meaning has been lost. They have nonetheless attracted a great deal of attention from modern mystics believing in earth magic.

*Return east along the B6341 to visit Cragside House, and then turn north east along the B6341 back to **Alnwick**.*

← • • • • • • • • • • • ①

### WITH MORE TIME

**Gateshead Millennium Bridge** *(left)* is the world's first and only tilting bridge. Linking Gateshead with Newcastle, the bridge not only serves a functional purpose as the River Tyne's only foot and cycle bridge, but its grace and engineering attract visitors from all over the world. En route south to Newcastle, stop off at **Seaton Delaval Hall**, Sir John Vanbrugh's masterpiece. One mile inland from Seaton Sluice, this impressive English baroque house was built for Admiral George Delaval between 1718 and 1728 and stands in fine gardens.

# Hadrian's Wall and the wilds of Northumberland National Park

The Roman occupation of Britain left a legacy of some extraordinary landmarks, especially along the northern frontier of their empire. This wild and rugged region has changed little in 2000 years: long stretches of their ancient wall, interspersed with original fort remains and latter-day restorations, still face north to the vast forest lands of Kielder and the Northumberland National Park.

## TOUR ROUTE

Hexham ①
Haltwhistle ②
Hadrian's Wall ③
Chipchase Castle ④
Bellingham ⑤
Northhumberland National Park ⑥
Kielder Water ⑦
Carter Bar ⑧
Otterburn ⑨
Corbridge ⑩

## TOUR LENGTH

**DISTANCE** approx. 125 miles (205km)

**DURATION** 3 days

## TOURIST INFORMATION CENTRES

**CORBRIDGE** Hill Street NE45 5AA;
01434 632815

**HEXHAM** Wentworth Car Park NE46 1QE;
01434 652220

**HEXAM** Northumberland, National Park Centre,
Barden Mill NE47 7A; 01434 344396

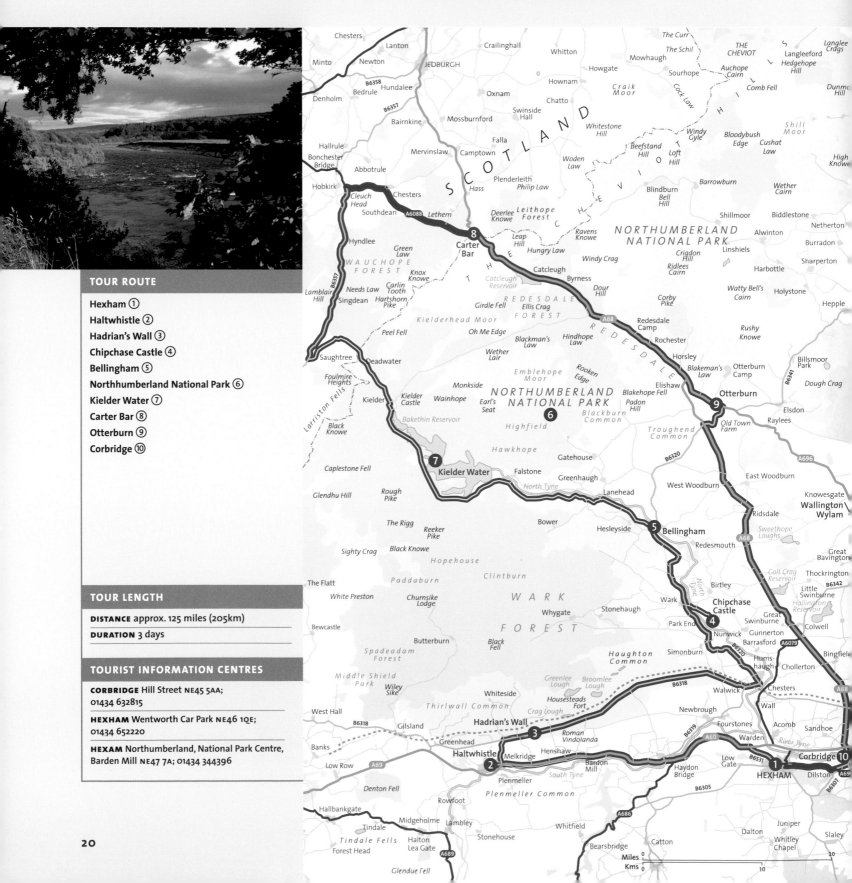

*Clockwise from far left:*
*River Tyne at Corbridge; view*
*of Hadrian's Wall; Hexham*
*Abbey; Roman Vindolanda,*
*Hadrian's Wall; St Wilfrid,*
*founder of Hexham Abbey*

# 1 HEXHAM

The handsome town of Hexham, on the banks of the River Tyne, was the headquarters of one of three border 'marches', or regions. Market day, held in the shadow of the abbey, is on Tuesdays, and is a lively affair. There has been a church at Hexham since Queen Ethelreda granted lands here to the Bishop of York (later St Wilfrid) in about AD674, but of his early monastery only the Saxon crypt and apse still remain. Destroyed by Viking raiders, the church was replaced by an Augustinian priory built in the Early English style, leaving the magnificent **abbey** you see today. The town is in the process of restoring many of its historic buildings including the **Old Gaol**. Built in 1332, it is the oldest in England, and now houses an interesting museum of border history.

*Leave Hexham heading*
*west along the*
*B6531, to reach the*
*A69. Turn left*
*following the A69*
*for 13 miles to*
*reach Haltwhistle.* ②

# 2 HALTWHISTLE

The traditional market town of Haltwhistle claims to be the geographical centre of Britain. First licensed in the 13th century, its busy **market** takes place every Thursday in the central market place, which overlooks the town's Early English church and an old-fashioned blacksmith's shop. Lying in the beautiful South Tyne valley, between the North Pennines Area of Outstanding Natural Beauty and Hadrian's Wall, Haltwhistle is a popular centre for walkers and is within easy reach of the Pennine Way and the South Tyne Trail.

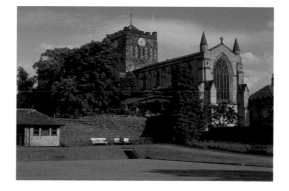

*Use local roads heading*
*north to intercept the*
*B6318, and follow this east*
*to visit Hadrian's Wall with*
*stops at Roman Vindolanda,*
*Housesteads Fort and*
*eventually Chesters.*
→ • • • • • • • • • • • ③

*Clockwise from above:*
view of Hadrian's Wall;
Roman Vindolanda;
Chipchase Castle

## 3 HADRIAN'S WALL

Even those not remotely interested in history will be moved by an encounter with the mighty Hadrian's Wall. Named after the Emperor Hadrian, it is now Britain's principal Roman site. Construction on the wall, which was intended to mark the northernmost boundary of Roman Britain, commenced in AD122. Stretching from Wallsend in the east to Bowness-on-Solway in the west, many sections of the wall, which has World Heritage Site status, are still visible today, albeit in a fragile state.

Journey back 2000 years at **Roman Vindolanda**, a fascinating Roman fort and settlement just south of Hadrian's Wall. The superb on-site museum displays many Roman artefacts, including boots, shoes, armour, jewellery and coins. In the surrounding museum gardens there are full-sized reconstructions of a Roman temple, shop, house, and a section of the wall itself, as well as a humble medieval Northumbrian croft.

Garrisoned right up to the end of the Roman occupation of Britain in the early 5th century, **Housesteads Fort,** just north of Vindolanda, conjures up an evocative picture of Roman military life at this time. Known to the Romans as Vercovicium, it is the best preserved of the 13 forts along the wall. The fort had barracks for around 800 men, and was in use for nearly three centuries by soldiers from Tungria, present-day Belgium and Holland.

The Roman fort of Cilurnum, today's **Chesters**, just north of Hexham, was one of the more central strongholds guarding Hadrian's Wall. Built in AD123, just after the wall was completed, Chesters is the best preserved Roman cavalry fort in Britain. But if you're feeling overloaded with all things Roman, then adjoining is the 18th-century **Chesters Walled Garden**, surrounded on three sides by woods of beech and yew, and laid out as a herb and herbaceous garden. This is a peaceful place and, growing within neatly clipped box hedges, boasts one of the largest collections of herbs in the country.

### THE BUILDING OF HADRIAN'S WALL

Many mistakenly believe that Hadrian's Wall was built by slaves, but in reality it was constructed by Roman legionaries, men from all over the empire. The greater part of the 75-mile long wall was built of stone, but west of Carlisle it was made of turf blocks. It was originally 4.5m (15ft) high and topped by battlements. Milecastles, which could garrison between 10 and 30 men, were constructed at intervals of one Roman mile (1490m; 1620 yards) along the wall, and there were also a series of large forts and lookout turrets. The northern frontier of the Roman empire was protected by Hadrian's Wall for over 250 years, finally being abandoned in about AD 400 to leave the spectacular ruins we see today.

*At Chesters join the B6320
towards Bellingham. Leave
the B6320 at Wark to
follow unclassified roads
to Chipchase Castle.*

• • • • • • • • • • 4

4 **CHIPCHASE CASTLE**

The legacy of the border wars of the 14th–16th centuries has resulted in Northumberland having more castles than any other English county. Chipchase Castle, near Wark, was the ancient seat of the Lords of Tyndale and the middle marches: today it is the family seat of the Tordays. It is an impressive medieval tower house with Jacobean additions, set in formal and informal grounds. The later interiors are those of a comfortable mansion, the most remarkable of which is the billiard room with a vaguely rococo ceiling and a Flemish overmantel depicting the March of Time.

5 **BELLINGHAM**

Many visitors to Bellingham are likely to be hikers walking the Pennine Way or bound for the Cheviots and journey's end at Kirk Yetholm in Scotland. But it is well worth stopping off at this small, friendly market town on the North Tyne River. The lovely medieval parish **church of St Cuthbert**, consecrated in 1180, has a unique barrel-vaulted roof capped in stone, the only one of its kind in England. The use of stone gives a clue to its history: it was in response to the repeated burning of its wooden roof. In the first part of the 1800s, a weekly market was held at Bellingham, and there is still an open-air farmers' market on Saturdays and Wednesdays during the summer months, with regular 'festival days' when musicians and entertainers mingle among the stalls.

*Return to Wark and continue along the B6320 north to Bellingham* ⑤

*North west from Bellingham there are several access points along unclassified roads into the* ***Northumberland National Park.***

→ • • • • • • • • • • • • ⑥

## 6 NORTHUMBERLAND NATIONAL PARK

⊘ From Bellingham follow
local roads (unclassified
but signposted) north west
to *Kielder Water*, and on to
⑦ the village of Kielder.

Stretching for over 60 miles from the Cheviot Hills to Hadrian's Wall in the south, North Northumberland National Park is an area of wild and rugged beauty. To the north, amid the breathtaking moors and grasslands of the Cheviots, lie as many as 50 pre-Roman hillforts. In the centre of the park is the Upper Coquet Valley with the Simonside Hills and the endearing villages of Harbottle and Holystone. To the west are the valleys of the North Tyne and Redesdale, wild, inspiring and once home of the Border Reivers, lawless clan-based bands who plagued the borders of northern England for hundreds of years. It is an area of peace and solitude, where you can walk for hours without encountering another soul. Information on the park is available from the main offices in Hexham.

⊘ Take local roads north west
to the junction of the B6357.
Follow this road north to
meet the A6088 and turn
⑧ right for *Carter Bar*.

## 7 KIELDER WATER

Kielder Water is the largest man-made lake in Europe, and is surrounded by Kielder Forest, one of Britain's biggest nature reserves. At the heart of this green swathe of countryside lies **Kielder** village which takes its name from Kielder Burn, a Norse word meaning violent water. A short walk away is a magnificent Victorian skew arch viaduct, which carried the former border counties railway line from the North Tyne to Riccarton Junction in Scotland. The viaduct now offers panoramic views over Bakethin Reservoir, a conservation area adjoining Kielder Water where many species of birds can be seen. Nearby **Kielder Castle** was built in 1775 by the Duke of Northumberland as a hunting lodge. It is now the visitor centre for the Border Forest Park, and the starting point for a range of pursuits from challenging mountain bike trails to gentle woodland wanders, fun family events to forest yoga classes.

### RED SQUIRRELS

The red squirrel (*Sciurus vulgaris*) is native to Britain, but its numbers have dwindled due to competition from the increasingly dominant American grey squirrel. There are estimated to be only 160,000 red squirrels left in the UK, of which perhaps 30,000 are in England, many in the woodlands of Northumberland. The Forestry Commission is working with partners in projects across Britain to develop a long-term conservation strategy that deters greys and encourages reds.

## 8 CARTER BAR

Located on an early turnpike road between England and Scotland, Carter Bar was where taxes and dues were collected to cross the border. It is often bleak and windswept, but it is the most spectacular crossing of the Anglo-Scottish border. On the English side the approach is through open moorland, but on the Scottish side the Lammermuir Hills roll away into the distance.

Follow the A68 south
east along Resdale
to *Otterburn*.

→ • • • • • • • • • • ⑨

## 9 OTTERBURN

Near the tiny village of Otterburn, on the edge of Northumberland National Park, is the site of an historic battle, today marked by a simple monument known as Percy's Cross. It commemorates an unusual turn of events. The war between the Scottish and English had turned into a feud between the families of Douglas (from Scotland) and Percy (from England). At Otterburn, their armies met in 1388. The Scottish leader, Douglas, was mortally wounded, and concerned that his death would encourage the English, his men concealed his body beneath a bush. The Scots went on to win the battle and capture the English leader Henry (Hotspur) Percy. When he offered to capitulate, he was directed to surrender to the bush under which Douglas was lying, and so the battle became famous because it was won by a dead man.

## 10 CORBRIDGE

The quaint town of Corbridge was renowned for its commerce as long ago as 1827. Several of the original decorated shopfronts still survive, as does its reputation for its specialist shops. The town was founded on its present site in Saxon times, and stones from the nearby garrison on Hadrian's Wall were used to construct many of the village buildings, including the church. Inside **St Andrew's** there is an original Roman arch as well as a fine Saxon tower. Today the streets remain much as they did in medieval times, and a wander along Front Street leads down to the river bank, where you can enjoy the views from the 17th-century bridge over the River Tyne. Remains of the Roman garrison of Corpustium lie just outside the town at **Corbridge Roman Site**, and the museum displays a fine collection of Roman sculpture and carving, including the Corbridge lion (*see p21*).

*Clockwise from above: bridge over River Tyne at Corbridge; Kielder Water*

*Head south on the B6320 until it meets the A68. Turn left and follow this road for 19 miles, to the junction with the A69. Cross over to enter Corbridge.* ⑩

*At Corbridge, head west on the A695, and follow this for almost 3 miles to join the B6305 into Hexham.*
← • • • • • • • • • • • ❶

## WITH MORE TIME

Dating from 1688, **Wallington** *(left)*, near Morpeth, is a splendid mansion that was home variously to the Blackett and Trevelyan families. The muted Palladian exterior contrasts well with the rococo plasterwork of the interior, which contains ceramics, paintings, needlework and a collection of dolls' houses. Closer to Newcastle is the birthplace of railway pioneer George Stephenson. This small stone tenement was built near **Wylam** in about 1760 to accommodate several mining families. The furnishings are from the time of Stephenson's birth in 1781.

25

# Durham: Land of the Prince Bishops

Much of the west of County Durham, including Teesdale, Weardale and the Derwent Valley, falls within the North Pennines Area of Outstanding Natural Beauty, where uncrowded roads crisscross some of the highest, wildest and least spoilt countryside in England. At the area's eastern edge lies Durham, the strikingly beautiful county capital, which is small enough to explore on foot. The panoramic view of its Norman cathedral and castle, home of the Prince Bishops, has been described as 'one of the finest architectural experiences of Europe'; together they are now a designated World Heritage site.

## TOUR ROUTE

Durham ①

Auckland Castle ②

Escomb ③

Raby Castle ④

Rokeby Park ⑤

Barnard Castle and Bowes Museum ⑥

Teesdale ⑦

Blanchland and Derwent Reservoir ⑧

Beamish ⑨

Finchale Priory ⑩

## TOUR LENGTH

**DISTANCE** approx. 105 miles (170km)

**DURATION** 3 days

## TOURIST INFORMATION CENTRES

**BARNARD CASTLE** Woodleigh, Flatts Road DL12 8AA; 01833 690909

**DURHAM** 2 Millennium Place DH1 1WA; 0191 384 3720

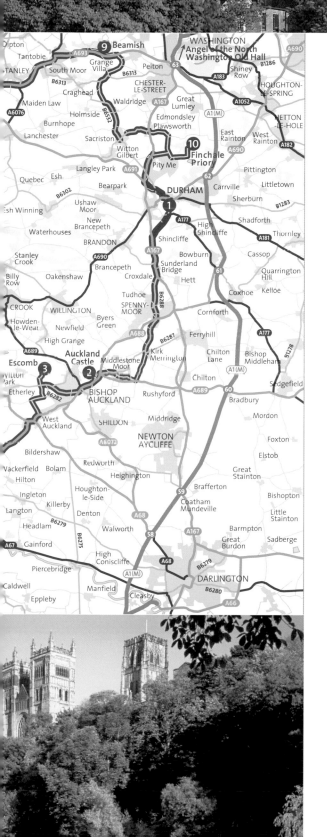

*Clockwise from far left:*
*Teesdale; view of Durham*
*Castle; stained-glass window*
*depicting the Prince Bishops,*
*Durham Castle; view of*
*Durham cathedral from the*
*River Wear; crest from*
*Durham Cathedral*

# 1 DURHAM

Perched dramatically above a loop of the River Wear, Durham is a compact city dominated by its renowned Norman cathedral and castle. **Durham Cathedral** is considered one of the greatest in Europe. Founded in 1093, it was built as a monumental shrine to Cuthbert (*see p28*), the canonised 7th-century bishop of Lindisfarne, and it also holds the tomb of Bede, the chronicler of Cuthbert's life and the first English historian. A stunning example of Romanesque architecture, the cathedral has geometrically decorated columns over 22m (72ft) high and the first example of transverse arches in England, which give the interior dramatic height. At the west end the Galilee Chapel is delightfully airy and its almost Moorish architecture is said to be inspired by the great mosque at Cordoba.

Even older, the **castle**, built on the site of a motte and bailey at the northern end of Palace Green opposite the cathedral, is intimate and a little eccentric in its mix of architectural styles. Dominated by its keep, it dates from 1072, built on the orders of William the Conqueror. It became the seat of the Prince Bishops, the powerful, virtually autonomous, leaders who ruled this region from the 1300s–1832; it now houses University College, the foundation college of England's third-oldest university.

Much of the city centre is pedestrianised, so it is easy to randomly explore the mish-mash of old and new: the cobbled market place, the Victorian Market Hall, the modern shops, and the 1850 town hall with its superb stained glass and magnificent fireplace of local stone. And if the majesty of it all becomes too much, then take one of many paths down to the riverbank, and watch rowers from one of the university teams, or board the *Prince Bishop* river cruiser for a gentle trip along the Wear, where you can enjoy outstanding views of the cathedral and castle.

*Leave Durham on the A177*
*south to its junction with*
*the A167 and follow this for*
*2 miles to a roundabout.*
*Take the B6288 south to its*
*junction with the B6287*
*and then take local*
*roads south west to reach*
***Auckland Castle.***

*Clockwise from above:*
Raby Castle; Bowes Museum;
Rokeby Park

## 2 AUCKLAND CASTLE

On the fringes of Bishop Auckland, overlooking the
River Wear, Auckland Castle is England's finest bishop's
palace. It was the seat of the Prince Bishops, and has
been home of the Bishop of Durham for more than
800 years. As you would expect of such men, who had
both secular and ecclesiastical authority, the castle is
sumptuous, though largely restored by James Wyatt in
1796 to create a Georgian home. The long dining room
holds Durham's most prized artistic exhibit, a collection
of 13 paintings depicting Jacob and his sons by the 17th-
century Spanish artist Francisco de Zurbarán. The
centrepiece of the castle is, however, the magnificent
chapel, reputed to be the largest private chapel in
Europe, with a good example of a medieval aisled hall.
The castle is set in 320ha (800 acres) of parkland,
where the Prince Bishops once hunted game.

## 3 ESCOMB

This gem of a village – and one that is easily overlooked
– has its houses arranged around a walled oval
enclosure. In the centre stands the simply designed
**Escomb Church**, first used for worship in the late 7th
century.  Unusually, the church is not dedicated and has
been left almost entirely as the Saxons built it, with
many of the stones salvaged from a nearby Roman
camp. This church has been used almost continuously
for worship during the centuries that Christianity has
been practiced in England.

## 4 RABY CASTLE

With soaring medieval walls and nine crenellated
towers, the first sight of Raby Castle is quite breathtaking. It began life as a 14th-century fortified house
and was converted into a country home in the 18th and
19th centuries. Raby houses a fabulous art collection
that includes important examples of Meissen
porcelain, musical intruments, tapestries, furnishings
and paintings by major artists like Munnings, Giordano,
Lely, De Hooch, Teniers, van Dyck and Reynolds. The
magnificent Baron's Hall is renowned as the venue for
the plotting of the 1569 'Rising of the North'. As many
as 700 knights gathered here in allegiance to the
Nevilles in a disasterous Catholic rebellion to usurp
Elizabeth I. In addition, the castle is surrounded by a
80ha (200 acre) deer park.

---

*Follow the A688 then the
B6282 west and then
unclassified roads north to*
**③ Escomb** *village.*

*Drive south on unclassified
roads to reach the A688,
following this south west*
**④** *to Raby Castle.*

*Leave Staindrop south on
the B6274 to its junction
with the A67, and there
turn right for just over 2
miles. Then turn south on
local roads to the A66 west
and Rokeby Park near
Greta Bridge.*

→ • • • • • • • • • • ⑤

### ST CUTHBERT

Born in Melrose on the Scottish borders, Cuthbert
became bishop of Lindisfarne and one of the
most venerated of English saints. He converted
Lindisfarne from Celtic to Roman Christianity,
following the Synod of Whitby in AD664. After
his death, his body was removed from the island
following continuous Viking raids and laid to rest
in Durham cathedral *(see p27).*

## 5 ROKEBY PARK

Rokeby (pronounced Rookaby) Park is an imposing 18th-century country home built in the Palladian style. It was the setting for Sir Walter Scott's ballad of the same name, and it has some fine period furniture and a print room, an example of the custom at the time of papering rooms with prints. But its most treasured possession is the unique collection of 18th-century 'pictures' by Anne Morritt, a Georgian needlewoman who specialised in re-creating paintings in complex embroideries.

## 6 BARNARD CASTLE AND BOWES MUSEUM

Barnard Castle is the 'capital' of Teesdale and one of the most attractive towns in Northumbria. Known to locals as 'Barney', it owes its origins to Bernard Balliol, who built a **castle** here in the 12th century, and whose descendants included Edward and John Balliol, kings of Scotland, and John Balliol, founder of Balliol College, Oxford. Today the castle is a striking ruin perched on a high bank overlooking the River Tees. It has been a home to many historic characters including Richard III, Henry VII, Warwick the Kingmaker and several of the Prince Bishops of Durham. The main streets of Barney are lined by beautiful stone-built houses. In the central market place is an intriguing octagonal building called the **market cross** dating from 1747. At different times in its history this building has served as a court, gaol, town hall and butter market.

From here, amble up Newgate to the gloriously ornate **Bowes Museum**, opened in 1892. Built in the style of a French chateau, it was commissioned by John Bowes, Earl of Strathmore, and his French actress wife Josephine, who spent most of their time collecting the 30,000 treasures now on display. Consequently, the museum has an impressive collection of pictures, ceramics, textiles, tapestries, clocks and costumes. Look especially for the life-size, mechanical silver swan. The 9ha (23 acres) of grounds feature a parterre garden designed by John Bowes himself.

*Continue north west from Rokeby Park on unclassified roads to **Barnard Castle**.* ⑥

*Follow the B6277 north west from Barnard Castle along **Teesdale** past Middleton-in-Teesdale, High Force and Cauldron Snout.*

→ • • • • • • • • • • ⑦

Clockwise from above:
High Force, Teesdale;
Beamish

*From High Force, head
north west along the B6277
for 3 miles, and then turn
right onto unclassified
roads for 5 miles into
Weardale and the A689.
Turn right on the A689 for
1 mile, and then turn left
on unclassified roads
towards Blanchland.*

## 7 TEESDALE

Extending 20 miles north of Barnard Castle, Teesdale is an area of unspoilt villages, moorland and dramatic waterfalls. It is within the North Pennine Area of Outstanding Natural Beauty and is often described as the northernmost of the Yorkshire Dales. The Pennine Way snakes along the bottom of the dale, but there are also other excellent walks in the area. The main centre is the attractive village of **Middleton-in-Teesdale,** which is known to have existed in the days of the Vikings, when it was owned by King Canute. The town did not grow significantly until the 19th century when it became an important lead mining centre: many of today's buildings have Victorian credentials, and give the village a bright and welcoming air, which is appreciated by the weary Pennine walkers who pass through. At the top of the dale, the River Tees has its source in a boggy hollow near Cross Fell, the highest of the Pennine summits. It soon runs into Cow Green Reservoir, from which it flows into a spectacular series of cataracts over a long rocky 'stairway' called **Cauldron Snout,** making this the highest waterfall in England. Reaching the source of the Tees is for experienced walkers only, but there is an easy walk to Cauldron Snout from the viewpoint overlooking the reservoir on its northern edge. As the Tees descends down the dale, it is fed by more streams, and drops dramatically to form the thunderous **High Force.** This is undoubtedly England's largest waterfall, and a most impressive sight. It is best seen from the south bank of the river after a heavy downpour, when the sound of the Tees roaring over a vertical drop of 21.5m (70ft) is quite deafening. There is a visitor centre at Bowless, and from here it is a 3-mile round trip to High Force along a stretch of the Pennine Way.

## 8 BLANCHLAND AND DERWENT RESERVOIR

With its mellow golden stone and its location in the deep, atmospheric Derwent Valley beneath the brooding North Pennine moors, **Blanchland** has been called one of the most perfect villages of England. The nearby **Derwent Reservoir**, the second-largest inland body of water in the North East of England, provides excellent facilities for sailing and fishing. Yet in spite of this recreational role, it is an important location for birdlife, too. Teal, tufted duck, pochard, goldeneye, wigeon, goosander and greylag geese often roost and feed here, as well as more uncommon visitors like the red-throated diver, gadwall, whooper swan and smew.

## 9 BEAMISH

The open-air museum at Beamish is an interactive, 'living' museum that brings Britain's industrial past to life. Most of the houses, shops and other buildings were victims of urban clearances in the North East and have been carefully reconstructed here. The most popular attraction is the re-creation of the high street of a typical market town in the early 1900s. The Dentist's House is always a big draw, with a 'dentist' who is all too keen to pull your teeth. The Music Teacher's House is occupied by a certain Florence Smith, who ekes out a living teaching Gateshead young ladies to sing and speak properly. Pockerly Manor House is the only original building on the site and has been furnished as a yeoman farmer's property of the type common throughout England in the 1820s. It should come as no surprise to find pit cottages here, but these examples once formed part of Francis Street in Hetton-le-Hole. Today, they are furnished as they were during Durham's great boom time for the mines, in the early part of the 20th century.

## 10 FINCHALE PRIORY

The ruins of the 13th-century Finchale Priory have a beautiful setting, lying as they do in a bend of the River Wear. It was built as a retreat for monks from Durham and founded by St Godric, who was a somewhat flamboyant character. An itinerant pedlar, he travelled to Rome and from there became a pirate sailing the Mediterranean. However, he renounced his piratical ways and turned to God, and at the age of 40 settled at Finchale, where he lived as a hermit for an incredible 65 years until his death in 1170. You can also reach the priory by a lovely riverside and woodland walk from Durham.

*Take the B6306 east for 4 miles, turn left onto the B6278, crossing the A68 and the A694. Cut east across country to reach the A692 and then use the A693 and local roads east to reach **Beamish**.* ⑨

*Take unclassified roads and the B6532 cross country to reach **Finchale Priory**.* ⑩

*Return to the A167, and follow directions south back to **Durham**.* ① 

## WITH MORE TIME

Don't miss the chance to visit the landmark **Angel of the North** at the entrance to Tyneside. Its wide, open 'arms' greet travellers as they reach Gateshead, and it is visible whether arriving by road or rail. Britain's largest sculpture is the work of well-respected artist Antony Gormley OBE, though it was not without its critics when it was unveiled in 1998. Close by is **Washington Old Hall**, a manor house said to be the home of George Washington's ancestors. It contains mementoes of the American connection and the War of Independence.

# Cumbria and Lancashire

# The dramatic hills and dales of eastern Lakeland

The pastoral land of the eastern Lakes, fed largely by the meandering River Eden, was once part of the ancient counties of Cumberland and Westmorland. It is the bedrock of ancient kingdoms, stories of legendary giants, Arthurian mythology and valiant knights. Castles and busy market towns huddle below the highest of the Pennine mountains, and small lakeside settlements fringe Ullswater.

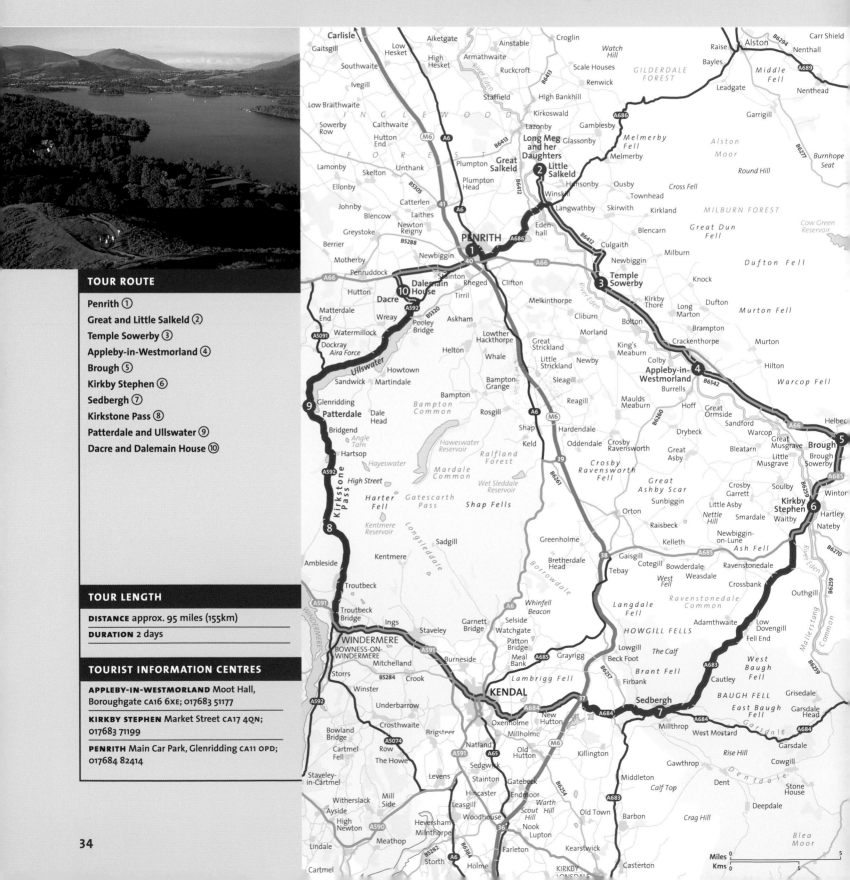

## TOUR ROUTE

Penrith ①
Great and Little Salkeld ②
Temple Sowerby ③
Appleby-in-Westmorland ④
Brough ⑤
Kirkby Stephen ⑥
Sedbergh ⑦
Kirkstone Pass ⑧
Patterdale and Ullswater ⑨
Dacre and Dalemain House ⑩

## TOUR LENGTH

**DISTANCE** approx. 95 miles (155km)

**DURATION** 2 days

## TOURIST INFORMATION CENTRES

**APPLEBY-IN-WESTMORLAND** Moot Hall, Boroughgate CA16 6XE; 017683 51177

**KIRKBY STEPHEN** Market Street CA17 4QN; 017683 71199

**PENRITH** Main Car Park, Glenridding CA11 0PD; 017684 82414

*Clockwise from far left:*
*Ullswater lake; Ullswater*
*village; Martindale, near*
*Ullswater; daffodils at*
*Ullswater; River Eden*

# 1 PENRITH

Penrith is a bustling market town, and around its market place is a labyrinth of lanes, yards and alleyways leading to attractive cottages, gardens and curious specialist shops. The town is built largely of local red sandstone, the same material that was used to build **Penrith Castle** in 1399, when William Strickland (later the Archbishop of Canterbury) extended an earlier pele tower. The castle was improved and added to over the next 70 years, and became a royal fortress for Richard, Duke of Gloucester, later King Richard III. High above the town is **Penrith Beacon**, built in 1719 on a spot where beacons have been lit in times of war and emergency since the days of Henry VIII. You can walk up to the beacon, from where there is an invigorating view across the Eden Valley to the Lakeland hills. On the outskirts of town, housed in Britain's largest earth-covered building, lies **Rheged – The Village in the Hill**, a place of art, craft, local culture and history. Among the attractions in this subterranean world are an IMAX cinema screen the size of six double-decker buses, which shows films of world exploration from the Grand Canyon to Everest. An exhibit showcasing British mountaineering illustrates how Britain's great mountaineers tackled the world's highest summits.

*Leave Penrith on the A686*
*to Langwathby. Follow*
*unclassified roads to Little*
*Salkeld. Park in the village*
*and walk up to Long Meg*
*and her Daughters.* ❷

# 2 GREAT AND LITTLE SALKELD

The villages of Great and Little Salkeld face each other across the River Eden, the 'little' linked to the 'great' only by bridges at Lazonby, to the north, and Langwathby, to the south. They are worth seeking out for the standing stones known as **Long Meg and her Daughters**, mute witnesses to the whole history of man in the Eden Valley. Unlike many stone circles, Long Meg and her family survived the anti-pagan fervour of the 18th century. Legend has it that they are witches turned to stone by the 13th-century magician Michael Scott for holding orgies and dancing on the sabbath. A short walk away are **Lacy's Caves**, created by Colonel Lacy, the 18th-century owner of Salkeld Hall. Quite why, is not clear, though it was more than likely in pursuit of the fashion of the time to build 'antiquities' and 'romantic' caves.

*Return south to the A686*
*and turn left and shortly*
*right onto the B6412, going*
*south east through Culgaith*
*to reach Acorn Bank at*
*Temple Sowerby.*

➔ • • • • • • • • • • ❸

## APPLEBY HORSE FAIR

Appleby Horse Fair – the largest traditional horse fair of its kind – was set up by charter under the reign of James II in 1685 and has been an annual event ever since. Originally, the fair was a venue for all types of trading, but its popularity with Romany people who came each year led to the occasion becoming a specialist horse fair. Held during the second week of June, Appleby Fair is today the largest gathering of Romany people in the UK.

## 3 TEMPLE SOWERBY

A pleasant, neat and attractive village of Georgian houses centred around a large green, Temple Sowerby was owned by the Knights Templar and later the Knights Hospitaller until the Dissolution under Henry VIII. Among the lovely buildings here is **Acorn Bank**, a fine 18th-century manor house, and former home of Dorothy Ratcliffe, who wrote in the Yorkshire dialect. In the sheltered garden, surrounded by ancient oak trees, there is a captivating display of herbaceous borders, roses and flowering shrubs. The herb garden here is renowned for the largest collection of medicinal and culinary plants in the north of England, and there's also a pleasing woodland walk beside Crowdundle Beck to the watermill, which is open to visitors.

*Take the A66 south east for 6 miles, and then branch right onto the B6542 into* **Appleby-in-Westmorland.**

## 4 APPLEBY-IN-WESTMORLAND

Formerly the county town of Westmorland, Appleby is a market town of great character. It is divided by the River Eden into two parts: old Appleby around St Michael's church and new Appleby centred around Boroughgate, a fine high street flanked by lime trees and attractive red sandstone houses that give the town a mellow, warm appearance. Appleby is overlooked by its imposing Norman **castle**, located on a steep bank above the river. Largely restored and rebuilt in the 17th century, it is surrounded by moats that define an inner and at least two outer baileys. Today, Appleby is most renowned for its lively horse fair (*see box*).

*Continue south east along the B6542 and rejoin the A66 to* **Brough.**

## 5 BROUGH

Brough (pronounced 'Bruff') comprises Market Brough, Church Brough and Brough Sowerby. Church Brough is a collection of stone houses centred around a village green. Market Brough, where a market cross tops a clock tower, grew around a 14th-century bridge spanning Swindale Beck; and Brough Sowerby lies one mile to the south. Located on the important stagecoach routes from London to Carlisle and Glasgow, and from York to Lancaster, the town prospered during the 18th and 19th centuries, employing a large number of stable boys, ostlers, cooks, innkeepers, blacksmiths and wheelwrights to service the needs of travellers. The ruins of a Norman **castle** stand in a dominant position above the river, and occupy the northern part of the site of the Roman fort of Verterae of which nothing remains. As at Appleby, each September sees an annual gathering of Romany people who come to Brough Hill Fair, an event that has taken place for the past 600 years.

*Leave Brough heading south on the A685 for 4 miles to* **Kirkby Stephen.**

## 6 KIRKBY STEPHEN

In response to continuous border raids, the old market town of Kirkby Stephen is a maze of narrow, high-walled passages and spacious squares into which cattle could be driven in times of trouble. The central market square is surrounded by a ring of cobblestones that demarcate the area used until 1820 for bull baiting. Just off the square, the church of **St Stephen's**, known locally as the Cathedral of the Dales, bears traces of Saxon and Norman handiwork, and Dalesfolk have worshipped on this site for over 1,500 years. It contains the 8th-century Viking **Loki Stone**. Named after a Norse god, it depicts a bound devil and is one of only two such stones in Europe. Kirkby Stephen is a staging post for walkers undertaking the Coast-to-Coast Walk. There is also an easy, uphill moorland walk from the town to Nine Standards Rigg on the Cumbrian border.

Dotted around the Eden Valley landscape are a number of carved stone sculptures, which double as seats. Part of a millennium scheme, they are known as 'Eden Benchmarks'. If you're not expecting them they can take you quite by surprise, but they offer delightful spots to sit quietly and contemplate the landscape. In Kirkby Stephen itself you'll also find a number of sculpted stones along a 'Poetry Path', which was devised to highlight the landscape of the Eden Valley.

## 7 SEDBERGH

The small, stone-built town of Sedbergh became part of Cumbria in 1974, even though it clearly has many 'Dales' affinities: it is in fact located in the Yorkshire Dales National Park and its western gateway. An ancient market town, its fame rests on the laurels of Sedbergh School, set in parkland on the edge of town. Among its memorable pupils was Will Carling, former captain of the England rugby team. To the north of town rise the rounded Howgills, a fine and compact group of fells that provide excellent walking country.

## 8 KIRKSTONE PASS

Rising from the urban sprawl of Windermere, a long and winding road climbs through the increasingly austere landscape to Kirkstone Pass, a long-established route into Patterdale. In winter, the 457-m pass (1490-ft) can become blocked with snow, but at any time it is a wild place, and takes its name from a nearby boulder that has the rough outline of a church, or 'kirk'.

*Continue south on A685, and then branch left onto A683 to **Sedbergh**.* ⑦

*Take the A684 west to Kendal and drive through the town to join the A591 for Windermere. Stay on the A591 until you can branch right onto the A592 north for **Kirkstone Pass**.* ⑧

*Continue over Kirkstone Pass and descend via Hartsop to **Patterdale** and **Ullswater**. Continue north east up the dale to pass the junction with A5091, and reach Aira Force.*
→ • • • • • • • • • • • ⑨

## 9 PATTERDALE AND ULLSWATER

Patterdale may be named after St Patrick, one of three missionaries thought to have travelled in this region during the 5th century. Located at the southern end of Ullswater, the village, buttressed by high fells, was described by Baddeley in his *Guide to the English Lake District* as 'one of the most charmingly situated in Britain, and in itself clean and comely'. Many of these remote villages were presided over by one dominant family. In Patterdale it was the Mounseys, who were described as the 'kings of Patterdale', and lived at **Patterdale Hall**, now rebuilt, but dating from around 1677. Nearby, the grounds around the impressive waterfall of **Aira Force** are now owned by the National Trust, and are a prime example of a landscaped Victorian park.

Many regard Ullswater as the most beautiful lake in the region. Its gently curving shape is the result of glacial action gouging out a trough 8 miles long and one mile wide, sinking to a depth of 61m (200ft). It was along the shores of Ullswater and at the foot of Gowbarrow Fell that Dorothy Wordsworth noted the daffodils that later inspired William to write his famous poem. During the summer months, you can take boat trips on the lake at Glenridding on the two recently restored 19th-century steamers *MY Raven* and *MY Lady of the Lake*, an excellent way of experiencing this stunning dale. Most walkers who come to ascend Helvellyn do so from Glenridding or nearby Patterdale by way of Striding Edge. But there are plenty of fells that offer energetic days out: Place Fell, St Sunday Crag, the valley of Grisedale and, across the lake, Martindale, one of the few places in the Lakes where red deer still abound.

*Continue on the A592 past Pooley Bridge, and take the turning left to **Dacre**. If visiting **Dalemain**, return to the A592 and turn left where signposted a little further on.*

→ • • • • • • • • • • • ⑩

### LADY ANNE CLIFFORD

Lady Anne Clifford, who lies buried in the churchyard in Appleby, was a remarkable woman. The daughter of George Clifford, 3rd Earl of Cumberland and a naval commander, she was born in Skipton in 1590. She inherited the Clifford estates in 1643, at the time of the Civil War, and moved north. She then became a royalist thorn in Cromwell's side, frequently defying his express orders and rebuilding and restoring her castles at Appleby, Bardon Tower, Brough, Brougham, Pendragon and Skipton. Lady Anne's influence was felt throughout these northern parts of England, and many buildings in the area, particularly churches, are well-restored due to her dedication and determination.

*Clockwise from far left:*
*Patterdale; Ullswater*

## 10 DACRE AND DALEMAIN HOUSE

A little off the beaten track, the village of Dacre is a gem. The name is derived from the Welsh for tear, *daigr*, though there is nothing to be sad about in this quiet village set in splendid isolation along the crystal waters of Dacre Beck. On the site of a Saxon monastery it is believed to have been here that pagan kings swore allegiance to Aethelstan, and were baptised into Christianity. At the four corners of the churchyard stand the enigmatic **Dacre Bears**, four large stone sculptures, now largely weathered, and thought to commemorate the marriage between Thomas de Dacre and Philippa Neville, though their true origin is unknown. The monuments seem to depict an encounter between a bear and a cat: one shows the bear sleeping, then the cat awakens the bear, which seizes the cat, kills it and promptly eats it.

In the lakeland fells east of Dacre stands **Dalemain House**, a mainly 18th-century mansion that was built around an earlier house and a Norman pele tower. It was purchased in 1680 by Sir Edward Hasell, the son of the rector of Middleton Cheney in Northamptonshire, and has remained in the same family ever since. The interior features marvellous oak work, mostly originating from the estate, and portraits by van Dyck, bequeathed by Lady Anne Clifford (*see p38*), adorn the walls. The gardens have flourished since the 12th century, but today the real floral treat is the May to June display of Himalayan Blue poppies that thrive here.

*Join the A66 north of*
*Dacre or Dalemain to*
*return east to Penrith*

⟵ • • • • • • • • • • • ❶

### WITH MORE TIME

The border city of **Carlisle**, once a crucible of murder, mischief and mayhem, is now the administrative centre of Cumbria, and worth a detour. The medieval fortress of Carlisle castle sits squarely at the heart of the city. The simplicity of the building contrasts hugely with the stone filigree Victorian adornment that adorns Carlisle's mainly 19th-century cathedral. The modern red-brick Tullie House Musem and Art Gallery hosts regular exhibitions and permanent displays reflecting the Roman and Reiver history of the city and border area.

# The rugged fells of western Lakeland

Beyond the high road passes such as Honister and Hard Knott, the landscape of western Lakeland becomes more rugged and austere. Keswick, the largest town in the Lake District, is the gateway to this part of western England where sights include neat Cumbrian villages and craggy fells that brood over magnificent lakes and vales, vestiges of the ice age when creeping glaciers gouged out the landscape. Today, this remote area retains an originality, a touch of 'otherness' that both intrigues and attracts.

## TOUR ROUTE

Keswick ①
Derwent Water ②
Borrowdale ③
Honister Pass ④
Buttermere ⑤
Crummock Water ⑥
Lorton ⑦
Cockermouth ⑧
Isel ⑨
Wigton ⑩
Caldbeck ⑪

## TOUR LENGTH

**DISTANCE** approx. 65 miles (105km)

**DURATION** 2 days

## TOURIST INFORMATION CENTRES

**COCKERMOUTH** Town Hall, Market Street CA13 9NP; 01900 822634

**KESWICK** Moot Hall, Market Square CA12 5RJ; 01787 72645

**MARYPORT** Maryport Town Hall, Senhouse Street CA15 6BH; 01900 812101

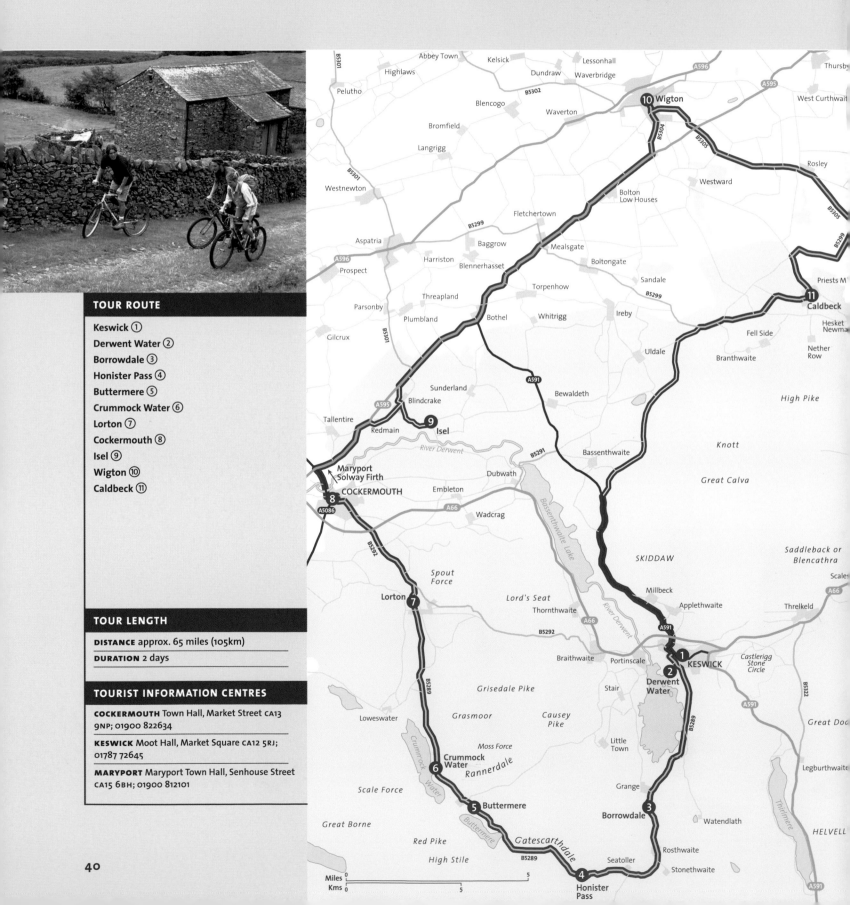

# 1 KESWICK

Centered on its bustling market place, Keswick is the pretty 'capital' of Western Lakeland. The town's superb setting at the head of Derwent Water at the northern end of Borrowdale, arguably Lakeland's most beautiful valley, makes it a big centre for fell walkers, climbers and holiday makers.

Built from local Skiddaw slate, Keswick's handsome buildings line its winding streets. The Moot Hall (now the tourist information centre) was built in 1813 on the site of an earlier building and, even until fairly recently, was used as the town hall. Keswick grew in importance from Elizabethan times, when it became a prosperous mining centre: as well as copper and lead, graphite was mined in the Borrowdale fells, and from the late 1800s pencils were manufactured locally in factories. The **Cumberland Pencil Museum** tells the story of pencils from the discovery of graphite to present-day methods of manufacture. Four miles north of Keswick along the shores of Bassenthwaite lake stands the 17th-century **Mirehouse**, which had strong literary connections, being visited by Southey, Tennyson and Wordsworth. It was during Tennyson's stay here that he was moved to write a poem describing the passing of King Arthur, later published as part of *Idylls of the King*.

On the fells just to the south east of town, **Castlerigg Stone Circle** enjoys a dramatic setting and is believed to date from 3000 BC, older than the great circles at Stonehenge and Avebury. It is commonly regarded as Cumbria's most superb stone circle.

*Clockwise from far left: cyclists near Keswick; mists over Derwent Water; Borrowdale; walkers on Cat Bells; Castlerigg Stone Circle; Ashness Bridge, near Keswick*

*Leave Keswick following signs to the B5289. Head south in the direction of Borrowdale: **Derwent Water** lies to your right.*

→ • • • • • • • • • • ❷

⊕ *Continue along the B5289*
• *into* ***Borrowdale***, *past the*
• *bridge at Grange. Just over*
• *one mile further on, keep*
• *an eye open for the parking*
③ *place for the Bowder Stone.*

## 2 DERWENT WATER

From the popular water's-edge viewpoint of Friar's Crag, the view over Derwent Water and into the hazy blue-green depths of Borrowdale is quite stunning. On a calm day, the brackeny slopes of Cat Bells and Maiden Moor are faithfully mirrored in the lake offering two spectacular images for the price of one. There are four islands in the lake, and one that early writers believed to be a floating island – in reality a mass of submerged vegetation that appears when the water level is low. In the late 1700s the eccentric Joseph Pocklington, known as Lord Pocky, lived on the largest island, **Derwent Isle**. Considered a man who never understood the concept of restraint, he built several picturesque extravaganzas on his island, including a chapel and a Druid's Circle, though only the chapel remains today.

One of the least taxing and most enjoyable ways of appreciating lower Borrowdale is to join a boat cruise on Derwent Water. The launches start their journey from the Keswick boat landings and cruise around the lake stopping at seven different jetties. You can start or break your journey at any of these, and pick up a later boat to resume the tour; the round trip takes 50 minutes.

*Keep on the B5289, passing through Rosthwaite to Seatoller. The road will then climb very steeply to the top of the* ***Honister Pass***.

⊖ • • • • • • • • • • • ④

## 3 BORROWDALE

The valley of Borrowdale is staggeringly beautiful, many of its tree-cloaked sides looking now much as they would have before man appeared. As you look south towards Grange, the valley seems blocked by a huge wooded crag named Castle Crag. But there is a way past the so-called tooth in the 'Jaws of Borrowdale'. A wooded path and the valley road follow the River Derwent and are flanked on both sides by high fells, which offer a network of routes for walkers.

Concealed high above the Borrowdale valley, the ancient hamlet of **Watendlath** was used by writer Hugh Walpole (who lived locally from 1924 to 1941), as his setting for *Judith Paris*, one of his *Rogue Herries* titles; Foldhead Farm in Watendlath is thought to be the model for Rogue Herries Farm. Then, as now, the hamlet is remote and unspoilt, a cluster of whitewashed cottages beside a trout-laden tarn that is popular with anglers.

No one seems quite sure whether the **Bowder Stone** near the hamlet of Grange, and easily accessible by constructed pathways, fell from the crags above or was left by a retreating glacier. The name comes from the Middle English 'bulder-stan', meaning a large boulder. Nearby is a small cottage built by Joseph Pocklington as a home for a local guide. In the base of the boulder, reputed to weigh about 2,000 tons, is a small hole, also the responsibility of Pocklington, who created it so that visitors could shake hands through it with their guide.

*Clockwise from far left:*
**Derwent Water; Buttermere**

## THE MAID OF BUTTERMERE

In the early 19th century, Buttermere's Fish Hotel was kept by a couple called Robinson who had a stunningly beautiful daughter, Mary. When only 14, Mary was remarked upon by Captain Budworth in his book *A Fortnight's Ramble in the Lakes*, and she became something of a local celebrity as the 'Beauty of Buttermere'. When she was 24, Mary caught the eye of a personable visitor to Buttermere, the Honourable Alexander Augustus Hope, Lieutenant-Colonel in the 14th Regiment of Foot. The colonel wooed and won the Beauty of Buttermere, and they were married in Lorton church in 1802. Ironically, poet Coleridge, a long-standing admirer of Mary, wrote a piece on the wedding for the *Morning Post*, where it eventually came to the notice of the genuine Colonel Hope, who had been abroad all that summer, for Mary's husband was an impostor. Local broadcaster and writer Lord Melvyn Bragg published a popular novel based on the story in 1987.

## 4 HONISTER PASS

The onward route through Borrowdale passes through the village of **Seatoller** (one of the wettest places in England), and up to Honister Pass 356m (1168ft) above sea level. **Honister Slate Mine** is still being worked for its much-prized slate and offers guided visits into the mine. In stormy weather, Honister is a dramatic and exciting spot, and the descent into Buttermere valley is breathtaking. Long-distance walkers undertaking the Coast-to-Coast Walk pass through Honister on their way from Ennerdale to Borrowdale.

*Descend steeply into Gatescarthdale, continuing on the B5289 until the village of **Buttermere**.* **5**

## 5 BUTTERMERE

Throughout Buttermere the whole scene is one of nature in her most benevolent mood, for here she has bestowed great riches of scenic beauty – swelling peaks, wooded fellsides, grey crags, oases of vivid green. The poet Robert Southey wrote of Buttermere: 'The hills that, calm and majestic, lifted their heads in the silent sky... Dark and distinct they rose. The clouds have gathered above them, High in the middle air, huge, purple, pillowy masses.'

The hamlet of Buttermere, little more than two hotels and a farm, is a good base from which to tackle the easy circular walks around either Lake Buttermere or Crummock Water *(see p44)*. Experienced fell walkers may tackle the steep and friable route onto Red Pike, a superb vantage point, but it is not for the fainthearted.

*Continue on the B5289 to* **Crummock Water**.
**6**

*Clockwise from above:*
**Derwent Water; Wordsworth memorial, Cockermouth; Crummock Water**

## 7 LORTON

Two small hamlets, High and Low Lorton, combine to create Lorton, a peaceful community of traditional Lakeland character. John Wesley preached here between 1752 and 1761, while 100 years earlier George Fox, the founder of the Quaker faith, preached in High Lorton beneath an ancient yew tree. The tree is more than 1,000 years old, and is immortalised by Wordsworth in his poem *Yew-Trees*.

**Lorton Hall**, set apart from the hamlets near a loop in the river, is built around a 15th-century pele tower, though the rest of the hall dates from 1663. Charles II stayed here in 1653, when he was out rallying support for his cause. One of his favourite trees, the beech, was planted by the lady of the manor, at the time of the Restoration, and still survives. The hall is only occasionally open to the public.

## 8 COCKERMOUTH

The town of Cockermouth is where William Wordsworth and his sister Dorothy were born. Their birthplace, a Georgian townhouse built in 1745, still stands in Main Street. **Wordsworth House** is now a museum containing furniture and effects of the family and the original staircase, fireplaces and panelling. As a child, Wordsworth played among the ruins of the 12th-century **Cockermouth Castle** that was built with stones from the nearby Roman settlement at Papcastle.

The town is a bustling place with a complex and seemingly random arrangement of lovely old cobbled streets, alleyways and yards. The **Lakeland Sheep and Wool Centre** on the edge of town is an excellent way of getting to know the woolly residents of Lakeland, and the part they played in the lives of Lakes people.

*Continue north towards Cockermouth on the B5289* **7** *to reach* **Lorton.**

*Head north from Lorton, turning left on the B5292* **8** *to reach* **Cockermouth.**

## 6 CRUMMOCK WATER

The larger Crummock Water is more open and less dominated by fells than Buttermere, though the huge bulk of Grasmoor to the north has immense presence. It is, however, every bit as beautiful. There's a delightful walk between **Scale Force**, the highest waterfall in the Lake District, and the village of Buttermere across the neck of land that links Buttermere lake and Crummock Water. Scale Force has been a popular excursion since Victorian times, when visitors would sail across the lake to see it. Though a little rocky underfoot, the base of the waterfall is nevertheless a lovely spot to have a picnic. Also on the lake's eastern shore is **Rannerdale** – a valley, that for all its undoubted beauty, has something of a sinister history. It was here at the end of the 11th century that the people of Buttermere ambushed and slew invading Normans, leaving their bodies to rot at the entrance to the dale. Today, this spot bursts into an intensely bright carpet of bluebells each spring.

*Take the A595, where you turn north. Then follow an unclassified road to the right at Redmain and continue to Blindcrake. Here, turn right until you reach the River Derwent at* **Isel.**

→ • • • • • • • • • • **9**

### LAKELAND'S HIGHEST SUMMITS

Although there are over 200 fells in the Lake District, few of them rise above 914m (3,000 ft), but those that do have a majesty of their own, and each is quite distinct. In the north, **Skiddaw** (*above*; 931m, 3,054ft) is composed of slate, and has a smooth almost conical profile. To the east, **Helvellyn** (950m, 3,116ft) has a dramatic ice-carved, east-facing corrie, but displays a rather plain rump to the waters of Thirlmere. The two highest, **Scafell Pike** (978m, 3,210ft) and **Scafell** (964m, 3,162ft) stand side by side, rugged and crag-ridden, but are separated by a near impassable gap, forcing walkers to descend to a rocky, scree-laden track that rises across the north-facing cliff face of Scafell before finally ascending to its summit.

## 9 ISEL

Perched close to the wooded banks of the River Derwent, the tiny hamlet of Isel is notable for its squat, Norman church of **St Michael's**, built in 1130. The setting is both exquisite and typical of the times when much of Lakeland was densely wooded, and travellers resorted to the rivers and woodland tracks to move about. Places of worship were often established where routes crossed, such as at St Michael's.

Around the nearest village, **Blindcrake**, the landscape reveals an unusual Lakeland farmscape that mixes the open spaces of the ancient Isel deer park with the rarer pattern of traditional strip fields.

## 10 WIGTON

Wigton is an unassuming and attractive market town on the Solway Plain, with a medieval layout and much Georgian architecture. In the triangular **Market Place** is a granite fountain with a pyramid spire, and on its sides are depicted four Acts of Mercy in bronze relief. Nearby, at the end of the main street, **Wigton Hall** is neo-Tudor in design with Georgian windows. Wigton is the birthplace of Robert Smirke (1752–1845), the painter and book illustrator, as well as the renowned Cumberland poet Ewan Clark and present-day writer and broadcaster Lord Melvyn Bragg.

## 11 CALDBECK

Most widely renowned for its local association with 18th-century huntsman John Peel, Caldbeck is a pleasing village surrounded by farmland near the slopes of the northern Lakeland fells. The manufacture of bobbins for the mills of Lancashire was a major Lakeland industry, and the **Howk Bobbin Mill** just a short distance from the village is a relic from an era that saw many of the local rivers lined with woollen, cotton, corn, bobbin and paper mills.

The church, dedicated to **St Kentigern**, dates from the 12th century, and was restored in the 1930s. Mary, the Beauty of Buttermere *(see p43)*, who in later life was happily married to a Caldbeck man, lies buried in the churchyard, as does John Peel, the huntsman forever immortalised in the verses of *D'ye ken John Peel*, written by his friend John Woodcock Graves.

In nearby **Hesket Newmarket,** to the south east of Caldbeck, is one of the England's smallest breweries, producing a wide range of real ales.

*Return to Blindcrake and turn right on the A595 for 13 miles, and then turn left on the B5304 into* **Wigton**. 10

*Take the B5305 and, at the A595, turn right and then immediately left back onto the B5305. Follow this to its junction with the B5299. There, turn right to* **Caldbeck**. 11

*Take the B5299 for 3 miles, then follow unclassified roads south west across country to reach the A591 at Bassenthwaite, and turn south towards* **Keswick**.
1

### WITH MORE TIME

The **Solway Firth** is an atmospheric place of salt marsh and huge skies. On its southern shore, Silloth is a pretty Victorian seaside resort with a splendid promenade. It was here that J M W Turner painted his *Sunset over the Solway Firth*. Allonby has a lovely shingle and sand beach and free-roaming Allonby ponies. On the Atlantic coast, **Maryport** celebrates its maritime history with both a museum and the Maryport Steamship Museum, while the Roman occupation of north west Cumbria is the focus of the town's Senhouse Roman Museum.

# The charms of southern Lakeland

The area of the southern Lake District is distinctly different from Lakeland's central, landlocked region. Here, limestone dominates the terrain, and this produces a more subtle and verdant landscape. There are few sizeable towns, but numerous villages and hamlets. There are also more wooded areas, and the weather in the south is tempered by the coastal influences from the Kent Estuary and Morecambe Bay. This is also a part of England that is well endowed with stately homes, many of which are still occupied by the same families who have lived in them for centuries.

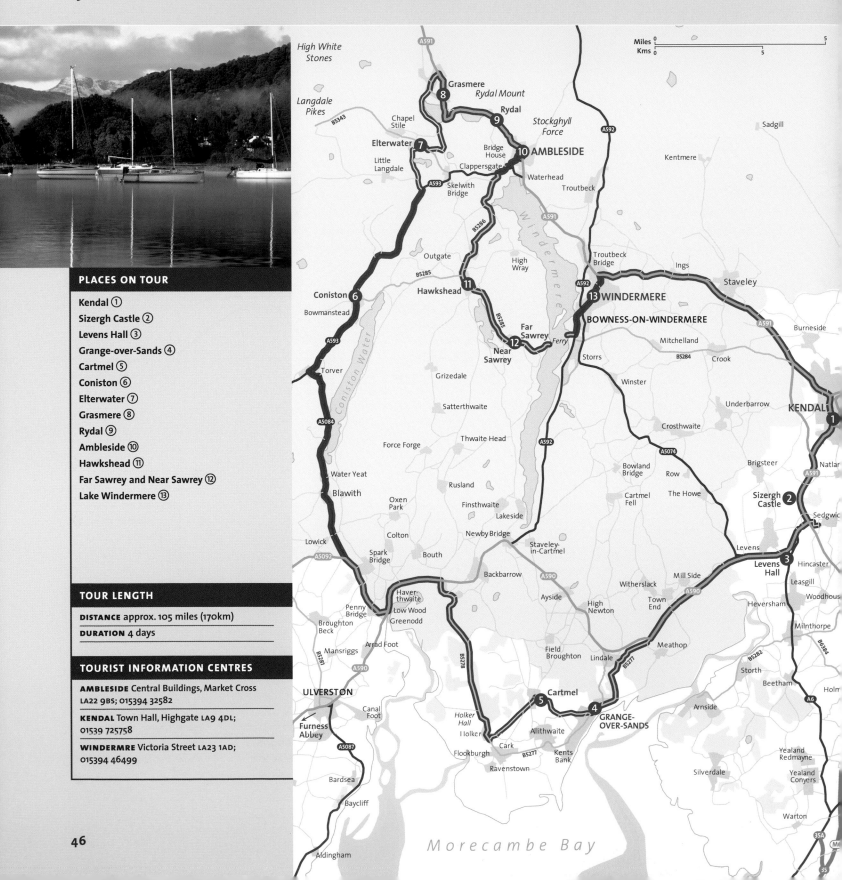

## PLACES ON TOUR

Kendal ①
Sizergh Castle ②
Levens Hall ③
Grange-over-Sands ④
Cartmel ⑤
Coniston ⑥
Elterwater ⑦
Grasmere ⑧
Rydal ⑨
Ambleside ⑩
Hawkshead ⑪
Far Sawrey and Near Sawrey ⑫
Lake Windermere ⑬

## TOUR LENGTH

**DISTANCE** approx. 105 miles (170km)

**DURATION** 4 days

## TOURIST INFORMATION CENTRES

**AMBLESIDE** Central Buildings, Market Cross LA22 9BS; 015394 32582

**KENDAL** Town Hall, Highgate LA9 4DL; 01539 725758

**WINDERMRE** Victoria Street LA23 1AD; 015394 46499

*Clockwise from far left:*
*boats on Lake Windermere;*
*Lake Windermere, Cumbria;*
*tomb at Cartmel Priory;*
*Kendal Castle*

## 1 KENDAL

Formerly an important woollen textile centre, the flourishing market town of Kendal is set amid a low-lying limestone landscape attractively crisscrossed by drystone walls and dotted with farmsteads. Today it is the southern gateway to the Lake District National Park, though the valley of the River Kent and the surrounding limestone scars offer plenty of easy walks.

Leading off Kendal's main thoroughfare is a series of parallel 'wynds' or narrow alleyways and courtyards, which developed to meet the increase in population that came with the rapid growth of the local textile industry from the 17th–19th centuries. Just outside town, **Kendal Castle** dates from the 12th century. In the 1500s, it was owned by Sir Thomas Parr, father of Katherine Parr, the last wife of Henry VIII, who was born here. It is an easy uphill walk from the banks of the River Kent and offers a splendid view over the town.

At Kendal's southern edge and housed in an imposing Georgian House, **Abbot Hall Art Gallery** has a highly acclaimed programme of contemporary exhibitions. Located in the former stables, the **Abbot Hall Museum of Lakeland Life** shows how the Cumbrian people have worked, lived and entertained themselves over the past 300 years. The adjacent church of the **Holy and Undivided Trinity** is Cumbria's largest parish church and dates from the 13th century: it is unique in having five aisles.

*Leave Kendal heading south*
*to join A591, and then*
*follow local signs for*
*Sizergh Castle.* ②

## 2 SIZERGH CASTLE

Some two miles south of Kendal stands the imposing ancestral home of the Strickland family, Sizergh Castle. The Great Hall, which was remodelled in the 1600s, and two Elizabethan wings are built around a 14th-century pele tower. Many of the rooms display a lavish use of oak panelling, and walls are decorated with family and royal portraits. There is also a collection of English and French oak furniture and fine porcelain that was acquired over the family's 750-year history. Numerous footpaths wind through the 638-ha estate (1,600 acre) to viewpoints overlooking the Kent Estuary and the fells.

*Return to the A591 and*
*head south. At the*
*intersection with the A590*
*bear right and then follow*
*local signs to Levens Hall.*
⊕ • • • • • • • • • • ③

⊕ *From Levens Hall, return to*
  *the A590 and head west*
  *for 5 miles to a roundabout*
  *and branch left on to the*
  *B5277 to Lindale. Turn*
  *left again to reach*
④ *Grange-over-Sands.*

## 3 LEVENS HALL

This magnificent home, owned by the same family for 700 years, was built onto an earlier pele tower. It is by far the largest Elizabethan house in the Lake District, yet has managed to keep an intimate scale. Beautiful paintings and fine panelling, plasterwork and family memorabilia adorn the rooms. The gardens and landscape that surround Levens have changed little since they were created in 1690 by Beaumont, a gardener to the aristocracy and much in demand. The topiary gardens are especially breathtaking, but don't miss the rose garden, the splendid herbaceous borders and the fountain garden with its display of ornamental limes. Part of the Levens estate is one of Cumbria's oldest deer parks, which contains some unusually dark fallow deer. Local legend has it that whenever a white fawn is born to the herd, the occasion foretells some change in the fortunes of the house of Levens.

## 4 GRANGE-OVER-SANDS

There is something truly relaxing about Grange-over-Sands. Situated on Morecambe Bay, its bracing sea air, mild climate and the arrival of the Furness Railway turned the former fishing village into a popular Edwardian resort. Part of its charm today is that it still retains this feel with a long, traffic-free promenade and attractive ornamental gardens. The surrounding countryside is especially appealing and popular with birdwatchers and walkers, having a wide variety of habitats.

⊕ *From Grange follow the*
  *B5277 south west and then*
  *turn right using local roads*
⑤ *to reach Cartmel.*

*Continue south west to the*
*B5278 using local roads and*
*head north to the junction*
*with the A590. Turn left*
*and then right on the*
*A5092 and later right*
*again onto the A5084.*
*Continue for 6 miles to the*
*junction with the A593*
*where you turn right to*
*reach Coniston.*

→ • • • • • • • • • • • ⑥

## 5 CARTMEL

One of south Lakeland's oldest villages, Cartmel grew up around its 12th- and 13th-century Augustinian **priory.** Much of the priory was destroyed at the time of the Dissolution, but the **church** was spared as its demolition would have left the parishioners without a place of prayer. Today, it is commonly regarded as one of Britain's most beautiful churches, and has a curious belfry set diagonally to the base of the tower. The pretty village, with its ancient streets and inviting cafes and inns is worth exploring too. The renowned Cartmel racecourse is just behind the square, with meetings held on both spring and summer bank holiday weekends.

Nearby **Holker Hall**, an attractive neo-Elizabethan mansion, is the home of Lord and Lady Cavendish. The exterior is stunning, but the interior is breathtaking in its design and decoration. Outside, part formal, part woodland gardens feature an observatory, an arboretum, terraces, a kitchen garden and a labyrinth set in a wild-flower meadow. The real highlight, though, is its **Lakeland Motor Museum**. Here, more than 20,000 cars, pedal cars and engines, tractors, motorcycles and bicycles are found in what is the most comprehensive collection of automobilia in England. For motorists, this is quite simply unadulterated nostalgia.

### QUEEN'S GUIDE TO MORECAMBE BAY

The vast expanse of Morecambe Bay is no place to linger without expert guidance. There are quicksands, and the tide comes in rapidly, as many have found to their cost. Some of those who have failed to beat the tide are buried in the church grounds at Cartmel, and it was the priory that introduced the services of a guide. Today, the guide is appointed by the Queen and runs guided walks from May to September, which must be booked in advance. Attempting to walk across the bay without a guide is not recommended given the risks involved.

## 6 CONISTON

Dominated by the Coniston Fells, which rise to the summit of the **Old Man of Coniston** (803m, 2,634ft), this village is one of the most popular destinations in the Lake District. Almost every day of the year sees walkers setting off to climb the 'Old Man', often continuing to circle high above Goat's Water, across Dow Crag and down to the Walna Scar road. For the less energetic, walks up to Tarn Hows, across Tom Heights and onto Monk Coniston Moor offer easier circuits. The development nearby of slate quarries and copper mines in the 19th century brought Coniston much of its prosperity, but it was the beauty of both the village and its valley that attracted many: Tennyson spent part of his honeymoon here; Arthur Ransome, the writer of children's books, made Coniston the setting for *Swallows and Amazons*; W G Collingwood, the English artist and archaeologist, was a resident as was the influential poet, art critic and social reformer John Ruskin. He lived at **Brantwood**, on the shores of

Coniston Water from 1871 until his death and according to his wishes, lies buried in the local churchyard. Brantwood is one of the most beautifully situated houses in the Lakes, enjoying stunning views. During Ruskin's time here, it became one of the greatest literary and artistic centres in Europe. Today Brantwood houses a museum commemorating his life and work.

Five mile-long **Coniston Water** was the setting for Donald Campbell's ill-fated attempt at the world jet-powered water-speed record in 1967. His boat, *Bluebird*, went out of control as he attempted to become the first man to exceed 300mph on water, and Campbell was killed. His death is commemorated in the village centre by a plaque. Before the advent of the automobile, Coniston Water was immensely popular with visitors who would arrive by rail. The Furness Railway Company also operated a steamer service on the lake: first launched in 1859, after years of disuse, *The Gondola* was rebuilt and brought back into service in 1980.

*Clockwise from far left:*
*topiary at Levens Hall;*
*view of Coniston Water*
*from Nibthwaite*

*Continue north east on*
*the A593 and after about*
*5 miles turn left along local*
*roads to Elterwater.*

→ • • • • • • • • • • • ❼

# 7 ELTERWATER

Standing at the entrance to Langdale, and with the craggy Langdale Pikes as a backdrop, Elterwater is a delightful cluster of attractive cottages, shops and an inn. The name of the village is said to mean 'swan lake' in Norse, and swans still grace the nearby Elterwater from time to time. Surrounded by waterfalls, volcanic crags and tree-clad slopes offering plenty of fell walking opportunities, the village is largely built of the attractive, local grey-green slate, and centres on a small green with an ancient maple tree. The manufacture of gunpowder came to be an important Lakeland industry during the 18th century, and the gunpowder works at Elterwater, responsible for the development of the village, did not close until the 1930s.

*Head north to reach the junction with the B5343. Take unclassified roads to the A591*
**8** *and **Grasmere**.*

# 8 GRASMERE

Associated forever with the poet William Wordsworth, and a tourist magnet as a consequence, Grasmere is nevertheless a delightful settlement located in a vast natural hollow at the foot of the steady rise to Dunmail Raise. Fells of varying heights and steepness enfold the village, and provide by far the best view of it, while the nearby lake of Grasmere adds a certain sparkle.

**Dove Cottage**, where the Wordsworths lived, was originally an inn called the Dove and Olive Bough. In Wordsworth's time it had no name, however, and was simply looked on as part of Town End, a small hamlet. The Wordsworths repaired and decorated the cottage themselves, and it was here that Dorothy, his sister, kept her *Journals*, written between 1800 and 1803, an almost daily account of the goings-on in their lives. Today, the cottage receives thousands of visitors annually, who come to see the miscellaneous household items, furniture, possessions and portraits from the poet's day, and to wander the small garden that William and Dorothy created. Wordsworth is buried in a quiet corner of the churchyard of St Oswald, along with Mary, his wife; Dorothy, his sister; and three of his children, Dora, Catherine and Thomas. The grave shelters beneath one of eight yew trees planted in the churchyard by the poet.

Immediately adjoining the church is the renowned **Grasmere Gingerbread Shop**, built in 1660 and formerly the village school. It was attended by the Wordsworth children when the family lived at the Rectory (1811–13) and was eventually taken over by a 19th-century entrepreneur, Sarah Nelson, who made gingerbread and other confectionery. Today, it is not unusual to find a long queue waiting patiently to buy the gingerbread, still made to a secret recipe.

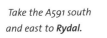

*Take the A591 south and east to **Rydal**.*
**9**

## 9 RYDAL

There is little to the scattered grey-stone village of Rydal, strung out along the main road running north from Ambleside; but the nearby lake, **Rydal Water**, was a favourite spot of the Wordsworths, who would often picnic on its island. It lies sandwiched between the slopes of Nab Scar and Loughrigg Fell, and would often freeze over, providing the Wordsworth household with another opportunity for enjoyment – skating.

In the village, **Rydal Mount** was home to William Wordsworth and his family from 1813 to his death in 1850. He was at the peak of his fame at this time, though his best work had all been accomplished, mostly at Dove Cottage. The Wordsworth family continued to live at Rydal after his death, and his descendants still own and live in the house, which is open to the public during summer months and receives many visitors – as it did when Wordsworth lived there. The adjoining garden is still very much as Wordsworth – who had strong views on how a garden should look – designed it.

## 10 AMBLESIDE

Lying half a mile north of Lake Windermere, Ambleside is a large Lakeland village almost entirely composed of slate; even new development in the centre of the town maintains this tradition.

The tiny and much photographed **Bridge House**, standing on what was probably an old packhorse bridge spanning Stock Ghyll, was immortalised by Turner and Ruskin, and is now an information centre. Built in the 18th century as a covered bridge and the summer house of the now demolished Ambleside Hall, it is said to have once housed a family with six children.

To the east of Ambleside lies Wansfell, an uphill but moderate walk that offers a truly fabulous view down the length of Lake Windermere and over the neighbouring valley of Troutbeck. Closer to town, in a wooded ravine, **Stockghyll Force**, an attractive waterfall and beck that for hundreds of years powered a wide range of mills, has been a popular stroll since Victorian times.

*Clockwise from top left:*
*Dove Cottage, Grasmere;*
*the pier, Ambleside; Bridge*
*House, Ambleside; Rydal*
*Mount; Wordsworth*
*memorabilia and portrait,*
*Dove Cottage, Grasmere*

*Continue south on the* ⊕
*A591 for 2 miles to* ⋮
*Ambleside.* ❿

*Head west out of the*
*village to reach the A593.*
*Follow this for half a mile,*
*and then branch left on*
*B5286 to reach **Hawkshead**.*
→ • • • • • • • • • • ⓫

⊕ Continue through
• Hawkshead and take the
• B5285 south east to reach
⑫ *Far* and *Near Sawrey.*

# 11 HAWKSHEAD

Set midway between Ambleside and Coniston at the northern tip of Esthwaite Water, Hawkshead is a timeless place. The village grew up at the junction of packhorse trails that were developed to link the early Windermere ferries with the Coniston valley. It was not until the 19th century that roads penetrated as far as the village, though today its centre, a snug arrangement of narrow cobbled streets and alleys leading to secluded courtyards, is banned to traffic.

Though born in Cockermouth *(see p44)*, Wordsworth attended the **grammar school** here (open to the public), and it is easy to see how the village and its setting would have inspired him in his earlier works. The **Beatrix Potter Gallery** contains a selection of original drawings by the artist, together with a display telling the story of her life. The building was once the office of her husband, solicitor William Heelis, and remains largely unaltered since his day.

To the south of Hawkshead, the landscape is dominated by the green mantle of **Grizedale Forest Park**. Walking and cycling are easy and popular here, with eight walking trails and five cycle trails to follow. The Ridding Wood Trail is surfaced throughout and passes 20 pieces of contemporary forest sculpture.

***Clockwise from below:***
**view across Esthwaite Water;**
**boats on Lake Windermere;**
**Hill Top Farm, Sawrey**

## BEATRIX POTTER

Beatrix Potter (1866–1947) was brought up in London but her parents took her on a summer holiday to Ambleside when she was 16. She loved Derwent Water, and explored the New-lands valley and watched wildlife in the woods, and made many sketches of the landscape. When back in London, Beatrix started a book that eventually became *The Tale of Peter Rabbit*, published in 1902. It was an instant success, and she went on to write two books a year for the next 10 years. Beatrix purchased Hill Top Farm near Sawrey with the proceeds and eventually moved there in 1913. After her marriage she wrote less and less and became more involved in conservation of the Lake District countryside, and left some 800ha (4,000 acres) to the National Trust.

## 12 FAR SAWREY AND NEAR SAWREY

The two small villages of Far Sawrey and Near Sawrey lie between the lake of Windermere and **Esthwaite Water** amid a rolling, wooded landscape and on a lane that runs down to the Windermere ferry. Near Sawrey is renowned for its association with Beatrix Potter. The 17th-century **Hill Top** farm was acquired with royalties from her first book, *Peter Rabbit*, and it was here that she created the world of *Jemima Puddle-Duck* and *Pigling Bland*. When she died in 1947, Potter bequeathed Hill Top to the National Trust subject to the condition that is was kept exactly as she had left it.

## 13 LAKE WINDERMERE

Windermere is the largest lake in England (10 miles long and one mile wide at its broadest point), and its surrounds are among the most beautiful in the country. Much of the shoreline is wooded, islands punctuate its middle reaches and high ground flanks much of the lake, providing excellent vantage points.

The lake is renowned for char and deep-water trout, the former, in its potted form, being a considerable delicacy among the wealthy families of the 17th and 18th centuries. By the middle of the 19th century, however, as Victorian tourists came to explore the 'Lake Mountains', sailing for pleasure here became an important attraction, and so it has remained. **Bowness-on-Windermere** is a sprawling tourist town that developed after the arrival of the railway at Windermere town in 1847. Before then this was no more than a small group of cottages and huts used by fishermen. Today it is a bustling place, with lake boats constantly coming and going. Bowness also marks the end of the Dales Way, a middle-distance walk that begins in Ilkley. To its north, at a place where barges used to unload gravel dredged from the lake bed, the Windermere **Steamboat Museum** houses a unique collection of historic steamboats and motorboats, including the *Dolly*, reputedly the oldest mechanically powered boat in the world.

*Continue east on the B5285 until you reach **Lake Windermere**. Take the ferry, and then turn left on the A592 to and then Windermere via Bowness-on-Windermere.* **13**

*From Windermere turn right on to the A591 to return to **Kendal**.*

## WITH MORE TIME

**Muncaster Castle**, set in beautiful gardens in Eskdale, west of Coniston Water, has been the home of the Pennington family since the 1200s. Open to the public, and said to be haunted, it contains a wide variety of historic furniture, some fine tapestries, and paintings by renowned artists such as Reynolds and Gainsborough.

To the south, the region of Furness (the hinterland of Barrow-in-Furness) owes most of its economic development to the exploitation of its natural resources by the monks of **Furness Abbey** *(left)*. The 12th-century abbey was and still is one of the most important monastic sites in the country.

# Lancaster and the rural uplands of the Forest of Bowland

North Lancashire is a verdant region, though the legacy of its industrial past still lingers in more than a few corners. The tussocky moorlands and flower-filled river valleys of the Forest of Bowland surround stone villages and characterful towns. Two rivers influence the region's landscape: the Lune to the north and the Ribble to the south, which takes a picturesque route through Clitheroe.

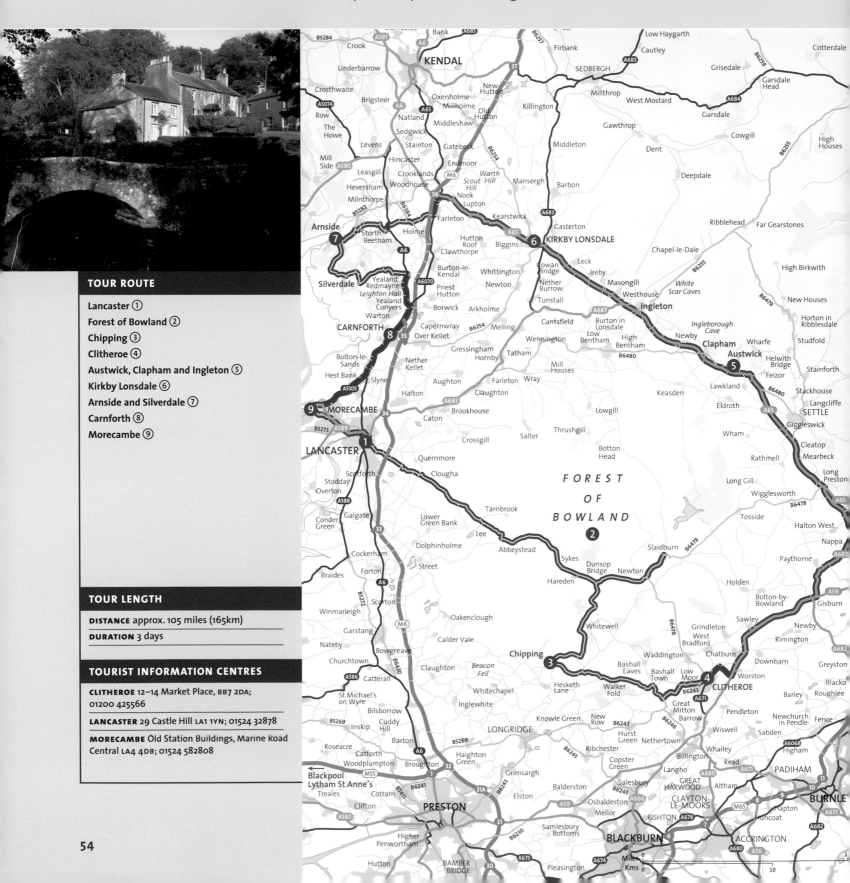

## TOUR ROUTE

Lancaster ①
Forest of Bowland ②
Chipping ③
Clitheroe ④
Austwick, Clapham and Ingleton ⑤
Kirkby Lonsdale ⑥
Arnside and Silverdale ⑦
Carnforth ⑧
Morecambe ⑨

## TOUR LENGTH

**DISTANCE** approx. 105 miles (165km)

**DURATION** 3 days

## TOURIST INFORMATION CENTRES

**CLITHEROE** 12–14 Market Place, BB7 2DA;
01200 425566

**LANCASTER** 29 Castle Hill LA1 1YN; 01524 32878

**MORECAMBE** Old Station Buildings, Marine Road
Central LA4 4DB; 01524 582808

*Clockwise from far left:*
*packhorse bridge at*
*Clapham; Littledale, Forest*
*of Bowland; statue of Eric*
*Morecambe, Morecambe;*
*view of Ashton*
*Memorial, Lancaster*

## 1 LANCASTER

Essentially Georgian, the vibrant city of Lancaster sits on the banks of the River Lune. Its 12th-century **castle,** known as John of Gaunt's castle, was an important stronghold and is still one of Europe's longest-serving operational prisons. Among the many individuals brought to Lancaster for trial , the most famous were the Pendle Witches *(see p57).* The Grand Jury Room includes some superb Gillow furniture *(see p58),* while the branding iron used on prisoners can still be seen in the Crown Court. Visitors can even briefly experience what it is like to be locked in a dungeon. Rising above **Williamson Park**, the elegant **Ashton Memorial** dominates the city skyline. The memorial was commissioned by Lancastrian millionaire Lord Ashton, in memory of his wife. The park has plenty to offer including a tropical butterfly house and an exotic birds enclosure, as well as beautiful parkland walks.

*Leave Lancaster south* ⊕
*on the A6, and on the*
*outskirts take unclassified*
*roads south east towards*
*Quernmore crossing the*
***Forest of Bowland*** *before*
*descending through*
*Dunsop Bridge to reach*
*Slaidburn via the B6478.* **②**

## 2 FOREST OF BOWLAND

An area of wild and windswept beauty, the Forest of Bowland is not a 'forest' as such, but a former hunting domain. This peaty, gritstone moorland landscape is networked by deep river valleys and where kings and nobles once hunted wild boar, deer and wolves. High on the moors, the road snakes through a pass known as the Trough of Bowland, a traditional packhorse way once used to convey the Pendle Witches to Lancaster for trial. The remote amber-stone village of **Slaidburn**, isolated and protected by the surrounding fells, and largely owned by the Fletcher family for almost 200 years, has remained virtually unchanged since the early 19th century. The church is distinctive for its unusual arrangement of Georgian box-pews, an 18th-century triple-decker pulpit, and exquisite carved screens.

*Return to Dunsop Bridge*
*and follow unclassified*
*roads south through*
*Whitewell to* ***Chipping.***
⊖ • • • • • • • • • • ❸

⊕ *Leave Chipping on local*
*roads signposted for*
***Clitheroe**, to reach the*
*B6243 on the outskirts*
④ *of the town.*

## 3 CHIPPING

Chipping, with its lovely mellow stone buildings and narrow streets, is tucked away beneath the Bowland fells in the heart of the Ribble Valley. The village retains much of its 17th-century layout, especially along Windy Street. It is worth looking inside the **Church of St Bartholomew** for its amusing figureheads carved on a pillar in the north aisle. Chipping thrived during the Industrial Revolution when seven mills were located along Chipping Brook, although only a chairmaking factory survives today.

⊕ *Take the A671 east out of*
*Clitheroe to reach the A59,*
*and follow this to Gisburn,*
*turning left onto the A682*
*to join the A65 at Long*
*Preston. Follow the A65*
*north to **Ingleton** via*
⑤ ***Austwick** and **Clapham**.*

## 4 CLITHEROE

One of the oldest towns in Lancashire, Clitheroe is centred around its 12th-century **castle**. Standing on a rocky outcrop of limestone above the River Ribble, the keep, one of the smallest in England, is nevertheless a prominent landmark. It is the only remaining castle in Lancashire that had a Royalist garrison during the Civil War. There is a small museum of local history adjoining the keep. Clitheroe itself has a delightful, traditional feel about it. A market has been held here since 1283 and still takes place three times a week. To the south of town rises the brooding dome of **Pendle Hill**, famed for its association with witchcraft, but also where George Fox supposedly had a vision that inspired him to found the Quaker movement.

*On leaving Ingleton, turn*
*right on to the A65, and*
*follow this for 6 miles to*
***Kirkby Lonsdale**.*

→ • • • • • • • • • • ⑥

## 5 AUSTWICK, CLAPHAM AND INGLETON

On the edge of limestone country, **Austwick** draws walkers who come to explore the surrounding countryside and the **Norber Erratics**. Deposited around 11,000 years ago by a retreating glacier, this group of boulders are a local geological curiosity. Set in beautiful Dales scenery featuring waterfalls and stands of ancient trees, nearby **Clapham** is a delight with its old stone houses and bridges. Within reach of the village are gorges and Britain's largest cavern, **Gaping Gill**, into which tumbles Britain's highest unbroken waterfall. It takes its name from its vast entrance, which swallows the waters of Fell Beck as they gather from the high grounds around Ingleborough. The main chamber is an incredible 140m (460ft) long and almost 30m (100ft) high and wide. **Ingleborough Cave**, also easily reached from Clapham through Clapdale Woods, is similarly spectacular with its impressive, 350-million-year-old stalactites and stalagmites, all atmospherically floodlit. The next village, Ingleton, capitalises on its limestone setting too: the underground world of **White Scar Caves** is Britain's longest show cave. The easy walk through woodland gorges at the edge of the village is spectacular all year round.

*Clockwise from top left:*
John Ruskin's view from
Kirkby Lonsdale; Clapham;
Devil's Bridge, Kirkby
Lonsdale; Clitheroe Castle

## THE LANCASHIRE WITCHES

One of the most famous events to take place in Lancashire occurred during the 17th century, and has since formed the basis of novels, and radio and television programmes. With the ascension of James I to the English throne in 1603, there came a new wave of persecution for those who were involved with witchcraft, such as the 13 so-called Pendle Witches, who were tried and hanged at Lancaster Castle in 1612. Two families were at the centre of the Pendle case. Significantly, both were headed by elderly widows who were known locally by their nicknames: Old Demdike and Old Chattox.

## 6 KIRKBY LONSDALE

The lovely and historic market town of Kirkby Lonsdale is set in an area of great natural beauty. From the medieval Devil's Bridge you can admire the views that so inspired John Ruskin and were painted by J W Turner, or simply get an excellent bacon 'buttie' and mug of tea from the bridge cafe. Don't be suprised to find hordes of amiable bikers congregating at the bridge on sunny weekends: over the years they have become a cult tourist attraction in themselves.

*From Kirkby Lonsdale return to the A65 heading north west for 5 miles to the junction with the A6070. Take the first left onto the A6070 for 1 mile, and then take local roads west cross country to Arnside and Silverdale.*

→ • • • • • • • • • • ❼

*Leave Silverdale east by
following signs for Yealand
Redmayne, and in the
village turn onto the
A6 south and follow the
road to Carnforth.*

**8**

## 7 ARNSIDE AND SILVERDALE

Located in an Area of Outstanding Natural Beauty, the
seaside town of **Arnside** looks out across the Kent
Estuary and the hills of the southern Lake District
beyond. From the wooded hill of Arnside Knott and the
neighbouring village of **Silverdale** to the south, there
are unrivalled views of the vast spread of Morecambe
Bay. There are lovely walks out of Silverdale to the headland of Jack Scout, owned mostly by the National Trust.

Nearby, **Leighton Moss Nature Reserve** is a vast and
popular nature reserve with some rare species of
breeding birds among the many thousands that flock
to its wetlands. Above the reserve stands the stately
neogothic **Leighton Hall**, owned and lived in by the
descendents of the furniture-making Gillow dynasty as
it has been for centuries. Consequently, the house has
all the atmosphere of a family home, and visitors are
invited to sit on the ancient chairs while knowledgeable
guides reveal the hall's history. You are even welcome to
take your place at the 18th-century dining table or to play
a tune on the Steinway! As well as landscaped parkland
and woodland walks, Leighton has a pretty 19th-
century walled garden – the passion of the present
owner – featuring rose-covered walls, a fragrant herb
patch and an overflowing herbaceous border.

*Take the A6 south through
Bolton-le-Sands, eventually
branching right onto the
A5105 for 3 miles to reach
Morecambe.*

**9**

## 8 CARNFORTH

This small Victorian market town is always busy
and gains all the breezy benefits of its location on
the edge of Morecambe Bay. But its fame rests on the
fact that in 1945 *Brief Encounter*, starring Celia Johnson
and Trevor Howard, was filmed in Carnforth **station**.
The film is a love story about a man and a woman,
both married but not to each other, who meet in the
refreshment room at a railway station. Carnforth
station cafe is now a nostalgic spot for film buffs. The
town also offers some nice walks along the River Keer,
the bay and the Lancaster Canal.

### THE GILLOWS OF LEIGHTON HALL

The Lancaster branch of the Gillows family has
been making furniture as well as architectural
joinery and billiard tables, encouraged by the
game's vogue, since the 1770s. The Gillows
were shrewd in producing a neat, rather
conventional range of furniture derived from
the designs of James Wyatt, the most
fashionable architect of the last two decades
of the 18th century, and from plates in the
pattern-books of George Hepplewhite and
Thomas Sheraton. They avoided the height of
fashion, supplying instead pieces that would
appeal to the burgeoning middle classes of
Liverpool and Manchester, who valued good,
solid, well-made furniture.

*Clockwise from top right:*
**Morecambe Bay;**
**Leighton Hall**

# 9  MORECAMBE

In the early 19th century, Morecambe was simply a small fishing village called Poulton-le-Sands, but it blossomed into one of the most attractive and popular holiday resorts in Lancashire. For years, there was a sense of rivalry with Blackpool, as Morecambe always had a lively character and style, one highlighted by the zany half of a famous comedy duo Morecambe and Wise. There is a lovely statue of locally born Eric Morecambe on the promenade. Another native, actress Dame Thora Hird, made her stage debut in 1911 at the age of two months when she was carried on stage at Morecambe's Royalty Theatre in a play directed by her father. The huge expanse of Morecambe Bay once offered the shortest route into Furness, or Lancashire-over-the-Sands as it was previously known. You need the company of a guide to cross safely today *(see p48)*, but the experience is unforgettable: vast skies, a seemingly limitless sprawl of sand and river, and an awesome sense of place.

*Leave Morecambe by following the B5274 east to the A589 and then take the A6 to return to **Lancaster**.*

⬅ • • • • • • • • • • ❶

## WITH MORE TIME

**Bright, brash and breezy is the only way to describe Blackpool *(left)*. A long-established holiday resort that formerly served the mill workers of Lancashire, the town now draws crowds from across Britain – anyone, really, who just wants to let their hair down for a few fun-filled days. In contrast, a short way south along the coast is Lytham – and St Anne's – two small genteel towns traditionally joined as one. Here you can enjoy the fine promenade, peaceful parks, beautiful gardens and admire the town's old half-timbered buildings.**

59

# The unexpected attractions of Lancashire's coastal plain

The flat expanse of the Lancashire coastal plain was created by draining once-inaccessible marshland, and most of this region is now farming country. The remaining fen-meadows are renowned for the large numbers of birds that roost here during the winter months. Along the dune-fringed coast lies the typical, fun-oriented seaside resort of Southport, which contrasts with workaday inland towns like Wigan and Preston.

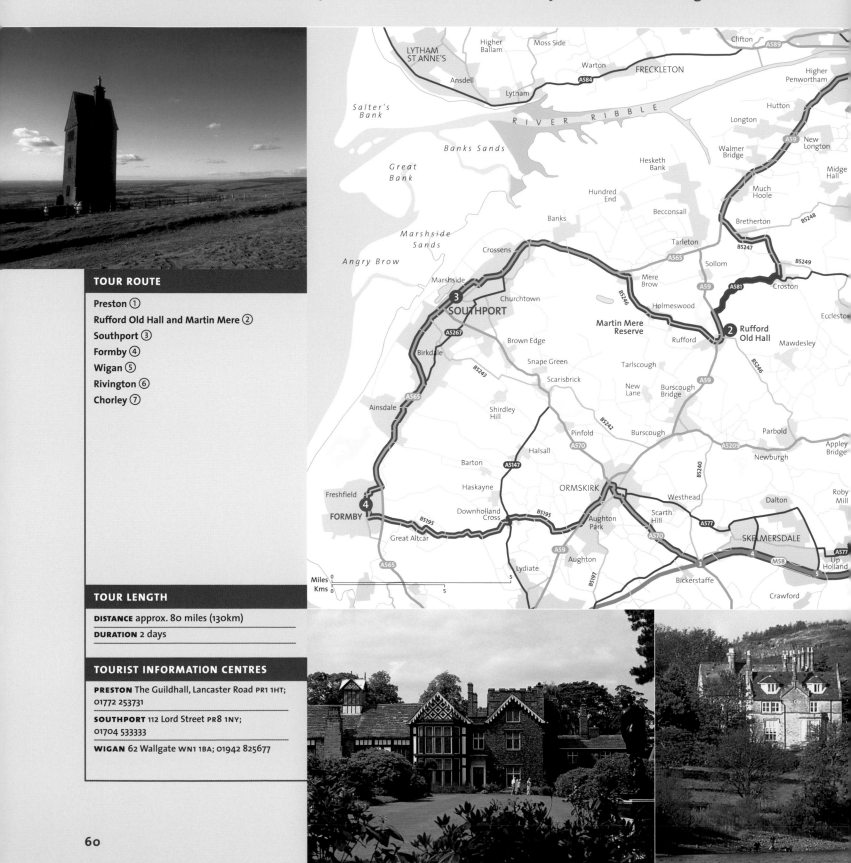

## TOUR ROUTE

Preston ①

Rufford Old Hall and Martin Mere ②

Southport ③

Formby ④

Wigan ⑤

Rivington ⑥

Chorley ⑦

## TOUR LENGTH

**DISTANCE** approx. 80 miles (130km)

**DURATION** 2 days

## TOURIST INFORMATION CENTRES

**PRESTON** The Guildhall, Lancaster Road PR1 1HT; 01772 253731

**SOUTHPORT** 112 Lord Street PR8 1NY; 01704 533333

**WIGAN** 62 Wallgate WN1 1BA; 01942 825677

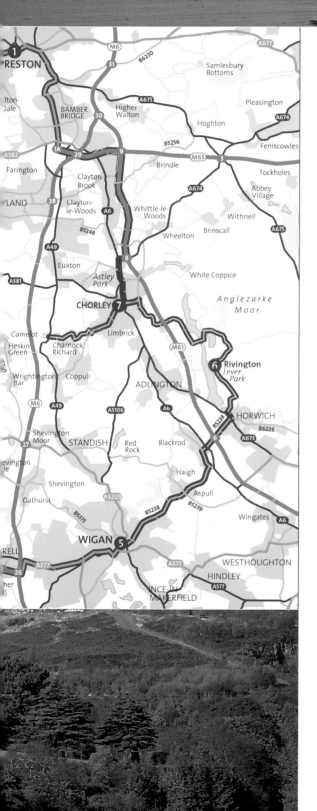

**Clockwise from far left:**
Rivington Moor; riding on
the beach near Southport;
Rivington reservoirs;
Rufford Old Hall

# 1 PRESTON

Granted city status as recently as 2002, Preston is a dynamic regional capital but one that still nurtures its splendid old buildings, like the 1893 **Harris Museum and Art Gallery**, one of the first Greek revival buildings in Britain. Today, it holds a wide-ranging collection of art and hosts regular exhibitions, which often explore the city's Asian heritage. In the city centre, the tiny Georgian oasis of **Winckley Square** is where Preston's wealthiest merchant's used to live, and close by is the expansive **Avenham Park**, whose wooded slopes lead down to the River Ribble. The city dates from the 7th century, but in 1179 this medieval market town received an important charter giving Preston the right to hold a 'Guild Merchant' every 20 years: the next meeting is in 2012, and it demonstrates the influence held by local traders. The city's football team – Preston North End FC – were founder members of the Football League, and the home ground of Deepdale is where you'll find the **National Football Museum**, arguably the finest collection of football memorabilia in Britain.

Leave Preston south west
on the A59 and after 7
miles branch left onto the
B5247 down to Croston.
From here, take the A581
west to rejoin the A59 and
turn left for **Rufford Old
Hall**. From Rufford take the
B5246 west towards
Southport and follow signs
to **Martin Mere**. ❷

# 2 RUFFORD OLD HALL AND MARTIN MERE

Home to the Hesketh family for 400 years, **Rufford Old Hall** is one of the finest buildings in Lancashire, with its impressive timber-framed Tudor hall. By the middle of the 18th century, manor houses such as this were considered unsuited to domestic life, and the family moved to Rufford New Hall, a more comfortable mansion half a mile away. The spectacular Great Hall has an intricately carved 'moveable' wooden screen and a dramatic hammer-beam roof, and the house contains fine collections of 16th- and 17th-century oak furniture, arms, armour and tapestries. The grounds are laid out in late-Victorian style and feature a herbaceous border, orchard, topiary, sculptures and a woodland walk.

En route to Southport, it is worth stopping at the **Martin Mere**, a wildlife reserve where visitors can get really close to some exotic species of birds, as well as more familiar ones. The surrounding marshlands – the mere – are an important wintering ground for swans and geese, as well as some rarer species.

Take the B5246 west to join
the A565 to Marshside and
on to **Southport**.
→ • • • • • • • • • • ❸

⊕ *Follow the A565
south along the
④ coast to Formby.*

## 3 SOUTHPORT

The coastal flats of **Marshside** to the north of Southport have some of the best wet grassland in the north west of England. This area along the Ribble Estuary is recognised as one of Britain's premier birdwatching locations, and to date some 300 bird species have been recorded here. Southport, by contrast, is a bustling seaside town: mile-long Lord Street is the main thoroughfare, with its attractive Georgian and Victorian buildings often bright with floral displays in summer. On the coast there's **Pleasureland**, the 'entertainment' zone, full of the excitement and thrills associated with a seaside fun park. Southport beach is expansive and one from which you can admire the recently restored Southport pier.

## 4 FORMBY

The coast around Formby is the largest area of undeveloped dunes and coastal woodland in England, and home to rare species like the natterjack toad and sand lizard. These windswept inter-tidal flats, which extend from Southport to the Mersey Estuary, are renowned for their Neolithic human footprints and those of animals that grazed the salt marshes in this period. The small and unremarkable town of Formby has been cut off from the sea by the shifting sands of Formby Point, now a two-mile stretch of dunes with extensive views across Crosby Channel and Liverpool Bay to the distant hills of north Wales. The nearby **Formby Point Squirrel Reserve** is one of the best places in England to see the red squirrel. Elsewhere they have declined due to disease and competition from grey squirrels, but here you can get up close, and even get them to eat from your hand.

⊕ *Take the B5195 to reach the
A59. Turn left into Ormskirk,
and then take the A570
and follow this south to
join the M58. Follow the
motorway east until you
reach the M6. Go under the
motorway, onto a slip road
to Orrell then take the A577
⑤ east into Wigan.*

*Take the B5238 north east
via Aspull, turn left and
then right onto the B6226
for Horwich then left into
Lever Park. Follow the
unclassified road through
Lever Park to Rivington.*
→ • • • • • • • • • • • • ⑥

## 5 WIGAN

Once the butt of music hall jokes and the unflattering subject of George Orwell's *The Road to Wigan Pier*, modern Wigan is an energetic town with a toe in Greater Manchester but its heart very much in Lancashire. It has a passion for football and rugby league, but has become popular for the imaginative development at **Wigan Pier**, on the Leeds and Liverpool Canal. The key attraction is here is The Way We Were, an authentic recreation of life in the 1900s in Wigan and surrounding Lancashire.

*Clockwise from above:*
*Wigan Pier museum;*
*Southport pier;*
*Astley Hall*

## LANCASHIRE CHEESES

General de Gaulle complained about the difficulty of governing a nation with 246 varieties of cheese; British prime ministers have an even more daunting task – Britain has over 450 specialist cheeses, and ten of them (plus a whole range of variants) come from Lancashire: Butlers Trotter Hill Tasty, Dew-Lay Creamy, Garstang Blue, Crumbly, Garlic, Lancashire with Black Pepper, Smoked, Lancashire Black Bombs, award-winning Mrs Kirkham's, and Sykes Fell. With the possible exception of Mrs Kirkham's, these cheeses are found only in Lancashire.

## 6 RIVINGTON

The wooded area around the village of Rivington is one of the most popular walking and cycling areas in south Lancashire. The focal point is the man-made reservoirs, extending northwards to Anglezarke, now a magnet for local birdwatchers. There are two contrasting landscapes around Rivington: one is the wooded remains of industrialist Lord Leverhulme's estate, which led to the creation of the gardens at **Lever Park**; the other is the wild, windswept uplands of the **West Pennine Moors**, a vast area that extends eastwards to Rossendale. An easily visible landmark is the modest hump of **Rivington Pike** perched on the flank of Winter Hill; there are splendid views from here reaching as far as the mountains of north Wales.

## 7 CHORLEY

The birthplace of Henry Tate, the sugar magnate and founder of the Tate Gallery, Chorley has a modern, buzzing centre that revolves around its traditional market. On the edge of town is Astley Park, a huge area of invigorating parkland surrounding the fine Elizabethan **Astley Hall**, with its beautiful if not quite symmetrical façade of mullioned windows set in red brick. Today, the hall houses changing displays and collections, and stages interactive events. The nearby theme park of **Camelot** at Charnock Richard, with its emphasis on King Arthur and the Knights of the Round Table, is hugely popular. For those interested in more tangeable history, the complex holds an extensive indoor antiques and collectables market each Sunday, as well as regular antiques auctions.

*Continue on local roads north to Chorley. Camelot is a few miles west of Chorley.* 7

*Leave Chorley on the ring road to the A6. Turn right to join the M61 (northbound). Turn left onto the M65, and follow this to its end and then take the dual carriageway north back to Preston.* 1

## WITH MORE TIME

The **Isle of Man** (*left*) – seat of the world's longest continuous parliament, the Tynwald – is still as popular a destination with Lancashire folk as it was in the days when mining and mill families would take their holidays there. The island, accessible by air from Liverpool, Manchester and Blackpool, and by sea from Heysham and Liverpool, is renowned for its scenery. In addition to its famous TT motorbike races, the Isle of Man now holds an annual walking festival to which the island is perfectly suited.

63

# Cheshire, Staffordshire and Derbyshire

# The ancient city of Chester and the Cheshire Plain

There's a great deal to see in and around the historic city of Chester, where gardens, grand houses, industrial archaeology and ancient monuments provide a sightseeing bonanza. Beyond the acclaimed jewels in Cheshire's tourism crown sparkle many lesser-known gems. The quietly prosperous Wirral peninsula combines industrial heritage with the tranquil calm of an uncommercialised coastline.

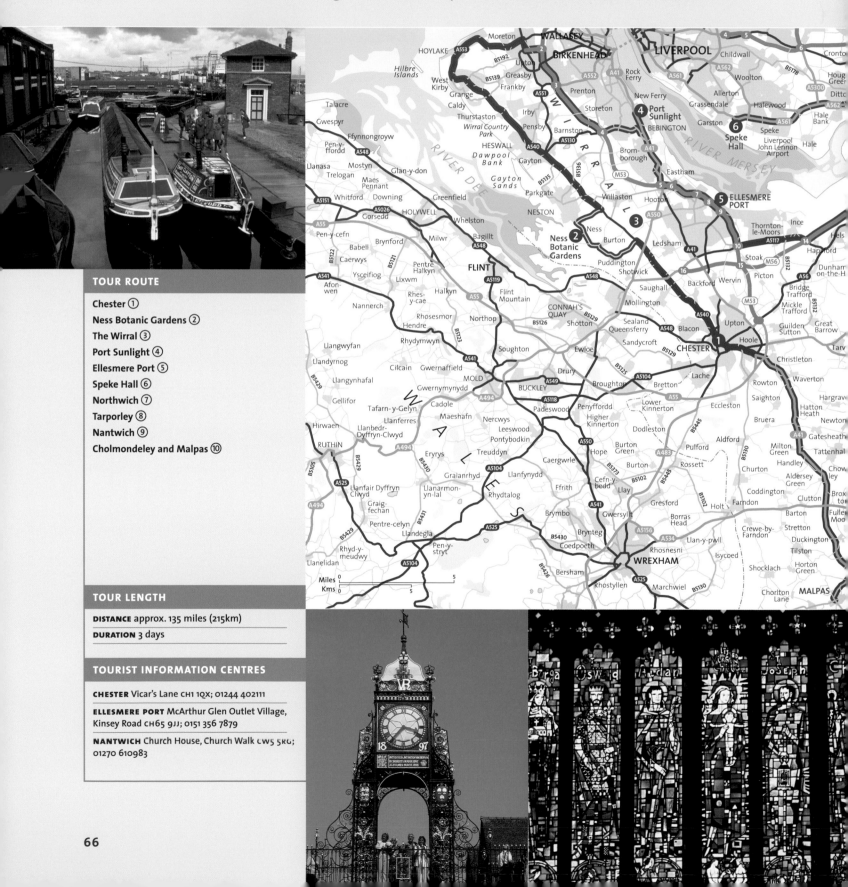

## TOUR ROUTE

Chester ①

Ness Botanic Gardens ②

The Wirral ③

Port Sunlight ④

Ellesmere Port ⑤

Speke Hall ⑥

Northwich ⑦

Tarporley ⑧

Nantwich ⑨

Cholmondeley and Malpas ⑩

## TOUR LENGTH

**DISTANCE** approx. 135 miles (215km)

**DURATION** 3 days

## TOURIST INFORMATION CENTRES

**CHESTER** Vicar's Lane CH1 1QX; 01244 402111

**ELLESMERE PORT** McArthur Glen Outlet Village, Kinsey Road CH65 9JJ; 0151 356 7879

**NANTWICH** Church House, Church Walk CW5 5RG; 01270 610983

66

Clockwise from far left:
Ellesmere Port; the Rows,
Chester; Ness Botanic
Gardens; stained glass,
Chester cathedral;
Chester city clock

# 1 CHESTER

Without a doubt, Chester is Cheshire's most rewarding
all-round visitor experience. Besides its Roman and
medieval heritage, it has excellent shops and
restaurants, a charming waterfront setting, Britain's
oldest racecourse and an award-winning **zoo**. Chester's
helpful visitor centre contains an exhibition on the
city's history, and a boat trip on the River Dee is not to
be missed. The Romans first set up camp here in AD79,
when it became home to the 20th legion. The old
Roman crossroads is still the hub of the city, its compass-
point streets radiating out to the intact **medieval walls**
that follow the lines of the original Roman fort. Chester
backed the royalist cause during the Civil War, and
suffered much damage at Parliamentarian hands.
During the 1700s, the walls were rebuilt as a fashionable walkway rather than as a defensive structure. The
admirable **Grosvenor Museum** and **Dewa Roman
Experience** give an entertainingly coherent picture of
Chester's past. History jumps out at you at every turn –
from the half-concealed Roman amphitheatre to the
hypocaust pillars visible on Bridge Street. Perhaps the
most striking architectural set piece is the handsome
half-timbered complex in the centre known as **The
Rows**. These double-decker shopping arcades are
mostly a late Victorian reconstruction of what existed
here during the 13th and 14th centuries. Notice the
ornate carving on **Bishop Lloyd's House** in Watergate
Street – a genuinely ancient building. The best features
in the **cathedral** are the carved misericords.

*Leave Chester north west on
the A540, following signs for
Hoylake and the Wirral. Turn
left after 8 miles for Ness
Botanic Gardens.* **2**

# 2 NESS BOTANIC GARDENS

Liverpudlian cotton magnate Arthur Bulley converted
most of his profits into these imaginative gardens at
the end of the 19th century. His great passion was
Asiatic flora (such as azaleas and magnolias), and he
financed several pioneering botanical expeditions to
China and the Himalayas in search of prized species.
These thrived in the mild, damp climate on acidic
sandstone soils above the Dee Estuary, where Bulley
could survey them in all their late spring glory from his
house at Mickwell Brow.

*Return to the A540
and continue north west
around The Wirral.*

**3**

⊥ You can by-pass
• Birkenhead's sprawl by
• taking the M53 from
• Wallasey as far as junction
• 4. Then follow signs for
④ **Port Sunlight**.

## 4 PORT SUNLIGHT

Depending on your political standpoint, you may regard this leafy model village near the old Sunlight soap factory as an enlightened attempt to provide an industrial workforce with agreeable living conditions, or a dastardly capitalist exercise in social engineering. Either way, it is worth a visit. Lord Leverhulme closely monitored the design and layout of these neat red-brick cottages with their trim gardens and airy tree-lined streets. More than 30 architects worked on the 900 or so houses here, which were built mostly during the 1890s. The majority of the houses are now privately owned, but Port Sunlight lives on in its present guise of Unilever, still churning out soap and washing powder by the truckload. The diamond at the heart of the village is the site of the **Lady Lever Art Gallery**, a memorial to Lord Leverhulme's wife. It contains a formidable art collection of mainly 18th- and 19th-century works, particularly pre-Raphaelite paintings and porcelain.

⊥ Take the A41 south and
: then the M53 south east to
⑤ **Ellesmere Port**.

## 3 THE WIRRAL

This wedge of land jutting between the Dee and Mersey estuaries is administratively part of Merseyside. Intensively industrialized along its north eastern shores, the Wirral's more rural, westerly stretches like to consider themselves an extension of Cheshire's favoured acres, and have suitably elevated property prices. **Parkgate**, now stranded some way inland by the silting Dee, retains its seaside charm, though its Regency esplanade overlooks tussocky salt marshes frequented by seabirds instead of open water. Views from the **Wirral Country Park** at Thurstaston stretch across the Dee marshes towards Wales. The tiny **Hilbre Islands** at the mouth of the river are renowned birdwatching sites and can be reached at low tide from West Kirby. A central ridge carries the Wirral Way footpath, while the little Victorian resort of **Hoylake** makes a welcome break from Birkenhead's refineries and chemical works. The urban district of Birkenhead is worth braving for the trio of **historic warships** berthed at the docks, which give a lively hands-on-deck insight into modern naval warfare. The frigate *HMS Plymouth* and the submarine *HMS Onyx* both saw active service during the Falklands War, while *HMS Bronington* was commanded by Prince Charles.

## 5 ELLESMERE PORT

The huge dock complex at the junction of the Shropshire Union and Manchester Ship canals is now occupied by a fascinating **Boat Museum**. Its floating contents are a world-class collection of inland and inshore craft. Narrow boats and coracles jostle for attention amid an atmospheric setting of quayside wharves and warehouses. Exhibitions reveal how multifarious cargoes were loaded from one vessel to another for inland or overseas transportation, and guided tours include a summer boat trip. Another popular attraction at Ellesmere Port is the **Blue Planet Aquarium**, which features a dramatic viewing tunnel allowing alarmingly close encounters with sharks and stingrays.

*From Ellesmere Port, take the M53 and then the A5117 to the M56 at junction 14. Follow the motorway north east to junction 12 and then follow signs for Liverpool across the Mersey. **Speke Hall** is next to John Lennon Airport off the A561.*

→ • • • • • • • • • • • ⑥

## CHESHIRE CHEESE

Cheshire is one of the oldest and most popular of English cheeses, first recorded in the Domesday Book. It was produced in commercial quantities from the early 17th century onwards, a by-product of the county's flourishing dairy industry. From 1739, the British Navy gave its seal of approval to Cheshire cheese and ordered it exclusively for the fleet. Today, some 6,500 tonnes of this firm but crumbly cheese are sold each year. It is made in three varieties: white (the natural colour), red (tinted with annatto, a natural dye, but essentially tasting much the same), and blue (pierced into veins like Stilton). The region's underground salt deposits impart a characteristically tangy flavour.

## 6 SPEKE HALL

Speke Hall takes you right back to the reign of Henry VIII. Despite the priest's hole and the thunderbox WC, Speke Hall's rich interior is mainly Victorian, with weighty oak panelling and William Morris wallpapers. The kitchen and servants' hall give a sense of life below stairs. From the attractive landscaped gardens, magnificent views stretch across the Mersey to the distant hills of Snowdonia.

*Clockwise from above: Lady Lever Art Gallery, Port Sunlight; Speke Hall; Hilbre Islands; old poster for Sunlight soap, made in Port Sunlight*

*Retrace your route back across the Mersey to Runcorn via the A562, and follow signs to **Northwich** south east along the A533.*

→ • • • • • • • • • • 7

*Clockwise from above left:*
St Mary's church, Nantwich;
sandstone trail, Bickerton
Hill, Malpas; Cholmondley
gardens; view from
Beeston Castle

# 7 NORTHWICH

Vast beds of rock salt lie beneath the red sandstone of
the Cheshire Plain, a source of great prosperity from
earliest times. Northwich is most closely associated
with the industry today which is explained, using
models and microscopes, at the **Salt Museum** on the
London Road. Subsidence caused by over-zealous salt
extraction affected Northwich town centre in the late
19th century and much was rebuilt in fashionable
mock-Tudor. One mile north of town is the **Anderton
Boat Lift**, the earliest one of its kind, constructed in
1875. An ingenious system of pulleys, pistons and
counterbalanced caissons shifts hefty canal boats 15m
(50ft) between the River Weaver and the Trent and
Mersey Canal using gravity and hydraulic pressure.
This recently restored Victorian engineering triumph is
once again fully operational, and visitors can
experience the lift in a special glass-topped boat.

*Take the A556 south west
from Northwich and turn
left onto the A49 to
Tarporley.*

→ • • • • • • • • • • • 8

## CHESHIRE'S SALT INDUSTRY

Cheshire's salt-beds lie only about 50m (150ft)
below the ground. They have been exploited
for more than 2,000 years – at least since
Roman times. Ground water dissolves the rock
salt into brine, which is extracted from bore-
holes and evaporated in shallow open pans.
Huge quantities of salt were transported from
Cheshire to the nearby Potteries *(see p80)* for
use in glazes for the ceramics industry, initially
by packhorse, later by canal or railway.
The Lion Salt Works at Northwich continued
in production until 1986, when the loss of
the Nigerian market during the civil war
forced its closure. It has since been restored
as a heritage centre.

## 8 TARPORLEY

While outsiders may consider this desirable little place a mere village, locals insist it is a proper town, complete with bank, post office and an enviable array of speciality shops (one sells enticing home-made chocolate). The historic high street consists of handsome brickwork, a notable landmark being the venerable Swan Hotel, whose oldest sections date back to the 16th century. A short distance south of Tarporley are the evocative 13th-century ruins of **Beeston Castle,** looming above an isolated sandstone crag in a woodland setting. It was originally part of a defensive chain on the Welsh marches, and incorporated all the latest technology gleaned from the Earl of Chester's experience in the Crusades.

## 9 NANTWICH

This is one of the most attractive towns on the Cheshire Plain. The salt industry in Nantwich declined long ago and much of its period character remains in a fine collection of buildings with typical black-and-white timbering. Some were built after a disastrous fire in 1583, when Elizabeth I donated £1,000 towards the reconstruction. Clocks, shoes and cheese kept Nantwich afloat after the demise of the salt trade, as recorded in the local **museum**. Today's prosperous-looking shops sell antiques and other tourist-oriented wares. Nantwich **marina** on the Shropshire Union Canal is a lively pleasure-boating centre in summer. In July, Nantwich holds the world's largest Cheese Show, exhibiting plenty of home-grown Cheshire *(see p71)*. The 14th-century **Church of St Mary** is worth investigating for its decorative ribs on the stone chancel roof, drawing the eye heavenwards, while the wooden choir stalls have splendidly carved misericords featuring quirky scenes. At Hack Green on the south side of town, watch for signs off the A530 to the **Hack Green Secret Nuclear Bunker**. This unusual visitor attraction, humdrum from outside, discloses the contingency plans drawn up during the Cold War by civil servants and military commanders appointed to think the unthinkable.

## 10 CHOLMONDELEY AND MALPAS

The ornamental gardens around the elegant **castle** belonging to the Marquess of Chomondeley make an enjoyable wander. Woodland and lakeside walks take you past an aviary and an assortment of domesticated rare breeds, including llamas and pygmy goats. Nearby **Malpas** is a pretty village with castle ruins and an ancient hilltop church with an extraordinary oak-panelled ceiling gleaming with a series of gilded bosses and angels. To the north, **Bickerton Hill** is the most extensive area of lowland heath in Cheshire, on a sandstone ridge largely owned by the National Trust. It is notable for rare insects and reptiles, including adders, so watch where you put your feet if you take this popular walk.

*Take the A51 south east direct to **Nantwich**.* 9

*Take the A534 westwards, take the A49 south and then unclassified roads to **Cholmondeley Castle** and **Malpas**.* 10

*Take the A41 north back to **Chester**.*
1

## WITH MORE TIME

The Stone road south east from Nantwich (A51) passes several interesting gardens. Greenfingered visitors will be in their element at **Bridgmere Garden World** *(left)*, but the ornamental gardens and glasshouses can be enjoyed by the least horticulturally-minded of visitors. Four miles further on, the **Dorothy Clive Garden** is a beautifully landscaped plantsman's garden created by Colonel Harry Clive in memory of his wife. Stunning views complement its gloriously varied collections of roses and rhododendrons.

# Cheshire's grand houses

Few counties can match the dense concentration of des-res housing as the county of Cheshire. For centuries, the landed gentry built stately homes in this rich farmland region, while today's successful captains of industry from Manchester and Merseyside still choose to settle in surroundings rather different from those that generate their wealth. The industrial heritage of Quarry Bank Mill and the silk town of Macclesfield show where some of this wealth originated, while Jodrell Bank Observatory ponders questions well beyond the range of human hearing.

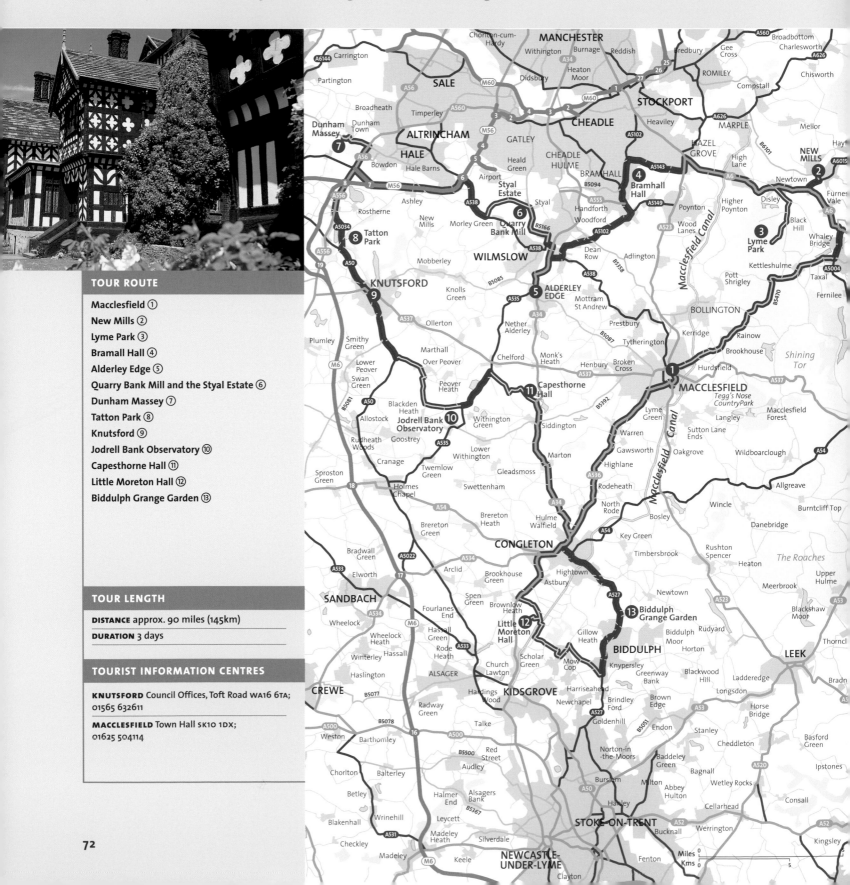

## TOUR ROUTE

Macclesfield ①
New Mills ②
Lyme Park ③
Bramall Hall ④
Alderley Edge ⑤
Quarry Bank Mill and the Styal Estate ⑥
Dunham Massey ⑦
Tatton Park ⑧
Knutsford ⑨
Jodrell Bank Observatory ⑩
Capesthorne Hall ⑪
Little Moreton Hall ⑫
Biddulph Grange Garden ⑬

## TOUR LENGTH

**DISTANCE** approx. 90 miles (145km)

**DURATION** 3 days

## TOURIST INFORMATION CENTRES

**KNUTSFORD** Council Offices, Toft Road WA16 6TA; 01565 632611

**MACCLESFIELD** Town Hall SK10 1DX; 01625 504114

*Clockwise from far left:*
Bramall Hall; Biddulph
Grange; Alderley Edge; Little
Moreton Hall; Tatton Park

# 1 MACCLESFIELD

There is a reason that the route from Macclesfield to Manchester is known as the Silk Road, and members of its football team as the Silk Men. For more than 200 years from the 18th century, this was Britain's leading centre of silk production. It specialised in high-quality handwoven textiles and silk buttons. The **Silk Museum** at the heritage centre recounts the history of the industry, and weavers' cottages with large garret windows still remain in Paradise Street. **Paradise Mill** contains some of the old Jacquard looms and spinning machines that are still in working order.

The affluent suburbs and villages of this large borough, handily situated for the London to Manchester transport routes, contain some beautiful houses. The pretty streamside village of **Prestbury** is especially popular and claims to have more millionaires per mile than any other village in England. **Tegg's Nose Country Park** to the south east of Macclesfield offers extensive views across the Cheshire Plain. Long-distance footpaths head into the Macclesfield Forest and on to the open moors from here.

*Take the B5470 north east from Macclesfield. Turn left onto the A5004 through Whaley Bridge, and join the A6 north west as far as New Mills.* 2

# 2 NEW MILLS

This rewarding canal-side mill town has an interesting **heritage centre** containing exhibits on the valley's historic water mills and textile industry. The recently opened **Millennium Walkway** in the Torrs Gorge Country Park is an exhilarating way to experience the River Goyt, swirling through a rocky ravine 6m (20ft) below. The elegant stainless steel structure extends for 160m (175yds) along the cliff face; only a handrail separates brave walkers from the roaring waters.

*Keep on the A6 west, turning left at Disley for Lyme Park.*
3

*Clockwise from above:*
Lyme Park; Alderley Edge;
Dunham Massey

## 3 LYME PARK

If this place looks oddly familiar, you may have seen its
backdrop role as Mr Darcy's covetable property
'Pemberley' in the BBC's dramatisation of Jane Austen's
*Pride and Prejudice*. Home of the Legh family before it
passed into the care of the National Trust, this
remodelled Tudor house is regarded as one of the
finest English examples of the Palladian style. The
Venetian architect Giacomo Leoni orchestrated its
transformation in 1725. Some Elizabethan interiors
survive, contrasting with the later style of Baroque
ceilings, exquisite limewood carvings by Grinling
Gibbons and a fine collection of clocks. The surrounding
formal gardens and medieval deer park are as gracious
as the house, being planted with roses, herbaceous
borders and rare specimen trees. A curious gibbet-like
structure called The Cage (an 18th-century hunting
tower) was occasionally used to imprison poachers.

*Return to the A6 and
continue westwards as far
as Hazel Grove. Turn south
on the A523, taking the first
turning on your right on
the A5143, which will bring*
④ *you to **Bramall Hall**.*

## 4 BRAMALL HALL

One of the finest houses in the area, Bramall Hall is a
splendid timber-framed medieval building set in
extensive parkland originally designed by 'Capability'
Brown. The house was originally built in about 1350 and
was the home of the Davenport family for nearly 500
years. It was sympathetically renovated in the 19th
century, but some rare Elizabethan wall-paintings still
survive. Confusingly, the name of the house is spelt
differently from the local village, which is Bramhall.

*Take the A5102 south and
west to join the A34,
following signs for
**Alderley Edge**.*

→ • • • • • • • • • • • ⑤

## THE SILK INDUSTRY

In 1743, Charles Roe built the first water-powered
silk loom in Macclesfield, and a new industry
was launched. The textile trade took a leap
forward when the French engineer Jacquard
developed his revolutionary weaving technique
in the early 1800s. It could take days to thread
and load the Jacquard looms, but once set up,
they rattled away non-stop and production
surged. The Napoleonic Wars interrupted the
supply of French silk, which further boosted
Macclesfield's economy. But in the 20th century,
after a wartime boom in parachute silk, the
industry declined. Ironically, it was the Chinese,
who first unlocked the secrets of the silkworm
thousands of years ago, who put paid to the
English silk industry by flooding the market with
cheap mass-produced artificial fibres. Today, only
silk ties and ribbons are made in Macclesfield.

## 5 ALDERLEY EDGE

Views extend to the Peak District and the Pennines from this sandstone escarpment above the Cheshire Plain. Designated a Site of Special Scientific Interest (SSSI) for its unusual geology and wildlife, Alderley Edge is a place of great natural beauty. Abandoned mine-workings here (occasionally open for escorted potholing expeditions), date back to Roman times or even earlier, when deposits of lead, copper and cobalt were exploited and the summit beacon was used when the Spanish Armada was sighted in 1588. An enjoyable walk through the woods leads to **Hare Hill**, a National Trust garden, best visited in early summer. Nether Alderley's 15th-century **watermill** displays an impressive cat's cradle of structural timbers beneath a sloping stone roof.

## 6 QUARRY BANK MILL AND THE STYAL ESTATE

In the mid-19th century, the Greg cotton empire was one of the most successful in Britain. In 1956, the family donated their water-powered Georgian cotton mill to the National Trust, along with the workers' village and woodland estate of Styal. Today it forms an authentic industrial heritage attraction. Quarry Bank Mill is still operational, producing souvenir quantities of cotton calico sold in the shop. The huge 50-tonne waterwheel driven by the River Bollin measures 7m (24ft) in diameter and is the most powerful in Europe. The **Apprentice House** reveals the grim and blighted lives of the pauper children who snatched a few hours sleep on straw-filled mattresses before their long days at the mill. The main mill building contains a series of multimedia interpretative 'galleries' showing many aspects of cotton processing. The award-winning **Power Gallery** shows the dazzling ingenuity of those early textile engineers who invented ever more efficient ways of transforming raw cotton fibres into finished cloth. All the processes of spinning and weaving, bleaching and dyeing are demonstrated in reconstruction displays.

## 7 DUNHAM MASSEY

The elegantly proportioned Dunham Massey is surrounded by an ornamental lake. The mellow brickwork and low-slung, shallow roofline are classic early Georgian, but the original house was built during the reign of Elizabeth I on the site of a Norman motte and-bailey castle. An early 20th-century refurbishment bequeathed a sumptuous Edwardian interior: its treasures include fine walnut furniture and Huguenot silver, along with a series of family portraits and a grand state bed. The handsome grounds consist of plantsman's gardens and a deer park containing a Jacobean mill restored to working order.

*Retrace your route north on the A34, turning off near Wilmslow on the B5166 north for **Quarry Bank Mill**.* ⑥

*Continue through the Styal Estate back to the A538 and turn right towards Hale and Altrincham. Join the M56 west at junction 6 and continue to the next exit, taking the A556 and signs for **Dunham Massey**.* ⑦

*Return to the A56 and head south, forking left about one mile beyond the M56 on to the A5034. Within another mile or so, you will see the entrance to **Tatton Park** on your left.* ⑧

*Clockwise from above:*
Japanese Garden, Tatton
Park; Jodrell Bank
Observatory;
Little Moreton Hall

## 8 TATTON PARK

This great estate belonged to the Egerton family for 360 years until it was passed to the National Trust in 1958. The stone-built neoclassical Wyatt mansion makes a splendid showcase for collections of paintings, porcelain and glass, as well as some exquisite Gillow furnishings (*see p58*). The house contains more than 200 specially commissioned pieces designed by the famous Lancaster cabinet-making firm, and represents the most important single collection of its work anywhere in Britain. The 405ha grounds (1,000 acres) are just as impressive, ranging from Victorian gardens (don't miss the fernery, pinetum and splendid glass-houses) to parkland where red deer roam. Restored to their original Edwardian interpretation, the Japanese gardens are especially interesting. **Home Farm** in Tatton Dale was once the heart of the estate, feeding the entire Egerton household and its staff. Rare animal breeds, cooking demonstrations and old-fashioned range and original tools and implements can be seen.

*About 1 mile further south on the A50 from Tatton is Knutsford.*

⑨

## 9 KNUTSFORD

There is a definite period costume feel about the cottages along Knutsford's main street, and you can see how they inspired Mrs Gaskell's 19th-century novel *Cranford*. But a perceptive onlooker may notice a few bizarre notes among the classic Georgian and Victorian shopfronts. Enthused by his Grand Tour in Mediterranean climes, Manchester glove magnate Richard Watt commissioned several eccentric Italianate buildings that defy classification: for instance, a campanile tower is incorporated into what is now the Belle Epoque restaurant. A **heritage centre** in a former smithy contains an exhibition about Knutsford. Just south of town, the charming village of **Lower Peover** is worth a detour and has a rare 14th-century black-and-white church. Nearby, **Peover Hall** is a brick-built house dating from 1585 with a palatial Stuart stable block.

*Follow the A50 south and take signs along minor roads south east to Jodrell Bank Observatory.*

↪ • • • • • • • • • • • • ⑩

## 10 JODRELL BANK OBESERVATORY

Amid historic homes, futuristic structures loom unexpectedly from the quiet Cheshire countryside: the giant Lovell Radio Telescope and a network of smaller ones aim their steel ears at faint radio waves from far corners of the universe. Visitors can get a closer view of the 76-m dish (248-ft) rotating on its Meccano stilts from the observatory pathway beneath. The visitor centre expounds on the mysterious extra-terrestrial studies carried out here by the School of Astronomy and Physics at Manchester University on quasars and pulsars and cosmic microwave background radiation. A simulated spacecraft ride with polarized glasses is part of the 3-D theatre experience. The surrounding arboretum includes thousands of species of trees, interspersed with nature trails and picnic areas.

## 11 CAPESTHORNE HALL

The Bromley-Davenports have lived on this estate since Domesday times, but the house was rebuilt after a disastrous fire in 1861. The former redbrick hall was flamboyantly remodelled by the Victorian architect Anthony Salvin in turreted Gothic. Among the paintings inside, note Lowry's version of the house, and many classical antiquities. The Georgian chapel is also worth a look for its box pews and double-decker pulpit. The 45 ha grounds (100 acres) contain an ice house.

## 12 LITTLE MORETON HALL

One of the most familiar and best-loved of all Cheshire houses, this is a glorious example of the local 'magpie' style of ornate half-timbering. Building work began on the manor house in the late 1400s and continued well into the next century. After that, its Royalist owners ran out of money for any further improvements. Somehow or other, this crazy mishmash of drunken angles and jettied, bulging walls is still standing, rambling round inner courtyards and lawns. The moat and bridgehouse are decorative rather than defensive. Don't miss the wall paintings, the knot garden and the fully fitted dog kennel. A mile or two south from the hall, right on the Staffordshire border, is a strange abrupt hill crowned by an 18th-century folly named **Mow Cop**.

## 13 BIDDULPH GRANGE GARDEN

These strange Victorian gardens, restored by the National Trust, are full of surprises – stone sphinxes, secret tunnels, a rainbow of rhododendrons. They were designed in the mid-19th century by James Bateman, a keen plant collector, to house specimens from all over the world in appropriate settings. Various sections of the gardens have been made into 'outdoor rooms', each reflecting a different geographical zone. Fiery maples and bamboos grow in the tranquil Chinese garden with its jaunty scarlet bridge, while clipped yew pyramids and obelisks grace the Egyptian Court. Flowering periods last virtually all year. On the return road to Macclesfield you will pass **Gawsworth Hall**, another fine half-timbered property still in private hands. It contains lovely pre-Raphaelite stained glass and a noteworthy collection of needlework. Open-air theatre performances take place here in summer.

*Take local roads to the A535 and follow this north. Turn right along local roads to* ***Capesthorne Hall.*** ⑪

*From here head for the A34, and turn south on this road through Congleton to* ***Little Moreton Hall.*** ⑫

*Follow signs cross country south to Mow Cop and then join the A527 north. Take signs to the right to* ***Biddulph Grange.*** ⑬

*Keep north on the A527 to Congleton, and then return to* ***Macclesfield*** *on the A536.*

## WITH MORE TIME

For 26 miles between Kidsgrove and Marple, **the Macclesfield Canal** *(left)* traverses the attractive countryside on the western fringes of the Peak District. It links the Trent and Mersey Canal in the Potteries with the Peak Forest Canal near Stockport. First opened in 1831, the canal was designed by Thomas Telford and provided a vital means of transporting raw materials to the textile mills, many of which specialised in the manufacture of silk. Today, the canal is a scenic backwater used by pleasure craft and towpath walkers.

# Lichfield and the historic Potteries

Two giant conurbations catch the eye on a map of the county of Staffordshire: Stoke-on-Trent (known as the Potteries) and Wolverhampton (also called the Black Country). The fringes of these built-up areas seem scarcely obvious choices for a scenic drive, but luckily it is only a short step to some of the prettiest scenery imaginable. The ancient hunting woods and heaths of Cannock Chase or The National Forest, the verdant valleys of the Churnet, Dove and Dane, and the wild and dramatic gritstone edges of the Staffordshire moorlands provide all the ingredients for a grand tour.

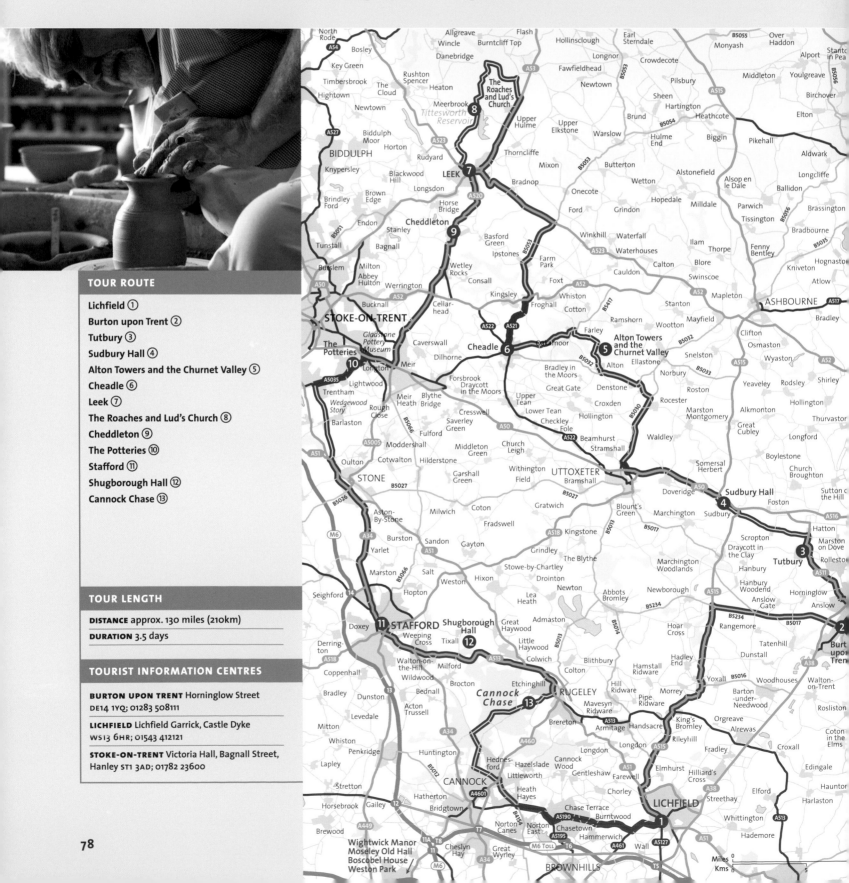

### TOUR ROUTE

Lichfield ①
Burton upon Trent ②
Tutbury ③
Sudbury Hall ④
Alton Towers and the Churnet Valley ⑤
Cheadle ⑥
Leek ⑦
The Roaches and Lud's Church ⑧
Cheddleton ⑨
The Potteries ⑩
Stafford ⑪
Shugborough Hall ⑫
Cannock Chase ⑬

### TOUR LENGTH

**DISTANCE** approx. 130 miles (210km)
**DURATION** 3.5 days

### TOURIST INFORMATION CENTRES

**BURTON UPON TRENT** Horninglow Street
DE14 1YQ; 01283 508111

**LICHFIELD** Lichfield Garrick, Castle Dyke
WS13 6HR; 01543 412121

**STOKE-ON-TRENT** Victoria Hall, Bagnall Street,
Hanley ST1 3AD; 01782 23600

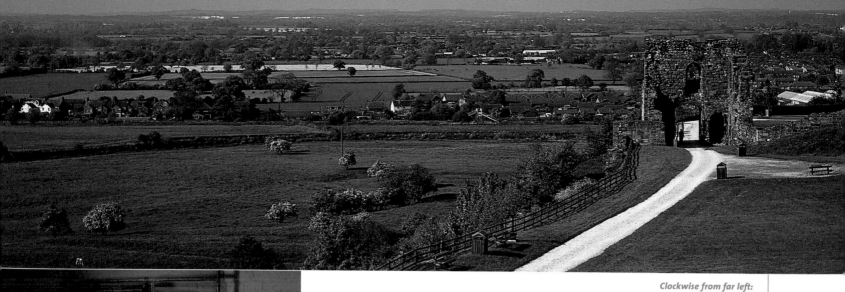

*Clockwise from far left:*
Wedgwood Centre; view
of Tutbury; Cannock
Chase; Johnson
memorabilia, Lichfield

## 1 LICHFIELD

A trio of stately spires graces the skyline of this historic market town. The 'three ladies' mark the site of Lichfield's ancient **cathedral**, dedicated to St Chad, a Saxon bishop of Mercia. The 13th-century sandstone building took a terrible hammering from the Parliamentarians during the Civil War, but was restored to its former glory, lavishly embellished by Gilbert Scott in the 19th century. Its oldest treasure is on display in the Chapter House – a gorgeously illuminated manuscript known as the **Lichfield Gospels,** completed in AD730. Samuel Johnson is Lichfield's celebrity resident: the Age of Enlightenment's most illustrious man of letters was born to a local bookseller in 1709. The **Samuel Johnson Birthplace Museum** occupies the house on Breadmarket Street where he spent his first 25 years before setting off with his actor friend David Garrick to seek fame and fortune in London. Another Lichfield luminary was Erasmus Darwin, grandfather of the evolutionist and an equally brilliant scientist and scholar. The **Erasmus Darwin Museum** traces his life and inventions, and stands near the exquisite Vicar's Close, a medieval square adjoining Darwin's herb garden. The route to Burton upon Trent takes you through the Norman hunting ground known as **Needwood Chase**, part of a woodland patchwork spreading into three counties and designated as The National Forest.

*From Lichfield, take the A515
north, turning right after 10
miles on to the B5234 to
Burton upon Trent*. ②

## 2 BURTON UPON TRENT

Brewing has been the economic mainstay of this riverside town since the 18th century. The pure Trent Valley water, filtered through gypsum beds, was ideal for beer-making, and easy transportation along the Trent and Mersey Canal boosted the industry's success. At one time there were some 30 local breweries, and an alehouse on every other corner. Many of Burton's Victorian civic landmarks were funded by the hugely wealthy Bass family. Today, Bass is in foreign hands, and the monumental smokestack of the **Coors Visitor Centre** (formerly the Bass Museum) dominates the urban horizon. A lively brewery tour relates the history of the industry, assisted by the famous Bass shire-horses.

*Leave Burton on
the A511 north and follow
signs to Tutbury.*

## 3 TUTBURY

The gap-toothed **castle** that commands a wooded ridge overlooking the Dove Valley was where Mary Queen of Scots ached and shivered in damp, draughty quarters during three separate spells of imprisonment. Despite the 60 attendants who cared for her, Mary always hated 'mouldy Tutbury', and was little impressed by grandstand views of the serpentine river looping through its green floodplain. Records indicate this strategic site has been fortified for some 5,000 years, and many crowned heads have visited the castle since medieval times when John of Gaunt lived here. Oliver Cromwell accelerated its disintegration, but subsequent restoration has left plenty to see. Look out for the Tudor privy garden, and the secret staircase to the Great Hall. Near the castle entrance stands Tutbury's fine priory **church**, whose west door is carved with multiple tiers of strange beak-headed creatures in typical Norman style. Tutbury's high street has some handsome architecture; while around town factory showrooms display the famous local lead crystal.

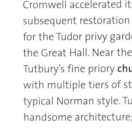

Take minor roads west to Scropton and continue to Sudbury. On the far side of the village is **Sudbury Hall.**

## 4 SUDBURY HALL

This late 17th-century property is one of the finest examples of the Stuart style. Charles II was a notably extravagant monarch, and the richness of Sudbury indicates that the Vernon family followed the royal example, sparing no expense during its construction. Outstanding features include a marvellous carved staircase and superb woodcarvings by Grinling Gibbons. The Victorian servants' wing houses a **Museum of Childhood** in which the pampered lifestyles of privileged children are contrasted with the unfortunate lot of those from poorer backgrounds in times gone by. Historic toys and games are also on display, along with a re-created Victorian schoolroom. Modern children can try their skill at a chimney climb.

Follow the A50 west as far as Uttoxeter, then head north on the B5030 for 3 miles. At Rocester, turn left on the B5032 for another 3 miles until you reach Alton, then turn right on to a minor road following signs for **Alton Towers.**

## 5 ALTON TOWERS AND THE CHURNET VALLEY

**Alton Towers** is by far the most popular attraction in Staffordshire; in fact, it is the UK's most-visited theme park. Screams from more than 100 gravity-defying thrill-rides echo for miles around, but for all its commercialisation, Alton Towers is more than a mere white-knuckle experience. A spectacular setting – the huge grounds of a ruined neogothic mansion containing lakes and gardens – is best viewed from a gentle cable-car ride that even the least adrenaline-hooked visitor can enjoy. Not far from Alton Towers's gates, the delightful **Churnet Valley** is a once-industrialised dell of woods and ponds. The best way to appreciate it is to walk along the Staffordshire Way through Dimmings Dale, past an old smelting mill and a cafe called the Ramblers Retreat. Near Oakamoor is a nature reserve called **Hawksmoor** with wooded trails along the banks of the Churnet.

Follow minor roads west to Farley then take the B5417 west through Oakamoor to **Cheadle.**

*Clockwise from top left: portrait of Mary Queen of Scots; Tutbury Castle; Alton Towers; The Roaches*

## 6 CHEADLE

The centre of Cheadle has some pleasing timbered buildings, but the unexpected glory of this small market town is the Roman Catholic **Church of St Giles**, designed by Augustus Pugin for the Earl of Shrewsbury in 1846. The crocketed spire soars from a forest of pinnacles. Beyond the west doors decked with golden lions glows a startling wonderland of brilliant neogothic decoration covering every square centimetre of the interior. The adjacent cloisters and school, also by Pugin, are in a similar style. Between Cheadle and Leek, the road offers grand panoramas over the lonely moors of the south western Peak District.

## 7 LEEK

As with other towns in this area, Leek's prosperity sprang from the silk trade. In the 19th century it specialised in the production of glossy black dyes used in Victorian mourning wear. Millshops in the town still sell clothing, but Leek has now become a popular touring base for visiting the Staffordshire moorlands to the north and the Potteries (*see p84*). James Brindley began his career here as a millwright before turning his genius to canals. The restored **Brindley Mill** once again grinds corn, and it contains a small museum to the great engineer. Both of Leek's churches have lovely Arts and Crafts stained glass.

## 8 THE ROACHES AND LUD'S CHURCH

A dramatic outcrop of weirdly shaped rocks, The Roaches is one of Staffordshire's most famous natural landmarks. A high ridge of gritstone, it is much revered by climbers, and the name is said to be a corruption of an old French word meaning 'rocks'. It forms an impressive edge to the south western Pennines, and provides splendid panoramas of the surrounding moorland. North west of the Roaches, you can take a fine walk from the youth hostel at Gradbach to a small but spectacular rocky gorge known as **Lud's Church**. During the 14th century it was used as a hiding place by religious dissenters called the Lollards. Ferns and mosses cloak the sheer walls of the chasm, reflecting an eerie green light.

## 9 CHEDDLETON

**Cheddleton Flint Mill** was used for grinding flints for the bone china works of the nearby Potteries. Cheddleton is the starting point for the **Churnet Valley Railway**, a nostalgia ride on restored steam locomotives following the Caldon Canal as far as Froghall. You can also follow the towpath from Cheddleton, past disused copper works and the wharfs where limestone from the quarries at Cauldon Lowe was loaded on to barges.

*Take the A521 to Froghall, cross the A52 and then turn left on the B5053 until you reach the A523. Turn left, following signs for Leek.* **7**

*Head north east from Leek on the A53. Take the fourth turning on your left and double back on minor roads past The Roaches and Lud's Church.* **8**

*Continue south past Tittesworth Reservoir back to Leek, then take the A520 south to Cheddleton.* **9**

*Keep on the A520 south until the crossroads at Meir and turn right towards Longton, following signs for the Gladstone Pottery Museum. Then take the A5035 west to Trentham and turn off for Barlaston to the Wedgwood Story.* **10**

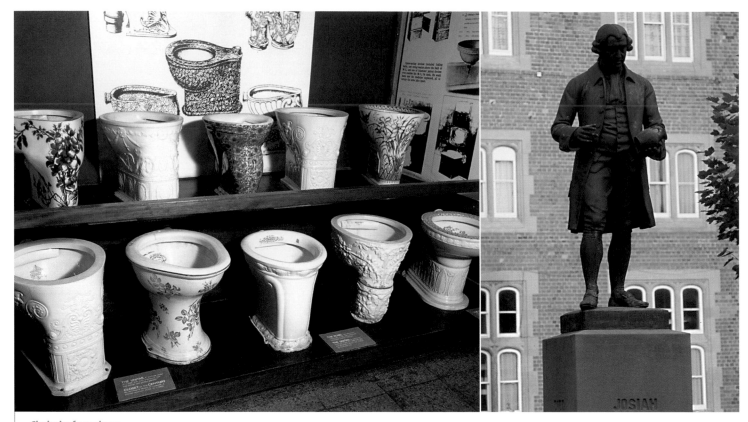

*Clockwise from above:*
Flushed with Pride section of the Gladstone Pottery Museum; statue of Josiah Wedgwood, Stoke-on-Trent; Shugborough Hall gardens

# 10 THE POTTERIES

For more than 250 years, the Potteries were the world's leading centre of ceramics manufacture. Production has declined in recent decades, and the distinctive old bottle ovens have been replaced by more environmentally-friendly modern kilns since the Clean Air Act of 1956, but firms such as Wedgwood, Doulton and Spode are still the area's biggest employers. The sprawling urban district around Stoke-on-Trent officially consists of six separate towns – Tunstall, Burslem, Stoke, Hanley, Fenton and Longton. Several excellent attractions are connected with the local industry (*see box*).

Longton's **Gladstone Pottery Museum** is a Victorian complex complete with bottle ovens and workshops arranged around cobbled courtyards. Lively demonstrations and interactive exhibitions reveal the history of the industry. The 'Flushed With Pride' section on sanitation through the ages attracts plenty of attention (beautifully decorated bathroom furnishings were a local speciality); there is also a historic tile gallery and a re-creation of a doctor's surgery. The **Wedgwood Visitor Centre** is arguably Britain's best-known pottery firm: a self-guided audio tour takes you through the entire production process, and recounts the life and legacy of the original Josiah Wedgwood, whose instantly recognizable jasperware is perhaps the most timeless of all Stoke's pottery. If you have an appetite for yet more examples of china, take a look at Hanley's wonderful **Potteries Museum and Art Gallery**. It has a world-class historical collection of ceramics, plus an original Spitfire designed by local resident R J Mitchell.

*Take the A34 and head southwards via Stone to **Stafford**.*

→ • • • • • • • • • • • ⑪

## STAFFORDSHIRE CERAMICS

Few households do not possess at least one piece of china or porcelain that was manufactured in the Staffordshire Potteries. Abundant local resources of clay, coal and water provided the essentials of the trade, along with lead, salt and iron to make the glazes. The arrival of the Trent and Mersey Canal in the late 18th century boosted the industry, but it was the perseverance and experimental genius of men such as Wedgwood and Spode that ensured success.

From primitive earthenware, production was modified to create slipware, creamware and then stoneware. Eventually the supremely sophisticated bone china was manufactured by adding ground animal bone and powdered flint to kaolin to make it translucent and intensely hard. Wedgwood's famous jasperware, with its classical cameo designs, is a form of unglazed stoneware tinted with metallic oxides.

## STAFFORDSHIRE OATCAKES

Known variously as a 'Tunstall tortilla' or a 'Potteries poppadom', this oatmeal speciality is allegedly a variant on the flatbread of India that became familiar to the British in colonial times. Staffordshire oatcakes look very much like pancakes, though their texture is sometimes unkindly likened to a wet facecloth. Filled with any sweet or savoury filling, they make a quick and tasty snack, and miners used to pop them in their pockets for lunch. They're easy to make on a griddle, using a mix of flour, oatmeal and yeast made into a batter with warm water and milk, but you can also buy them ready-made locally. Most local bakers have their own secret recipes, and oatcakes can be found in most corner shops and bakeries in the area.

## 11 STAFFORD

This county town feels almost village like in comparison with its huge neighbour Stoke-on-Trent. On central Greengate Street stands the **Ancient High House**, claimed to be the tallest timber-framed townhouse in England, built in 1595. It contains period rooms with displays on the history of the building. The **Shire Hall Gallery** is the former county hall and crown court, and **Stafford Castle** on the south west side of town is a ruined Norman fortress rebuilt in Gothic Revival style and then abandoned again. It contains a visitor centre and is used for special events. A few miles north west of Stafford, Shallowford is home to **Izaak Walton's Cottage,** the birthplace of the author of *The Compleat Angler*. His family house, an idyllic 16th-century thatched cottage in period gardens, contains displays on Britain's best-known angler and his lifelong passion.

## 12 SHUGBOROUGH HALL

This 18th-century mansion is the country seat of the Earls of Lichfield, and was the home of the glamorous socialite photographer Patrick Lichfield, the fifth Earl. An exhibition of the late earl's work can be seen in the house. The estate dates from 1693 and contains a working farm run on Georgian lines with rare breeds and a restored cornmill. The grounds are famed for their romantic neoclassical monuments in the Greek Revival style designed by James 'Athenian' Stuart, including a triumphal arch and a Doric temple. The regal state rooms are richly decked with paintings, silver, ceramics and French-style furnishings. On a humbler note, a museum of rural life in the stable block has exhibitions on life 'below stairs'.

*Take the A513 east from Stafford towards Rugeley, and follow signs to* **Shugborough Hall**. ⑫

*Return to the A513 and head east towards Rugeley. Then take local roads south west across* **Cannock Chase**. ⑬

## 13 CANNOCK CHASE

Shugborough lies within the confines of the ancient hunting forest known as Cannock Chase. A mix of planted woodland, rolling heath and many springs and streams, it provides a popular breathing space for the heavily industrialized A5 corridor north of the Black Country. On quiet days, when not too many people are about, you may spot fallow deer, or hear nightjars chirring in the bracken on summer evenings. A **museum** at Hednesford, in the training pit of an old colliery, traces the wildlife and history of the area, including its mining activities.

*Return to* **Lichfield** *along the A5190 from Hednesford.*
⬅ • • • • • • • • • • • ①

## WITH MORE TIME

The north-western outskirts of Wolverhampton contain four grand properties worth visiting. **Wightwick Manor** is a Victorian house in the Arts and Crafts style, with William Morris interiors and lots of pre-Raphaelite paintings and stained glass windows. **Moseley Old Hall** and **Boscobel House** are both associated with Charles II, who hid here after the Battle of Worcester. **Weston Park** *(left)* is a 17th-century house with an elegant and richly decorated interior, and grounds landscaped by 'Capability' Brown.

83

# Chatsworth and the picturesque Derbyshire Dales

This tour explores the Peak District's southern limestone region, known as the Low or White Peak. Much of it seems very rural, accessible only via a maze of tiny lanes or walking trails along disused railway lines. But it also includes some of the national park's most popular destinations, such as Chatsworth, the grand home of the earls and dukes of Devonshire, and the classic limestone valley of Dovedale.

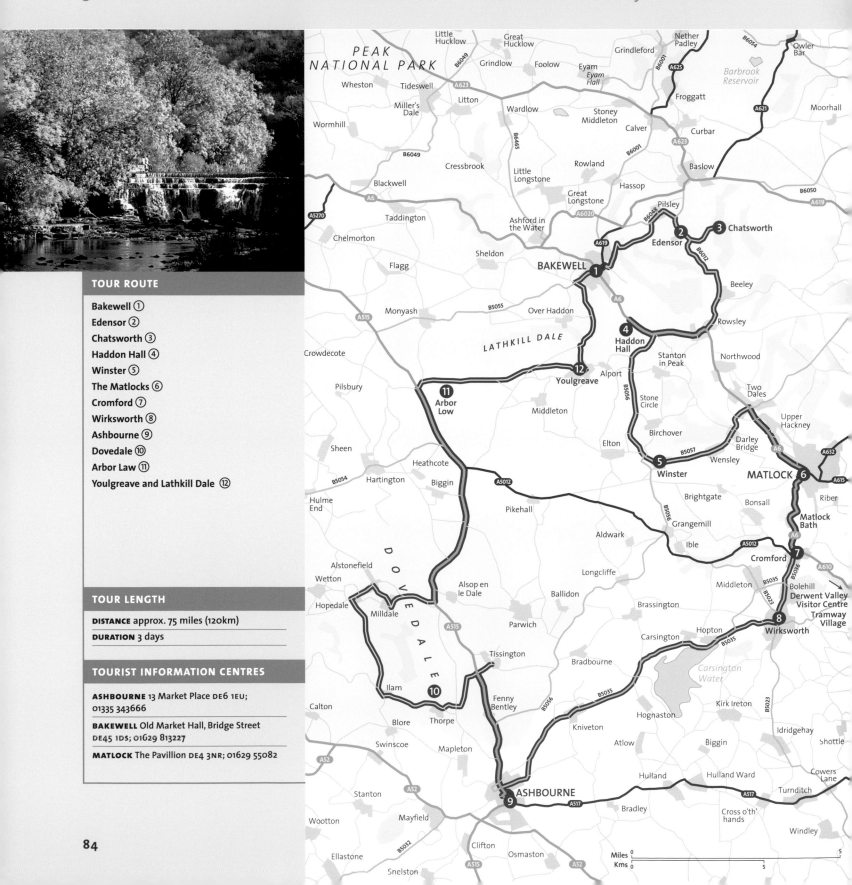

## TOUR ROUTE

Bakewell ①
Edensor ②
Chatsworth ③
Haddon Hall ④
Winster ⑤
The Matlocks ⑥
Cromford ⑦
Wirksworth ⑧
Ashbourne ⑨
Dovedale ⑩
Arbor Law ⑪
Youlgreave and Lathkill Dale ⑫

## TOUR LENGTH

**DISTANCE** approx. 75 miles (120km)

**DURATION** 3 days

## TOURIST INFORMATION CENTRES

**ASHBOURNE** 13 Market Place DE6 1EU;
01335 343666

**BAKEWELL** Old Market Hall, Bridge Street
DE45 1DS; 01629 813227

**MATLOCK** The Pavillion DE4 3NR; 01629 55082

*Clockwise from far left:*
The Wye at Bakewell;
Chatsworth; cable car at
Matlock Bath; drystone
walls near Ashbourne;
Holmebridge at Bakewell

## 1 BAKEWELL

To set the record straight – there are no tarts in
Bakewell. That eggy, almondy thing with jam in it is
properly called a pudding in this town. It originated as
a fortuitous mistake by a flustered cook, allegedly at
the Rutland Arms. You can buy an authentic version at
the **Old Original Bakewell Pudding Shop**.

Bakewell started life as a place to ford the River Wye,
and several ancient trading routes converge here. It
holds a time-honoured cattle market every Monday,
and a big agricultural show in August. This little town
with its multi-arched bridge of warm brown stone is
one of the most attractive and popular anywhere in the
Peak District National Park – as property prices attest.
The Old Market Hall provides premises for a well-
stocked information centre, and at the **Bakewell Old
House Museum** you can learn more about local life
from this rickety timbered cottage crammed with
household bygones and farm tools. The **parish church**
contains monuments to the Vernon and Manners
families, who hailed from nearby Haddon Hall (*see p88*).

*Take minor roads
north east and follow
signs to Edensor.* ②

## 2 EDENSOR

Some say that the sixth Duke of Devonshire had the
original village of Edensor (pronounced 'Ensor')
demolished simply to improve the view from
Chatsworth, but the replacement he provided for his
estate tenants and employees was an undeniable
showpiece. Built in the picturesque 'cottage orné' style
in about 1840, each house is individually designed with
elaborate flourishes such as oriel windows and lacy
bargeboards. Apparently the duke couldn't decide
which type he preferred in the architect's pattern book,
so he chose one of each. Gilbert Scott built the
Early English-style church in 1867. Both Joseph Paxton,
the duke's head gardener (designer of the Crystal
Palace), and Kathleen Kennedy, the late US
president's sister who married the Marquis of
Hartington, are buried here.

*Follow signs
across the B6012 east
to Chatsworth.*
→ • • • • • • • • • • • • ③

⊕ Return to the B6012 south
• towards Matlock. At
• Rowsley, turn right on to
• the A6, and follow signs for
• a couple of miles until you
④ reach **Haddon Hall.**

⊕ Retrace your steps briefly
• along the A6 towards
• Rowsley, then take the
• B5056 signed to Birchover,
• passing Nine Ladies on
• your left. Follow the same
⑤ road south to **Winster**.

Continue through Winster
along the B5057 towards
Darley Bridge, turning right
on to the A6 towards
**Matlock** and **Matlock Bath.**

→ • • • • • • • • • • ⑥

## 3 CHATSWORTH

Unquestionably one of England's grandest stately
homes, the 'Palace of the Peak' is simply not to be
missed. Within its 14,000-ha park (35,000 acres) lie
woods, lakes and amazing gardens, a working farm, an
adventure playground and more than five miles of
footpaths. The original house was built in the 16th
century by the redoubtable Bess of Hardwick and her
second husband William Cavendish, whose name passed
down to a dynasty of earls and dukes of Devonshire. In
the 1690s, the first duke replaced the then-outmoded
Tudor house with the present neoclassical version,
designed by one of Wren's contemporaries. The
following century, 'Capability' Brown landscaped the
grounds. No expense was spared as cash flowed freely
from the Ecton Hill copper mines. Brown diverted the
River Derwent to provide a flattering mirror on which
the honey-coloured mansion could apparently float in
its parkland bowl. Other ambitious water features
include a magnificent cascade down a 200-m stone
staircase (650ft), and Europe's second tallest gravity-fed
fountain. Architect Joseph Paxton added prototype
Crystal Palace hothouses, one with central heating.

   If the grounds are stunning, the house is a glorious
match. One highlight of the 26 rooms open to the
public is an eye-popping art collection, where Frink and
Freud rub shoulders with Rembrandt and Van Dyck.
There are priceless Blue John vases, and an astonish-
ingly realistic *trompe l'oeil* violin painted on the back of
the music room door. Choose a weekday to visit if
possible, when the crowds are smaller. Much of the
estate's recent success is due to the enterprise and
business sense of the dowager duchess (widow of the
11th duke) – one of the talented Mitford girls. The
Chatsworth farm shop just up the road at Pilsley is
well worth a visit.

## 4 HADDON HALL

If you're tired of the pomp and circumstance of
Palladian architecture, the subtle charm of this
exquisite medieval manor house on the banks of the
Wye will seem a breath of fresh air. Its mellow mullions
of gold-grey stone glimmer with diamond leading, and
climbing plants spill over the walled gardens. Haddon
Hall is the result of a long process of accretion that
began in the 12th century and stopped abruptly in the
16th, when the resident dukes of Rutland, weary of
antique plumbing, retreated to the fashionable comforts
of Belvoir Castle in north Leicestershire. So perfectly
preserved is Haddon, unmolested by Georgian
'improvements', that it often serves as a backdrop for
period costume dramas. *Peveril of the Peak*, Sir Walter
Scott's tale of the elopement in 1563 of the 18-year-old
heiress Dorothy Vernon with John Manners, son of a
local earl, fuels its romantic appeal. The Elizabethan
long gallery and the wall-paintings revealed during
20th-century restoration work are memorable features,
but it is Haddon's quintessentially English atmosphere
that lingers longest, swathed in the the scent of roses.

## 5 WINSTER

This hilly old lead-mining village is a place of great
character and well-preserved historic buildings. Many
of the well-to-do houses lining its steep streets date
from the 18th century, while the arcaded 16th-century
**Market House** was the National Trust's first property in
Derbyshire, now housing an information centre. North
of Winster, near Stanton Lees, is an ancient stone circle
called the **Nine Ladies**. Legend has it that these stones
are the tombs of Haddon women stricken down with
the plague, who danced their last here.

*Clockwise from above:
views of Haddon Hall;
Cromford canal; view of
the cascade and
Chatsworth House*

## 6 THE MATLOCKS

Matlock and Matlock Bath merge along a steep-sided gorge of the Derwent Valley. This fern-filled, craggy site has been a well-known beauty spot for centuries, prompting Byron to declare 'I can assure you there are things in Derbyshire as noble as Greece or Switzerland'. Warm springs became a focus of attraction as early as 1689, and a spa developed, promoted by local industrialist John Smedley. Today, an **aquarium** occupies Smedley's grand old hydro (hydropathy centre), and the thermal pipes have been turned into a petrifying well, where objects dipped in it acquire a hard coat of lime and look as if they have been turned to stone. The arrival of the railway determined Matlock's present character of a landlocked and slightly faded resort somewhat stranded by the tides of progress. But Matlock Bath's cheery amusement arcades and souvenir shops still pack in the crowds on sunny summer weekends. In September, the Matlock Illuminations brighten up the waterfront promenade with fireworks, lighting displays and decorated boats.

One of Matlock Bath's most popular diversions is a cable-car ride to the **Heights of Abraham**, rewarded by show-caves and spectacular views. These cliffs were named after the rocks scaled by General Wolfe's forces at the Battle of Quebec. The **Peak District Mining Museum** has lively and informative displays on the local lead-mining industry, including a huge steam pump and a mock-up of a typical mine shaft. You can combine the museum with a tour of the nearby **Mining Museum and Temple Mine**, where you have to stoop through ever-diminishing passages and try your hand at panning for gold. **Peak Rail** offers nostalgic steam train trips through Darley Dale from Matlock.

## 7 CROMFORD

In the late 18th century, Cromford saw the establishment of the world's first factory mills. It was here that Richard Arkwright pioneered his ingenious water-powered cotton-spinning loom and transformed textile manufacture from a cottage industry into a fully mechanised, mass production system. The multi-storey red-brick **mill**, with its handsome Venetian windows and rooftop cupola, produced cotton for more than 200 years. Some of the machinery (still in working order) and a huge collection of bobbins are displayed in the Working Textile Museum that now occupies the site. Horsedrawn narrowboats take passengers along the **Cromford Canal** in summer.

*Take the A6 south
all the way
to Cromford.* ⑦

*Follow the
B5023 south to
Wirksworth.*

⑧

## 10 DOVEDALE

The River Dove, running along the Derbyshire-Staffordshire border, dashes through a wooded, steep-sided ravine of classic limestone features, making Dovedale one of the most magical of any of the Derbyshire dales. It is consequently one of the Peak's honeypot visitor destinations and unfortunately suffers badly from overcrowding, but when there are fewer visitors you may spot dippers or kingfishers. The only way to see Dovedale is on foot; the official car park and entrance to the dale is at the southern end, beneath the stately pyramid of the hill called Thorpe Cloud, a popular local climb. A walk along Dovedale's banks from the famous stepping stones leads through dappled shade past caves and strange rock formations towards the packhorse bridge at **Milldale**, mentioned in Izaak Walton's *Compleat Angler* ('Why, a mouse can hardly go over it – it is but two fingers broad').

Several attractive villages deserve a look near Dovedale. **Ilam** is a fine estate village in the adjoining Manifold Valley. Its neogothic hall, **Ilam Park**, belongs to the National Trust and is used as a youth hostel, but the park is accessible to walkers. **Tissington**, east of Dovedale, is another immaculate estate village, some say the prettiest of any in the national park. Its Jacobean manor and Norman church form a perfect assembly around the duckpond beneath an avenue of venerable limes. It is well know for its association with the local well-dressing tradition (*see box*). The Tissington Trail from Ashbourne to Parsley Hay is one of several paths for cyclists and walkers on disused railtracks. **Alstonefield**, north of Dovedale, is another tidy stone village of mullioned cottages and a 16th-century hall around a tree-lined green. The church of St Peter's is in Decorated and Perpendicular style with a mainly 17th-century interior (notice the box pews and double-decker pulpit). Many visitors stop in **Hartington**, further up the dale, to stock up on cheese, sold at the factory shop opposite the duckpond on the village green. The village now produces more than 25% of the world's accredited Stilton.

## 8 WIRKSWORTH

Scarred by quarrying and mines on its outskirts, this town has a long and distinguished history, traced in its **Heritage Centre** in an old silk and velvet mill. The Barmote Court, set up to adjudicate on local mining disputes, still sits twice a year in the **Moot Hall**. Near the old grammar school in an attractive close of Elizabethan almshouses, the **parish church** contains glass by the pre-Raphaelite artist Burne-Jones, and a carved Saxon sarcophagus known as the Wirksworth Stone. Just outside the town is the **National Stone Centre**, an engaging place to learn about the uses of stone through varied activities. South west of Wirksworth is **Carsington Water**, England's newest and ninth-largest reservoir, which provides a much-visited outdoor activities centre with a sailing club.

⊕ *Head south west*
*towards Ashbourne*
⑨ *on the B5035.*

## 9 ASHBOURNE

Just outside the southern tip of the national park, Ashbourne is one of the main gateways to the Peak District. It is a thriving little market town of grey stone, regarded as one of the most desirable places to live in the Midlands and a good place to look for antiques. No visitor should miss a visit to the **Gingerbread Shop and Tea Rooms,** where the town's fiery speciality is made in a quaint, timbered building, allegedly to a recipe passed on by Napoleonic prisoners-of-war. Many historic buildings are preserved in the centre, including the Old Grammar School, dating from 1585, and the Georgian market place. A gallows beam also hangs over the main street between two old inns. In **St Oswald's Church,** notable for its pencil-slim, 65m-high spire (212ft), other monuments include the Cockayne Chapel and the touching memorial to Penelope Boothby, who died aged five in 1791, and is now immortalised in Carrara marble. A long-standing tradition in Ashbourne is the Shrovetide Football match between 'up 'ards' and 'down'ards'. With the goalposts set three miles apart and very few rules (apart from a proviso that you mustn't actually murder anyone), it's a bruising ritual.

⊕ *Head north on the A515,*
*turn left near Tissington*
*for Dovedale including*
*Thorpe, Ilam and*
⑩ *Hartington.*

*Return to the A515 and*
*continue north, turn*
*right on minor roads for*
*Arbor Low.*

⊖ • • • • • • • • • • • • ⑪

Clockwise from far left:
Dovedale; view of
Wirksworth; Arbor Low stone
circle, Ashbourne

## 11 ARBOR LOW

This is the Peak District's most impressive ancient
monument, a henge of about 50 recumbent limestone
slabs surrounded by an earthwork ditch and bank. It
lies in a farmer's field and is believed to be about 4,000
years old. Arbor Low's impact is in its high and lonely
setting amid wide sweeping horizons broken by an
occasional eerie clump of trees. In a neighbouring field
stands the conical hump of a Bronze Age tumulus
called **Gib Hill**.

Continue east on
minor roads to
**Youlgreave** and
**Lathkill Dale**. ⑫

## 12 YOULGREAVE AND LATHKILL DALE

**Youlgreave** is a picturesque lead-mining village on the
River Bradford, which races over a series of mini-weirs
beneath clapper bridges. Its Gothic church is one of the
best in the area, containing fine stained glass and an
ancient alabaster tomb. To the north of Youlgreave lies
**Lathkill Dale**, a lovely valley of coppiced woods and old
mine-workings. Most of it is a designated nature
reserve renowned for rare flora and insects. Part of the
river disappears into swallow holes, a classic feature of
limestone country.

Follow signs north to
the B5055 back
to **Bakewell**.

← • • • • • • • • • • • ❶

## WELL-DRESSING

The custom of decorating wells with colourful
pictures made from flowers and other natural
materials is believed to have originated in
Tissington, though exactly when is uncertain –
some think it stems from pre-Christian Celtic
times. The practice is a thanksgiving for the
gift of water (a precious commodity in a
limestone region where water sources often
vanish underground). Some also associate it
with deliverance from the plague. The designs
are often biblical, but sometimes feature
historical or modern-day themes. About 60
Derbyshire villages compete with each other
for the best-dressed well throughout the
summer between May and September.

## WITH MORE TIME

From Matlock, continue on the A6 down the 'National Heritage Corridor' (Lower
Derwent Valley) to see further evidence of Derbyshire's industrialised past. Just
off the road near Crich you'll find **Tramway Village** *(left)*, where visitors can take
penny rides on vintage vehicles. Belper's **Derwent Valley Visitor Centre** in a well-
preserved 19th-century cotton mill is the focal point for the industrial heritage
sites. Here you can sort out your spinning jennies from your water frames and
find out how textiles are manufactured in modern times.

# The glorious High Peak

North of Edale, the pallid limestone country of the southern Peak District surrenders to sterner landscapes of millstone grit. Meandering between the northern High or Dark Peak and the southern White Peak, this tour charts the complex effects of geology on the lie of the land. Surprises lurk among these windswept, sheep-strewn moorlands laced with drystone walls: vanishing rivers, shivering mountains, thermal springs and a subterranean labyrinth of mysterious caverns. The spa town of Buxton makes a civilised touring base with its handsome architecture, and the distinctive villages are suprisingly varied.

## TOUR ROUTE

Buxton ①
Miller's Dale ②
Tideswell ③
Castleton and the Hope Valley ④
Edale ⑤
Chapel-en-le-Frith ⑥
Hayfield ⑦
Snake Pass ⑧
Derwent Reservoirs ⑨
Hathersage ⑩
Eyam ⑪
Ashford-in-the-Water ⑫

## TOUR LENGTH

**DISTANCE** approx. 110 miles (175km)

**DURATION** 3 days

## TOURIST INFORMATION CENTRES

**BUXTON** The Crescent SK17 6BQ;
01298 25106

**MATLOCK** Crown Square DE4 3AT; 01629 583388

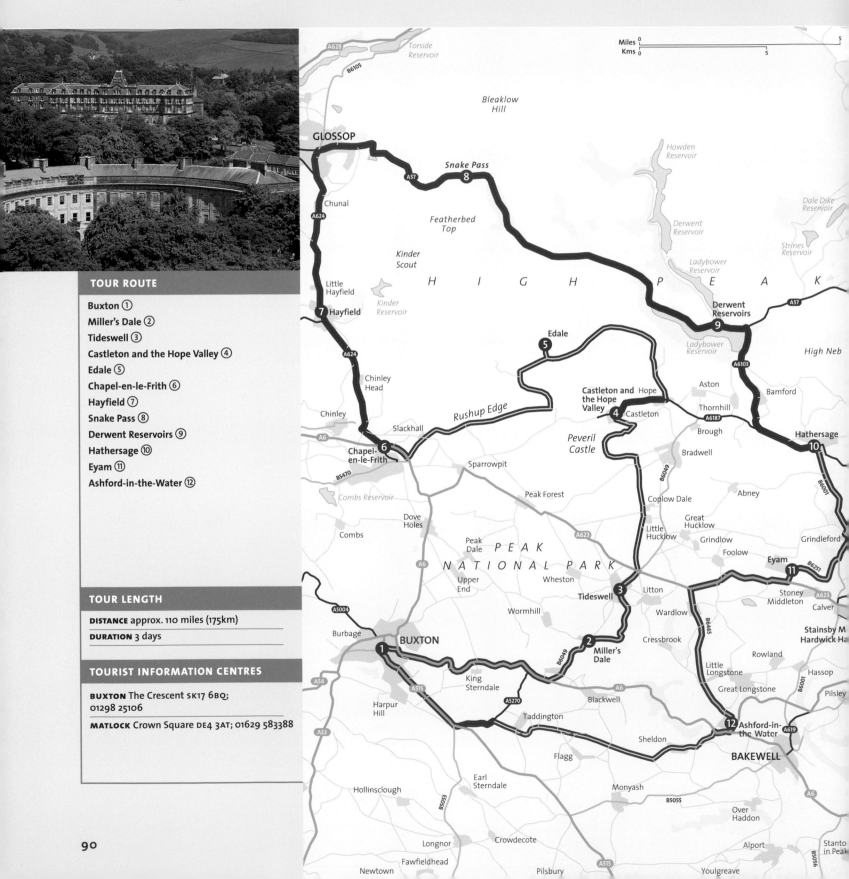

*Clockwise from far left:*
Buxton Crescent; Hope
Valley; Blue John caverns,
Castleton; hang-gliding
at Hathersage;
Peveril Castle, Castleton

## 1 BUXTON

Standing some 1,000m (3,260ft) above sea level, this elegant spa town certainly qualifies as a local highlight. Its handsome buildings are all the better for an ambitious restoration programme. The Romans discovered the merits of Buxton water, gushing steadily from underground springs at a pleasant 28°C (82°F); Mary Queen of Scots also soothed her rheumatism in these healing waters. Buxton is no longer an active spa, but its bottled spring water is now stacked on every supermarket shelf. Visitors can quaff it for nothing at the fountain of **St Ann's Well** by the tourist office. The **Old Pump Rooms** are now used as an art gallery and tourist information centre.

Buxton's fortunes revived during the 1780s, when the fifth Duke of Devonshire spent some of the profits from local copper mines on a fashionable neoclassical facelift. John Carr's stately Georgian crescent rivals the great set pieces in Bath, but Victorian architecture and landscaping left their mark too. The **Pavilion Gardens** surround an 1871 glass-domed pleasure palace on the banks of the Wye. Buxton is liveliest during its July festival, hosted at the Edwardian **Opera House** in a sumptuous but light-hearted setting of gilded marble and rococo plasterwork, with performances of work by Gilbert and Sullivan.

On the edge of town, **Poole's Cavern** is Britain's longest show-cave, named after a 15th-century outlaw who used it as a hideout. Its fast-growing 'poached egg' formations of fluorite pillars tinted by orange iron oxides are particularly striking.

*From Buxton, take the A6
east, turning off left on
the B6049 as far as
Miller's Dale.* ❷

## 2 MILLER'S DALE

This is the starting point for one of the most enjoyable of the White Peak walks, along a disused railway track called the **Monsal Trail** running between Buxton and Bakewell. Head west from the car park at the old station, and follow the path along the River Wye towards Chee Dale. Classic limestone scenery and flora characterise the route: great cliffs tower overhead and the path crisscrosses the river from time to time, avoiding some of the old railway tunnels.

*Continue east and then
north on the B6049
to Tideswell.*

→ • • • • • • • • • • • ❸

↓ *Take minor roads from the A623 just north of Tideswell, via Little Hucklow. Follow signs northwards through the lanes towards Castleton. From Castleton, head east along the A6187 and the* **(4)** **Hope Valley***.*

## 3 TIDESWELL

In medieval times, Tideswell prospered on lead-mining and wool, expanding to a sizeable community. Today, a steady flow of visitors swell the teashop coffers. The imposing church on the main street is known as the **Cathedral of the Peak**, a fine example of 14th-century Decorated Gothic, although the Perpendicular tower was added later. Inside, notice the old box pews, memorial brasses and the panels depicting the ten commandments. Some of the badly treated apprentices from nearby Litton Mill lie buried in the churchyard.

### POTHOLING

It is hard to believe that Derbyshire, now about as far from the coast as you can get in England, once lay beneath the waters of a warm, shallow sea. But its carboniferous limestone consists of the fossilised shells and skeletons of billions of tiny marine organisms. Soluble in water, the rock is gradually dissolving into Gruyère cheese-like fissures, passages and caverns. The area around Castleton is one of the best in the country for potholing. Some caves are hundreds of metres long and many have been artificially excavated or enlarged by mining but can be dangerous. Needless to say, you should never venture into these systems unescorted by an experienced caver, and permission to enter any cave should always be obtained in advance. The local tourist board can provide a list of accredited caving clubs. The **Giant's Hole** west of Castleton is a relatively easy system, and the **Bagshawe Cavern** near Bradwell offers novices an escorted adventure trip involving wading and scrambling through narrow chimneys. If the Agony Crawl appeals, potholing may be for you.

*Take minor roads north west towards Edale.*

→ • • • • • • • • • • • • **5**

## 4 CASTLETON AND THE HOPE VALLEY

Right at the heart of the Peak District, the Hope Valley is a great touring and walking centre, famed for its caves and always humming with visitors at weekends. The Norman fortress of **Peveril Castle**, immortalised in Sir Walter Scott's romantic novel, *Peveril of the Peak*, was built by one of William the Conqueror's favourite knights (believed to be an illegitimate son). Henry II added the keep in 1176. Not much remains of the ruins, but it is a splendid vantage point for the surrounding countryside. Below the hilltop castle gapes Britain's largest cave entrance, known until genteel Victorian times as the Devil's Arse, since when it has been called **Peak Cavern**. Ropes used in the mining industry were made here until about 1830 and one of the rope-maker's cottages survives. Demonstrations of rope-making are part of the guided visit to the cave. The **Speedwell Cavern** is a flooded lead-mine on the vertiginous Winnats Pass just west of the village. A boat tour takes visitors along a canal deep into the hill to an underground lake called the bottomless pit. The nearby **Treak Cliff** and **Blue John** caverns both have impressive limestone formations, and are the world's only source of the mauve fluorspar known as Blue John. The name comes from the French *bleu-jaune*, referring to its predominant bands of blue-yellow colour. The brittle stone is still extracted in small quantities and made into jewellery and trinkets, on sale in many of Castleton's souvenir shops.

*Clockwise from far right:* Edale; view of Castleton

## 5 EDALE

This tiny rural village is the northern limit of the White Peak, and the southern terminus of the Pennine Way. Edale consists of little more than one street of well-kept cottages, but its location and the spectacular hill scenery on its doorstep ensures it is never short of energetic-looking visitors. An exhibition about the national park can be seen in the local tourist information centre, along with a wide selection of maps and walking guides. Many walkers set off from the National Trust car park for **Kinder Scout**, highest summit in the Peak District (636m, 2,073ft), an irresistible beacon over Edale Moor to the north west. On Edale's southern side rise the green shoulders of **Mam Tor**, the Shivering Mountain, whose unstable layers of shale and gritstone are constantly subject to landslips. In the 1970s a massive slide caused the permanent closure of the Castleton end of the old A625 road, and traffic is now diverted through the steep Winnat's Pass (suitable only for light vehicles). Hang-gliders often soar over Mam Tor, enjoying amazing views over the White and Dark peaks.

## 6 CHAPEL-EN-LE-FRITH

The 13th-century **church** that gives its name to the small market town of Chapel-en-le-Frith was built by forest workers ('frith' means forest), and dedicated to St Thomas à Becket. Just east of town is the **Chestnut Centre**, an imaginative conservation park in 20ha (50 acres) of landscaped grounds beneath the wooded heights of Rushup Edge. It is dedicated to breeding otters and owls and releasing them into the wild, but other endangered species can be seen here too.

## 7 HAYFIELD

A traditional cotton-milling village, Hayfield is another popular launch pad for the Pennine Way. Weekend walkers head for the more attainable goal of **Kinder Downfall**, a dramatic reservoir waterfall dashing over a staircase of shattered rock. A plaque in Bowden Brook Quarry car park commemorates the trespassers who walked to Kinder Scout from here in 1932, defying local landowners and gamekeepers about the right to roam in Britain's wilderness places.

*Follow local roads east at the T-junction with the A6 turn right and follow signs for **Chapel-en-le-Frith**.* ⑥

*Take the A624 north to **Hayfield**.* ⑦

*Take the A624 to Glossop and then turn east on to the A57 – signed Hathersage – to **Snake Pass**.* ⑧

⊕ *Continue east along the*
*A57. After about 12 miles,*
*you will see the waters of*
*Ladybower Reservoir*
*parallel to the road. In*
*another mile or so, turn left*
*up the Derwent Valley to*
⑨ *the* **Derwent Reservoirs**.

*Return down the valley*
*back to the A57 and turn*
*left for a mile or so, then*
*take the A6013 south*
*and then the A6187 east*
*to* **Hathersage**.

⊖ • • • • • • • • • • • ⑩

## 8 SNAKE PASS

Thomas Telford's brilliantly engineered road gives
grandstand views of some of the most dramatic
High Peak landscapes between Manchester and
Sheffield. It is an austere scene, the moorlands
scattered with conifers, peat hags and isolated stone
barns. Out of season, you may have it virtually to
yourself, but in severe weather Snake Pass is often one
of the first roads in England to be closed. Much of the
countryside to either side belongs to the National Trust,
and is freely accessible, but only on foot. A good walk
leads from Alport bridge along an ancient Roman track.

## 9 DERWENT RESERVOIRS

Derwent Dale is one of the longest and least populated
of the Peak District's gritstone dales. In the late 19th
century its geology and topography made it suitable
for an ambitious water-retaining scheme to supply the
large Midland towns to the south east. Two formidable
dams designed like castle ramparts were built to form
the northern Howden and Derwent reservoirs. The
much larger Ladybower Reservoir was begun in the
mid-1930s. In drought conditions, the remains of farm-
houses and the drowned village of Ashopton emerge
above the waterline. Today, this daisy-chain of artificial
lakes is a magnet for walkers. The national park
information centre of Fairholmes, halfway up the valley,
is a good place to find out about local walks. Beyond
Fairholmes, motorised traffic is restricted at weekends,
but you can walk or cycle all around the wooded shores.

*Clockwise from far left:*
Derwent Reservoir; Eyam;
Celtic cross, Eyam churchyard

## TRAGIC EYAM

The story goes that the plague arrived in Eyam in September 1665, carried by fleas in a parcel of cloth. The tailor's assistant who unpacked the cloth soon became fatally ill, and the dreaded disease spread rapidly. Many villagers fled to the surrounding moorland, but in a bid to contain the infection, Eyam's rector, William Mompesson, consulted the remaining inhabitants and all agreed to cut themselves off from the outside world. Food and medicines were delivered to the boundary stones by the Earl of Devonshire and other well-wishers and money dipped in sterilising vinegar was left as payment. Each family buried its own dead, and outdoor sermons replaced church services to reduce infection. By the autumn of 1666, the outbreak had run its course, but not before about 260 of the 350 quarantined villagers had died, including the rector's wife Katherine. One woman lost her husband and six of her seven children within eight days. These Riley Graves lie just east of the village.

## 11 EYAM

The gruesome experiences of the mid-17th century make this village one of the best-known, and most visited, of any in the Peak District. Eyam (pronounced 'Eem') is the Plague Village (*see box*), immortalised by its brave self-imposed quarantine. With or without its heart-rending history, it is a remarkably seductive assembly of typical Peakland cottages against a backdrop of rolling hills. The main buildings are the fine Jacobean manor farm called **Eyam Hall** with its pretty gardens and craft workshops, and the **Church of St Lawrence**, which dates from Saxon times. A Celtic cross stands in the churchyard, and a plague register records the names of the victims. **Eyam Museum** tells the story of the plague, and other aspects of the village's history.

*Take the B6001 south from Hathersage, and follow the B6521 to **Eyam**.* ⑪

## 10 HATHERSAGE

This village is one of the main gateways to the Peak District from the Sheffield direction, and its proximity to awesome rock faces such as Stannage Edge makes it popular with climbers. Hathersage was the inspiration for 'Morton' of Charlotte Brontë's *Jane Eyre*, which the author partly wrote during a visit here in 1845. Graves in the churchyard bear the local family name of Eyre, along with the extraordinary 3-m grave (10-ft) of Little John, one of Robin Hood's merry men. Suggestions that Little John was more than mere legend were supported by the exhumation of a huge thighbone from the grave in the 1770s. David Mellor, the leading cutlery designer, has a factory **shop** in Hathersage, housed in the award-winning Round Building. Visitors are welcome to watch the finishing process. The high-quality steel for these stylish designs comes from nearby Sheffield, where Mellor learned his trade.

## 12 ASHFORD-IN-THE-WATER

The humpbacked **Sheepwash Bridge** over the shallow, babbling River Wye makes this classic White Peak village the stuff of postcards, despite the busy A6 running along its southern edge. Packhorses laden with malt once passed along this route. Ashford has no unmissable sights, just a charming collection of flower-decked 17th- and 18th-century cottages sprinkled along broad grassy verges. The 'black marble' monuments in the church are made from a prized type of dark limestone quarried locally.

*Take the A623 (signed Chapel-en-le-Frith) west from Eyam. After 2 miles, turn left down the B6465 to **Ashford-in-the-Water**.* ⑫

*From Ashford, follow signs west through the lanes to Sheldon, past Flagg Moor and follow the A5270 and the A515 back to **Buxton**.*
← • • • • • • • • • • • ①

## WITH MORE TIME

Just east of the M1 near junction 29 (take the A617 or B6039 south east from Chesterfield), lies **Hardwick Hall** *(left,* the Countess of Shrewsbury's last and greatest bid to stamp her name on history. The tall, symmetrical windows earned the building its oft-repeated tag 'more glass than wall'. The towers are crowned with the initials ES (Elizabeth Shrewsbury), better known as Bess of Hardwick. **Stainsby Mill**, on the Hardwick estate, is a remarkably complete water-powered flour mill. Reconstructed machinery still grinds flour that's sold to visitors.

# Yorkshire

# West Yorkshire's Brontë country

If you haven't tasted one of Betty's Fat Rascals, you haven't lived. Some might add Harry Ramsden's legendary fish and chips from Guiseley to a list of quintessential other Yorkshire experiences. For these and many other reasons, the slice of God's own country between Harrogate and Hebden Bridge is a tasty morsel. A varied menu includes the delights of the Brontë Parsonage Museum, Saltaire's industrial heritage and modern art, and the steam railway at Keighley – and the wide open moorlands at Haworth to work off all those calories.

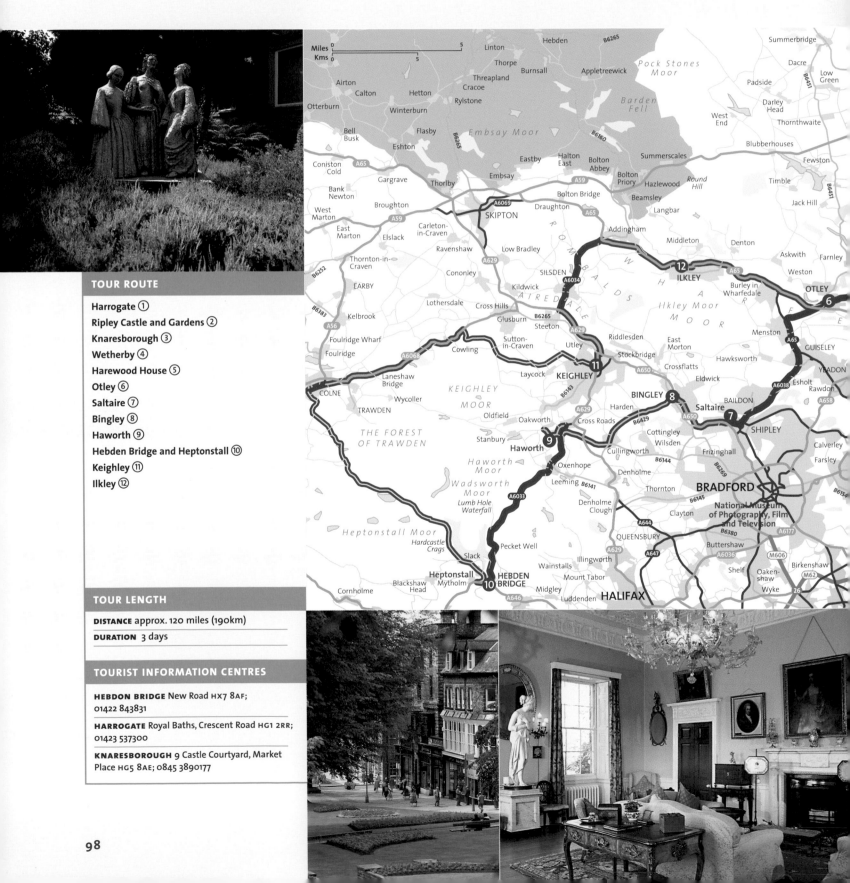

## TOUR ROUTE

Harrogate ①

Ripley Castle and Gardens ②

Knaresborough ③

Wetherby ④

Harewood House ⑤

Otley ⑥

Saltaire ⑦

Bingley ⑧

Haworth ⑨

Hebden Bridge and Heptonstall ⑩

Keighley ⑪

Ilkley ⑫

## TOUR LENGTH

**DISTANCE** approx. 120 miles (190km)

**DURATION** 3 days

## TOURIST INFORMATION CENTRES

**HEBDON BRIDGE** New Road HX7 8AF;
01422 843831

**HARROGATE** Royal Baths, Crescent Road HG1 2RR;
01423 537300

**KNARESBOROUGH** 9 Castle Courtyard, Market Place HG5 8AE; 0845 3890177

Clockwise from far left:
Brontë Parsonage Museum;
countryside round Haworth;
Turkish Baths, Harrogate;
drawing room, Ripley
Castle; Harrogate

# 1 HARROGATE

Harrogate is the archetypal English spa town, famed for its medicinal springs, public gardens and fine architecture. These days, revenue from hydropathic health cures has been largely replaced by a busy round of conferences, exhibitions and trade fairs hosted in the modern Harrogate International Centre. But many pleasing buildings survive from Harrogate's heyday in the late 19th century, notably its grand hotels. The sulphurous waters still run free of charge at the **Royal Pump Rooms Art Gallery and Museum** (1842), and still taste vile enough to do you a power of good. But the wells are enclosed by glass screens to reduce the typically sulphurous 'rotten eggs' smell. More modern, appealing water therapies are offered in the shape of a health and beauty spa in the extensively restored and exotically tiled late-19th-century **Turkish Baths**. The **Mercer Art Gallery** makes use of an early spa building too. A large stretch of open parkland called **The Stray** sweeps through the centre of town, while spring bulbs and formal beds brighten the typically Victorian **Valley Gardens**, where there is a boating lake, a teahouse and a bandstand. On the south western outskirts of town, the superb **Harlow Carr Gardens** are the Royal Horticultural Society's northern pride and joy – the Streamside Garden is a magnificent sight all summer long. The surrounding moors seem to encroach on the garden with a blaze of heather when not much else is flowering. You can stop for afternoon tea in one of **Betty's Cafe Tea Rooms** renowned teashops here as well as in town. The orginal Betty's was started in Harrogate by a Swiss confectioner in 1907 and has become a highly successful 'micro-chain' of Yorkshire teashops. Betty's still operates as a family firm, deliberately kept small so that every detail, down to the exact blend of tea, is monitored.

From Harrogate take the
A61 north for 3 miles to
**Ripley Castle and Gardens**.

→ • • • • • • • • • • • ②

*Clockwise from above:*
*viaduct at Knaresborough;*
*Harewood House; Bramham*
*Park, Wetherby;*
*Knaresborough Castle*

Head south east
on the B6165 to
**3** **Knaresborough**.

Head south to the A661
and then turn left
**4** towards **Wetherby**.

Head south from Wetherby
on the A58, and join the
A659 west following signs
to **Harewood House**.

→ • • • • • • • • • • • **5**

## 2 RIPLEY CASTLE AND GARDENS

Ripley Castle, set on the banks of the River Nidd, has
been the home of the Ingilby family for nearly 700
years. The interior is noted for its fine paintings,
furnishings, chandeliers and portraits, including one of
Sir John Ingilby holding plans of the house. The most
notable room is the library in the Tudor keep, where
'Trooper' Jane Ingilby supposedly held Oliver Cromwell
at gunpoint. However, the Knight's Chamber is by far
the most spectacular with its 16th-century oak ceiling,
a priest's hiding hole, and its superb collection of arms
and armour from the English Civil War. The castle
terrace offers fantastic views over the magnificent
gardens and the lakes beyond. You can follow a park
walk round the ornamental lake and into the deer park
itself. It is also worth taking a peek at the walled
kitchen garden with its extensive herb bed and an
extraordinary collection of rare vegetables. The quaint
village of Ripley was built by Sir William Amscotts
Ingilby in the 1820s and is modelled on a village in
Alsace-Lorraine that he so admired.

## 3 KNARESBOROUGH

Perched on the craggy lip of the Nidd Gorge,
Knaresborough enjoys one of the most striking settings
in North Yorkshire. Amid its ample stock of well-kept
period houses (many of them Georgian) crammed into
a maze of intricate alleys, there's a lot to see. Notice the
curious troglodytic folly known as the House in the
Rock, and the wonderful chemist's shop on the Market
Square (the oldest in England, dating from 1720), which
makes its own lavender water. There's an ancient castle,
a medieval hermitage, and a railway viaduct bestriding
the deep gorge. Knaresborough's colourful characters
also play a part in the tourism industry. Besides the red-
coated town crier keeping visitors up with the news on
market day, there's no avoiding Old Mother Shipton, a
16th-century soothsayer who narrowly escaped being
burnt as a witch for her uncannily accurate predictions.
Her spooky riverside cave dwelling pulls in the crowds,
along with a petrifying well whose mineral-rich waters
turn anything placed in them to 'stone' within weeks.

## 4 WETHERBY

The north western approach road to Wetherby takes
you past the picturesque ruins of Spofforth Castle
(Hotspur's birthplace, *see p18*), cunningly shoehorned
into a rocky, naturally defensive site. **Stockeld Park**, one
mile nearer the town, is a fine 18th-century house with
an extra-wide staircase designed to accommodate the
broad-beamed crinoline ballgowns of the time.
Wetherby itself is an agreeable former coaching stop
on the Great North Road with a well-preserved legacy
of period buildings and traditional speciality shops. It
holds regular produce and farmers' markets, and is well
known among followers of form as a steeplechasing
venue. **Bramham Park**, on the southern side of the town,
is a mini-Versailles with its formal cascades, lakes and
temples. The handsome Queen Anne mansion was
damaged by fire in 1828, but its ornate Baroque interior
still displays a fine show of French furnishings and
sporting pictures.

## 5 HAREWOOD HOUSE

The seat of the earls of Harewood was built in 1759 by John Carr. Clearly, no expense was spared to make this grand house outshine its local rivals, though the original design was modified in the 19th and 20th centuries. 'Capability' Brown landscaping deploys a cascade and wooded grounds, brilliant with rhododendrons and bog garden plants in early summer, that sweep down to a lake. Inside, Adam plasterwork and Chippendale furniture enhance outstanding collections of watercolours and porcelain. The restored state bed stands ready for any royal visitation. Modern art and a 'below stairs' exhibition add a welcome change of pace.

## 6 OTLEY

Thomas Chippendale's Wharfedale birthplace is a handsome little town, one of its attractions being that the pubs stay open all day long on Fridays (market day). Rumour has it that Cromwell's Ironsides drank the Black Bull inn dry on their way to the Battle of Marston Moor in 1644, yet still managed to win a decisive victory. Otley's older vernacular buildings are a well-kept mix of mainly Georgian and Victorian styles, making the town a suitable stand-in for Emmerdale's fictional Hotton. The four-faced Jubilee clock is a useful, if chimeless, timekeeper on the main street, while **Chevin Forest Park** on Otley's south eastern outskirts is a scenic place for a stroll. En route to Saltaire stop off at Guiselely for some of **Harry Ramsden's** famous fish and chips at the White Cross roundabout.

## 7 SALTAIRE

Now a World Heritage Site, this model factory township attracts many permanent residents as well as transient visitors. When the worker's cottages were first built here, Saltaire enjoyed a distinctly more rural outlook than it does today. It was developed in the mid-19th century by Titus Salt, an enterprising textile tycoon whose penchant for the Italian Renaissance gave his mill complex an unexpectedly Mediterranean appearance. Look for the llamas (alpacas) on Saltaire's ubiquitous coat of arms – those silky coats provided the cash for this ambitious project. The former mill, in the style of a Tuscan palazzo, once housed over a thousand clattering looms, today replaced by an upmarket shopping centre and the **1853 Gallery**, Europe's largest permanent collection of the works of Bradford-born artist David Hockney. The **Victorian Reed Organ and Harmonium Museum** has some eye-catching exhibits, and a few may bend your ear too.

Continue west
along the A659
as far as **Otley**. 6

Take the A65 and A6038
south to Shipley; turn right
on the A650, following
signs for **Saltaire**. 7

Continue north
west on the A650
to Bingley. 8

Clockwise from above
view near Haworth;
Five Rise Locks, Bingley;
Ilkley Moor

## 8 BINGLEY

Bingley's main claim to fame is a prodigious flight
of locks on the Leeds and Liverpool Canal. **Five Rise
Locks** presents a logistical challenge even to
experienced boat-handlers, shifting some 18m (60ft)
in height in just five ingeniously interconnected
stages. It is impossible to empty any of the locks
unless the one below it is also empty. The canal was
built between 1770 and 1816, encouraged by a
consortium of Bradford businessmen anxious to
transport goods to Liverpool. Until 2001 it remained
the sole waterway to cross the Pennines.

Take the B6429 to
Cullingworth, then turn
right on the B6144
following signs to
⑨ **Haworth**.

## 9 HAWORTH

Brontë fans know that this bleak moorland village was
the home of the famous literary sisters whose cruelly
curtailed lives and enduringly popular novels have
made it a place of pilgrimage. The Georgian parsonage
that is now the **Brontë Parsonage Museum** lies beyond
the craft and antique shops on the cobbled main
street. Here you can see the table where those tales of
repressed passion were penned, and the horsehair sofa
where Emily died. Other destinations on the Brontë
trail are the Sunday school where the sisters taught,
the family vault in the parish church, and the Black Bull
inn where brother Branwell drank himself into
insensibility. After the museum, you can head up the
path past the Brontë waterfalls to **Top Withens**, the
roofless ruin overlooking a panorama of windswept
moorland that many allege was the inspiration for
*Wuthering Heights*.

Take the A6033 south as
far as **Hebden Bridge** and
**Heptonstall**.

→ • • • • • • • • • • • ⑩

## THE BRONTË SISTERS

Irish-born Patrick Brunty changed his name to
the more distinguished-sounding Brontë as he
moved up in the world following his ordination
into the church. He moved to Haworth in 1820
with his Cornish wife Maria and their two
eldest children, who died soon afterwards. Their
surviving four children remained at home, the
girls creating imaginary worlds from books,
while their brother Branwell fell gradually into
debt and disgrace under the influence of
opium and alcohol. The novels *Jane Eyre*
(Charlotte), *Wuthering Heights* (Emily) and
*Agnes Grey* (Anne) were the result – all
published in 1847, catapulting the reclusive
sisters into fame. Sadly, Branwell, Emily and
Anne soon succumbed to the tuberculosis
induced by their damp and draughty
surroundings at Haworth, but Charlotte
survived to marry, although she too died
within a year. True classics, the greatest Brontë
novels are still read avidly today.

## 10  HEBDEN BRIDGE AND HEPTONSTALL

These miniature Victorian mill towns virtually merge above Calderdale. Down in the valley, Hebden Bridge was originally a packhorse stop on the Rochdale canal. Textiles brought prosperity in the 19th century, but since the 1960s it has become a sort of Yorkshire Hampstead, a haunt of artists and intellectuals seeking alternative lifestyles. Perched on steep terraces to the west, the older weaving community of Heptonstall is a handsome little place and claims the world's oldest Methodist chapel in continual use. The hexagonal building dates from 1764, when John Wesley visited the village. The poet Sylvia Plath is buried in the local churchyard. From Hebden Bridge you can gain access to the Mary Towneley Loop, a circular national trail that forms part of the Pennine Bridleway. Another enjoyable walk leads up the valley to **Hardcastle Crags**, a wild beauty spot of tumbling water and fern-filled woodland now managed by the National Trust. **Gibson Mill**, at the heart of the property, has recently been restored as a flagship environmental project and exhibition centre.

## 11  KEIGHLEY

'Keethly', as it's pronounced, is a solid, much-expanded Victorian town with pleasantly old-fashioned shops in Cavendish Street. Its main visitor attraction is the steam-powered **Keighley and Worth Valley Railway**, which makes a memorably nostalgic way of reaching Haworth, and has starred in many period films requiring a steam train setting (notably *The Railway Children*). **Cliffe Castle Museum** has a local history exhibition housed in the lavish mansion of a wealthy textile magnate. To the north east of town, **East Riddlesden Hall** is a mullioned manor dating from 1648, full of splendid plasterwork and panelling, but imbued with dark legends relating to the Murgatroyds who once lived here.

## 12  ILKLEY

The very mention of this place is almost certain to get that relentless Yorkshire ditty churning through your head; the tourist authorities even package Ilkley as *Baht' at* Country. If this evokes an image of cloth caps and whippets, you've been misled; Ilkley is a decidedly superior little town of literary festivals and smart teashops. It has plenty of history too, much of it related in the **Manor House Museum and Art Gallery**, a 16th-century building near the church (where there are three Saxon crosses). The Romans established a garrison called Olicana here, but Ilkley really came into its own right as a Georgian spa town. The luxury hydros that profited from its icy moorland springs left a core of Victorian and Edwardian architecture and some handsome villas behind. Ilkley's famous moors swell to a crescendo on both sides of the town. Mysterious 'cup and ring' markings (*see p19*) and a 'Swastika Stone' found here date from the Bronze Age.

*Take the minor road past Hardcastle Crags, over the exhilarating upland scenery of Heptonstall Moor, towards Colne. Turn right on to the A6068 towards Cowling, right again on minor roads, following signs for Keighley.* ⑪

*Follow the A629 north up Airedale, turning right on the A6034 to Addingham, then right again on the A65 to Ilkley.* ⑫

*Take the A65 east to Otley, and follow signs to Harrogate via the A659, B6161 and B6162.*

← • • • • • • • • • • • • ①

## WITH MORE TIME

On the eastern side of Leeds you'll find **Lotherton Hall**, near Saxton, an Edwardian house with fascinating contents and fine grounds. Leeds and Bradford are full of interest, and you don't have to stray far into the urban jungle to find **Kirkstall Abbey** *(left)*, one of Britain's best-preserved Cistercian monasteries, with the Abbey House Museum of recreated Victoriana in its gatehouse. Bradford's star sight is the splendid **National Museum of Photography, Film and Television** with interactive galleries on the many ways of image-making.

# The natural wonders of the southern Dales

On the south side of the Yorkshire Dales National Park, the Dales run mostly north to south, and road connections between valleys are sparse. But where your car cannot venture, hiking trails can often bridge the gaps across emerald-and-silver mosaics of whaleback hills, crystal waters and bare limestone. Sculpted over millennia, these tantalising glacial landscapes promise much more than a geology fieldtrip.

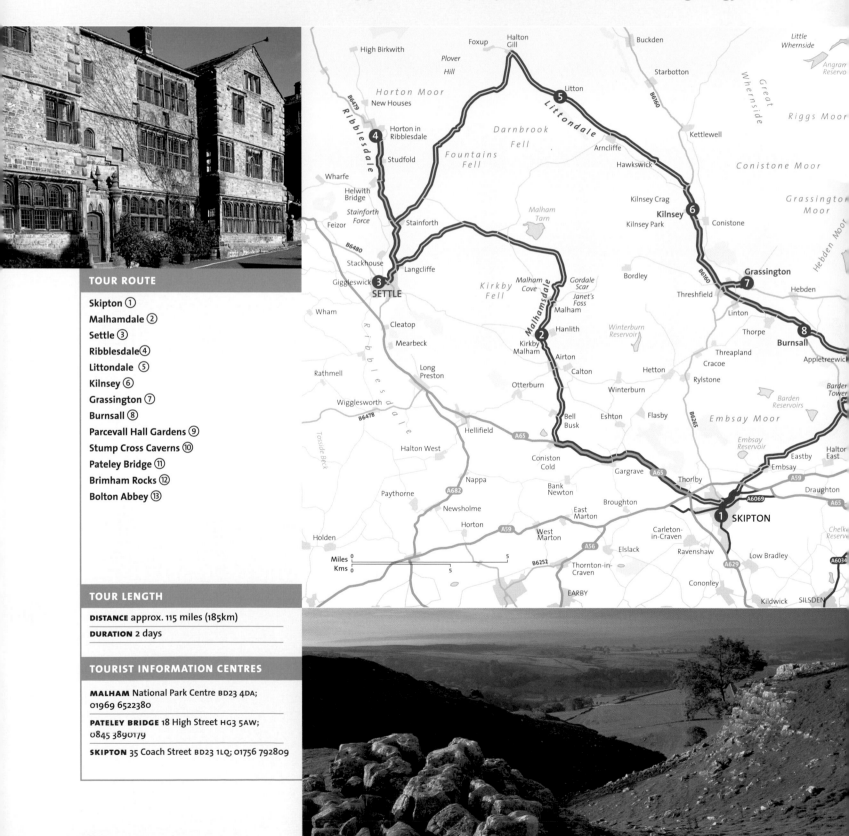

## TOUR ROUTE

Skipton ①
Malhamdale ②
Settle ③
Ribblesdale ④
Littondale ⑤
Kilnsey ⑥
Grassington ⑦
Burnsall ⑧
Parcevall Hall Gardens ⑨
Stump Cross Caverns ⑩
Pateley Bridge ⑪
Brimham Rocks ⑫
Bolton Abbey ⑬

## TOUR LENGTH

**DISTANCE** approx. 115 miles (185km)

**DURATION** 2 days

## TOURIST INFORMATION CENTRES

**MALHAM** National Park Centre BD23 4DA; 01969 6522380

**PATELEY BRIDGE** 18 High Street HG3 5AW; 0845 3890179

**SKIPTON** 35 Coach Street BD23 1LQ; 01756 792809

# 1 SKIPTON

All major routes to the southern Dales pass through Skipton, which makes it a popular touring base, even though it is located just outside the national park. The town centre, a mix of ancient inns, 18th-century houses and modern shops, swings into action four times a week with one of the best markets in the area (the biggest is on Saturday). The converted old High Corn Mill and the glass-roofed Craven Court with its Victorian-style ironwork are two of the town's attractive shopping complexes. Skipton means 'sheeptown' but it is still an important cattle-auction centre too, retaining the odd set of traffic lights specifically dedicated to the safe passage of livestock. In the middle of town, the Norman **castle**, bearing the royalist Clifford family's resolute motto 'Desormais' ('Henceforth'), is remarkably intact given it survived a three-year Roundhead siege. After the Civil War Cromwell gave permission for the roof to be replaced as long as it was not strong enough to withstand the weight of a cannon. Inside, spot the quaint medieval loo cantilevered over the moat, and the exquisitely mullioned Conduit Court added in Henry VIII's reign. The town's **Holy Trinity Church** contains Clifford family tombs and an ornate 16th-century chancel screen. For a rundown on local history and much else besides, visit the **Craven Museum** in the old town hall. Among its multifarious exhibits is a small display commemorating Thomas Spencer, a Skipton lad who teamed up with Mr Marks to found a vast retailing empire.

*Leave Skipton on A65, heading westwards out of town as far as Coniston Cold, then turn right up towards Kirkby Malham and **Malhamdale**.*

Horton-in-Ribblesdale is renowned among hill-walkers for the Three Peaks Challenge, a punishing race held in April up the three landmark summits of Ribblehead: Pen-y-Ghent, Ingleborough and Whernside are all around 700m high (well over 2,000ft). The fastest competitors can scale the lot in under three hours. Less masochistic hikers can tackle this gruelling 23-mile route at a more leisurely pace at any time of year; but even so, you need to be very fit and experienced. Many find that just one peak will amply suffice for a day's march, but if you can manage all of them in a single day, you can join the Three Peaks of Yorkshire Club. The official starting point for the Three Peaks ascent is the Pen-y-Ghent cafe. Log in here, and they'll send out a search party if you aren't back by nightfall.

## 2 MALHAMDALE

So well tramped is the area around the headwaters of the River Aire that this dale on the Pennine Way is generally named after its main village, rather than Airedale as one might expect. **Kirkby Malham**, near the entrance to Malhamdale, has a notable church – St Michael's – with fine box pews and 16th-century roof timbers. Malham's helpful information centre points many visitors in the direction of the spectacular limestone features further up the valley. The Malham Trail takes in **Malham Cove**, a crescent wall of rock rearing 90m (290ft) above a natural amphitheatre. Formed on a geological fault-line, it has all the drama of an outdoor IMAX cinema screen. At the end of the ice age, cascades higher than Niagara Falls plummeted over its brim; today, the more modest Malham Beck runs underground, emerging from sinkholes at the base of the cliff. Blackened lichen and moss etch frown-lines on the pale stone, and all around you can see where frost and acidic meltwater have carved deep fissures or 'grikes' into the flat, bare rock. This limestone pavement is a rare habitat for harts-tongue ferns, orchids and dog's mercury. **Malham Tarn** to the north is Yorkshire's second-largest natural lake, another haunt of unusual birds and plantlife. While most water hereabouts swiftly disappears into the porous limestone, this sedgy tarn rests on a bed of slate covered with impervious glacial drift. **Gordale Scar**, the subject of a famous Turner painting, is a dramatic rock cleft where a stream leaps beneath overhanging crags. The smaller waterfall of Janet's Foss spills over a mossy tufa screen into a pool once used for dipping sheep.

*Continue westwards on unclassified roads past Malham Tarn, following signs for* **Settle**.

→ • • • • • • • • • • • ③

## 3 SETTLE

Like Skipton, Settle has a large and lively **market**, held here on Tuesdays. The town hall and arcaded Shambles (the old slaughterhouse) occupy centre-stage on the main square; steep lanes and sloping yards ripple off it in all directions past 17th-century terraces with dated door-cases, and upmarket shops full of walking boots, antique silver and second-hand books. The **Watershed Mill** is a former cotton mill-turned-visitor centre selling Dales products. The Folly on School Hill in the town centre is Settle's grandest house, built for a well-to-do tanner in 1675. The town is renowned as the starting point for one of Britain's most scenic rail routes, the **Settle-to-Carlisle Railway**. This ambitious Victorian engineering project (opened in 1876) carves 72 miles through Ribblesdale over wild moorland to the bucolic Eden Valley.

The unassuming town of **Giggleswick** on the opposite bank of the Ribble seems almost a suburb of Settle on a map. Period houses line the shady streets around the market cross and its public school, topped with a dome of green copper, dates from 1512. The birds of prey at the **Yorkshire Dales Falconry and Conservation Centre** show off their skills at regularly held shows.

## 4 RIBBLESDALE

A fine riverside walk leads along the Ribble Way from Langcliffe on the northern outskirts of Settle to **Stainforth**, a pretty village with a 17th-century packhorse bridge and two waterfalls – **Stainforth Force** and **Catrigg Force**. Further up the valley, **Horton-in-Ribblesdale** dates back to Norman times. It is a straggling moorland village scarred in places by quarry workings. At the top of the valley, the scenery is austerely craggy, scattered with glacial drumlins and riddled with potholes. The **Ribblehead Viaduct**, built to carry the Settle-to-Carlisle Railway over a boggy stretch of Blea Moor, makes an unforgettable statement amid bleak surroundings. It strides across 24 arches rising 50m (165ft) above the valley floor, before disappearing into a long tunnel.

## 5 LITTONDALE

The unspoilt valley of Littondale takes its name from one of five villages on the River Skirfare, one of the River Wharfe's main tributaries. This is a haunt of keen walkers and nature lovers. If the light slants in a certain way along the valley sides, you may notice the pattern of ancient terraces known as lynchets, remnants of a medieval strip-farming system. **Arncliffe** is an idyllic village of stone cottages and porched barns arranged around a large oblong green, much in demand as a backdrop for the long-running Yorkshire 'soap' *Emmerdale*. Charles Kingsley wrote part of *The Water Babies* here, though the book is set largely in Malhamdale. The church commemorates local men-at-arms who fought and died at Flodden Field in 1513.

*Head up **Ribblesdale** on the B6479 towards Horton-in-Ribblesdale.* **4**

*Retrace your route down the B6479 to Stainforth, then turn left on the road signed for Halton Gill. Continue over open moorland to **Littondale**.* **5**

*Head south east on unclassified roads to join the B6160 near **Kilnsey**.* **6**

*Clockwise from far left: path to Malham Cove; Arncliffe, Littondale; waterfall, Horton-in-Ribblesdale; Malham Cove*

*Clockwise from above:*
Burnsall; Bolton Priory,
Bolton Abbey

⬇
*Continue south on the*
*B6160 and east on the*
⑦ *B6265 into Grassington.*

⬇
*Head south east on the*
*B6265/B6160 from*
*Grassington as far*
⑧ *as Burnsall.*

⬇
*Take a left-hand turn on an*
*unclassified road to Apple-*
*treewick, then follow signs*
*to Parcevall Hall Gardens,*
*just beyond the next*
⑨ *village of Skyreholme.*

*Head north to the B6265*
*and turn right for Pateley*
*Bridge. After a couple of*
*miles you will see Stump*
*Cross Caverns, signed to*
*your right.*
→ • • • • • • • • • • ⑩

## 6 KILNSEY

A remarkable natural feature marks this Wharfedale village. As the largest overhang in Britain, **Kilnsey Crag** presents an irresistible challenge to intrepid rock-climbers, who cling to its underside like insects. This limestone spur juts some 9m (30ft) from the valley wall, and is one of the country's toughest climbs. If this level of adrenaline isn't for you, head for **Kilnsey Park**, where there is a trout farm, nature trails and other family attractions. **Coniston**, just across the river, has another strange rock formation resembling a steak-and-kidney pie with a pastry funnel in its middle.

## 7 GRASSINGTON

Wharfedale's principal touring centre is a neat and gentrified little town of cobbled alleys and well-groomed Georgian buildings. The streets are liberally sprinkled with teashops and rustic hostelries. The riverside setting adds much to its charm, and the **Grasswood Nature Reserve** on its outskirts makes a pleasant escape from summer crowds. One of the national park's main information centres at Colvend is a useful place to find out about the local area. Nearby **Linton** on the opposite bank to Grassington is a quieter place with classical almshouses and an ancient church.

## 8 BURNSALL

The view of Burnsall's arched bridge straddling the River Wharfe has captivated many Dales visitors. The village's summer sports day and ancient fell-race up a neighbouring hill attracts a large crowd in August. In **St Wilfred's** churchyard stand Viking gravestones and the village stocks. Look out for a headstone to the Dawson family, carved by the renowned sculptor Eric Gill. The village benefited greatly from the generosity of Sir William Craven, a local worthy who was twice made Lord Mayor of London. He funded several projects such as the lovely bridge and the village school.

## 9 PARCEVALL HALL GARDENS

Enjoying grandstand views from a hillside setting, these extensive woodland gardens with skillfully planted rockeries and shrubberies are worth seeking out. The Elizabethan mansion isn't open to the public, but tearooms and picnic areas take advantage of an outstanding panorama over Wharfedale. To the south, a high fell called Simon's Seat (485m, 1591ft) adds a scenic craggy backdrop.

## 10 STUMP CROSS CAVERNS

These show-caves were discovered by lead miners in the mid-19th century. The intricate passageways were formed by underground watercourses, and contain impressive stalagmite and stalactite formations. Ancient fossilised bones of long-extinct reindeer, bison and wolverines have also been unearthed here. Unusually, you can visit the caves without a guide.

## 11 PATELEY BRIDGE

This attractive little market town, winner of many Britain-in-Bloom contests and plentifully stocked with cafes and shops, is another popular stop-off for visitors. Though it's well outside the national park, it makes the perfect base for exploring Nidderdale to the north (*see below*). The much-loved **Nidderdale Museum** in the former workhouse will fill you in on local history and customs. At the top of the high street on Old Church lane, the ruined church of **St Mary** is set in a pretty churchyard. Just outside the town is the Water Mill Inn, where an old flax mill has been restored to working order.

## 12 BRIMHAM ROCKS

These natural outcrops of gritstone in a high moorland setting of heather and bilberries have been worn into fantastic shapes by wind and weather. Many bear fanciful names – the Anvil, the Castle, the Sphinx and so forth. The sculptor Henry Moore said their influence on his childhood imagination helped to mould the strong, abstract forms typical of his work. The rocks are scattered over an extensive site owned by the National Trust.

## 13 BOLTON ABBEY

Given the name of the village, it's a bit confusing to discover that the atmospheric Wharfeside ruins here correctly belong to **Bolton Priory**. The building dates from 1154, and was founded by an Augustinian community that grew immensely wealthy on the proceeds of local sheep. Parts of the church, chapter house, cloisters and prior's lodging can still be seen. Immortalised by Turner in 1809 and restored by Pugin in the late 19th century, this lovely site now forms part of the Yorkshire estate of the dukes of Devonshire. It is predictably well kept with excellent visitors' facilities. A memorable woodland walk leads upstream to the **Strid**, where the river surges through a narrow crevice. The banks here are just 2m (6ft) apart – close enough to tempt a leap, but a missed foothold on the slippery rocks means almost certain death in the ferocious currents below. To cross the river more safely, use the stepping stones near the ruined priory. About three miles north east of Bolton Abbey is **Barden Tower**, a curious folly-like building that began life as a medieval hunting lodge. It was renovated by the redoubtable Lady Anne Clifford (*see p38*), who restored Skipton Castle after the Civil War, and who spent the last part of her life at Barden Tower. It now serves as a guesthouse and restaurant.

Continue along the B6265 into **Pateley Bridge**. ⑪

Take the B6165 south east out of town and turn off to the left after a mile or so, following signs to **Brimham Rocks**. ⑫

Return to the B6165 and head south east, forking right on to the B6451 at Dacre Banks. Continue as far as the A59 and turn right towards Skipton. **Bolton Abbey** is signposted to the right on the B6160. ⑬

Continue north along the B6160 and turn left to return to **Skipton** on local roads via Eastby.

⑥ • • • • • • • • • • • ①

## WITH MORE TIME

From Pateley Bridge, head up a minor road to **Nidderdale** *(left)*, an Area of Outstanding Natural Beauty. Beyond the Gouthwaite Reservoir lies a weird ravine of caverns and pot-holes called How Stean Gorge, with overhanging cliffs and dripping vegetation. It's spooky enough to have been chosen as a location setting for science fiction dramas such as *Doctor Who* or *Blake's Seven*. These strange landforms were carved over millennia by the How Stean Beck on its descent from upper Nidderdale.

# Richmond and the picture-postcard northern Dales

Two famous dales, Wensleydale and Swaledale, are the star attractions of this part of England. Studded with charming settlements and encased in beautiful scenery, they provide enough scope and interest for a stay of several days. But the minor sidetracks up lesser-known dales can be just as rewarding – all the more so once you escape the crowds and have this glorious countryside all to yourself.

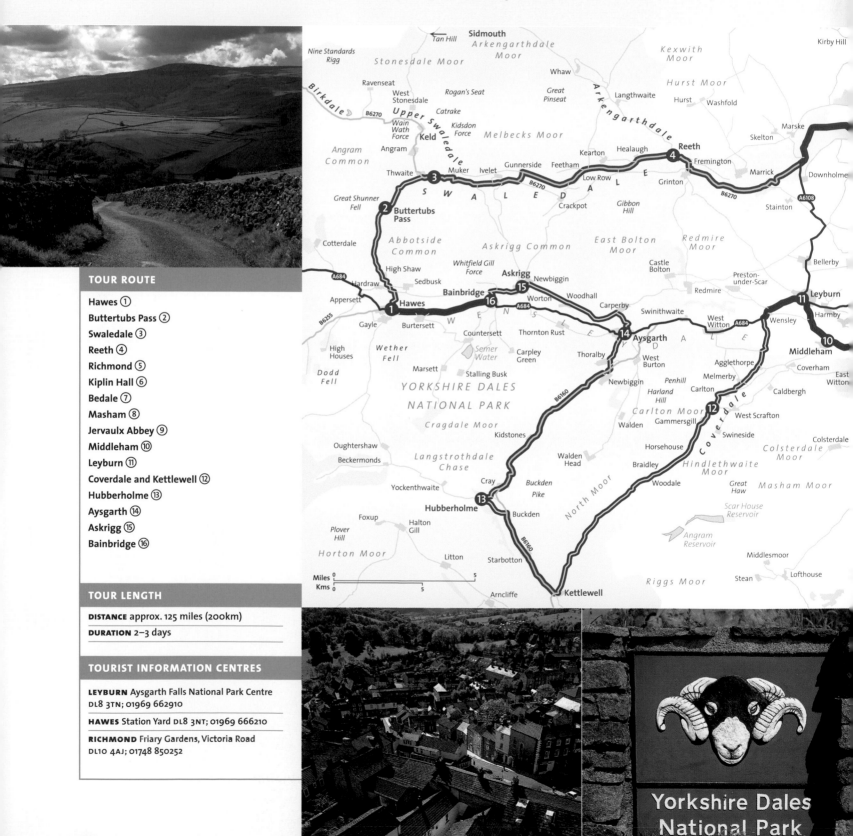

## TOUR ROUTE

Hawes ①
Buttertubs Pass ②
Swaledale ③
Reeth ④
Richmond ⑤
Kiplin Hall ⑥
Bedale ⑦
Masham ⑧
Jervaulx Abbey ⑨
Middleham ⑩
Leyburn ⑪
Coverdale and Kettlewell ⑫
Hubberholme ⑬
Aysgarth ⑭
Askrigg ⑮
Bainbridge ⑯

## TOUR LENGTH

**DISTANCE** approx. 125 miles (200km)

**DURATION** 2–3 days

## TOURIST INFORMATION CENTRES

**LEYBURN** Aysgarth Falls National Park Centre
DL8 3TN; 01969 662910

**HAWES** Station Yard DL8 3NT; 01969 666210

**RICHMOND** Friary Gardens, Victoria Road
DL10 4AJ; 01748 850252

*Clockwise from far left:*
*view of the Dales; Swaledale;*
*Hardraw Force, Hawes; Druid*
*Temple, Masham; national*
*park sign; Richmond*
*town centre*

# 1 HAWES

Appropriately enough, Wensleydale's principal town is the main outlet for its most famous product – cheese. You'll find this in abundance at its lively Tuesday market stalls, and also at the Wensleydale Creamery on Gayle Lane (*see p112*). A less well-known Hawes industry is demonstrated at the Hawes Ropemaker, former premises of W R Outhwaite & Son, the last traditional twine firm in town. Hand-made specialist products (dog-leads, skipping ropes, leading reins) are made in a purpose-built workshop. In the old railway station opposite is the **Dales Countryside Museum**, covering 10,000 years of local history with exhibitions on typical crafts and trades such as peat-cutting, lead-mining and knitting. Just out of town is **Hardraw Force**, one of England's highest single-drop waterfalls (best after heavy rainfall). You can walk behind the cascade on a rocky ledge.

Head north out of Hawes
on unclassified roads
towards Thwaite, pausing
at the Green Dragon pub to
walk to Hardraw Force
before reaching
**Buttertubs Pass**. ②

# 2 BUTTERTUBS PASS

High on the remote fells between Wensleydale and Swaledale are the strange rock formations known as the Buttertubs, where yawning fissures eroded by rushing streams have left flat-topped, circular pillars of limestone. In the past, farmers traversing this high pass (518m, 1,700ft) on their way to market would pause here for a breather, and dangle their dairy produce in these potholes to keep cool. The depths of some of them reach an impressive 30m (100ft).

Continue north on
unclassified roads to
Thwaite, and turn right
on to the B6270
along **Swaledale**.
→ • • • • • • • • • • ③

⬇ Keep going east
along the B6270
④ as far as **Reeth**.

## 3 SWALEDALE

Visitors encounter a scene of pastoral tranquility in this dale, whose most numerous inhabitants seem to be its sturdy sheep (*see p113*). The landscapes here are very ancient: the villages of Thwaite and Muker have Norse names dating back to Viking days. Old stone barns known as laithes are dotted around the valley, and the long-established meadows are ablaze with a rich tapestry of wild flowers from springtime onwards. In the 18th and 19th centuries, however, Swaledale was the heart of a thriving lead-mining industry. The remains of old smelting houses, crushing mills and rusty-grey spoil-heaps can still be seen around Gunnerside Gill, where streams were dammed to scour out the ore.

Swaledale is less widely visited than some other Yorkshire Dales, but is no less beautiful or interesting, and all the more enjoyable for being less crowded. Lovely walks lead along the bucolic valley floor and up into the wild fells to either side.

*Clockwise from far right:*
*views of Richmond Castle;*
*Thwaite, Swaledale*

## WENSLEYDALE CHEESE

The first cheese in Wensleydale was reputedly made by medieval monks, originally from sheep's milk. Following the Dissolution, the recipe changed and by the 1840s the sweet, crumbly cows'-milk version we know today was well established. The first commercial dairy was founded in Hawes at the beginning of the 20th century, and the Wensleydale Creamery is now a firm fixture on the tourism trail, much boosted recently by the well-known dietary preference of Nick Park's animated cartoon characters Wallace and Gromit. Cheese-making tours show you how it is made, after which you can sample and purchase a variety of white or blue-veined Wensleydale cheeses. It is sold in bandaged truckles or waxed miniatures, smoked or mixed with chives, cranberries, apricots – even papaya and mango. Whatever next, Gromit?

## DALES SHEEP

A classic feature of the northern Dales is the hardy, black-faced Swaledale sheep with curly horns. Able to withstand the most severe winter weather, the Swaledale's wool is densely textured and wiry. It is not so good for delicate next-to-the-skin knitwear, but ideal for hard-wearing carpets. Wensleydale also has a highly distinctive breed of sheep, blue-faced with an extraordinary dreadlocked fleece of fine curly ringlets up to 30cm (1ft) long.

## 4 REETH

Swaledale's largest settlement, dominated by its sloping village green, has a prosperous, upmarket air. With its national park information centre and plenty of craft shops and cafes, Reeth is a natural base for walks or tours up Arkengarthdale (*see p117*). The **Swaledale Folk Museum** contains an eclectic array of bits and bobs connected with bygone lifestyles. Just south east of Reeth is **Grinton**, whose church was for centuries the only one in Swaledale. Coffins were carried many miles along a rough track known as the Corpse Way to be buried here. Just east of Reeth stand the ruined priories of Marrick and Ellerton near the banks of the Swale. Ellerton dates from the 15th century and was orginally a Cistercian house. The tower and nave still stand.

## 5 RICHMOND

Yorkshire's Richmond is very different from its Surrey namesake, but it is just as full of civic pride, amply justified by its magnificent setting and admirable state of preservation. This Dales gateway is indeed a jewel, crammed with historic buildings that surround an enormous cobbled square. The splendid **castle** looming above the River Swale on a rocky outcrop dates from Norman times and is still largely intact as it saw very little military action. Behind its curtain walls lie England's oldest Great Hall and a keep over 30m (100ft) high. A heritage garden reflects the castle's lengthy past, and a walk beneath the walls gives a fine prospect of the river. Just off the market place is another noteworthy building, the authentically Georgian **Theatre Royal** dating from 1788. The exquisitely restored interior and a small museum can be visited. Displays on local crafts and a reconstruction of a medieval cruck house are among the items on show at the **Richmondshire Museum**, and the town's regimental associations are emphasized at the **Green Howards Regimental Museum** in a collection of more than 3,000 medals and bloodstained pistols. Army personnel are still much in evidence in Richmond due to the large garrison at nearby Catterick. There is a pleasant riverside walk to the 12th-century ruins of **Easby Abbey** on the south east edge of town.

*Continue along the B6270 east until you reach the A6108, turning left for **Richmond**.* ⑤

*Leave Richmond via the B6271 towards Brompton-on-Swale. On the east side of the A1, you'll find signs to **Kiplin Hall**.*
⑥

⊥
*Retrace your route along*
*the B6271 and join the A1 at*
*Catterick. Head south down*
*the A1 to Leeming Bar, then*
*turn west on to the A684*
**7** *to Bedale.*

## 6 KIPLIN HALL

Not far from Bolton-on-Swale, Kiplin Hall was built in the early 1620s as a hunting lodge for George Calvert, secretary of state to James I, later the first Lord Baltimore and the founder of Maryland, USA. Its design, unique in Jacobean architecture, uses mellow red brick instead of Yorkshire stone to construct a tall, compact, symmetrical, country house with central domed towers on each side of a pavilion. The interior has a great deal of Victorian influence, although there are some fine Georgian fireplaces and an 18th century staircase, which leads to a series of domestic rooms and the Long Gallery. Paintings by G F Watts and Angelica Kauffman adorn the dining room walls, while watercolours by Lady Waterford fill the decorative sitting room.

## 7 BEDALE

Another ancient market town, Bedale first gained its charter in 1251, and its market cross dates from the 14th century. The **Church of St Gregory** dominates the wide main street, the clock on its tower curiously off-centre. It contains a bell rescued from nearby Jervaulx Abbey after the Dissolution. Also on the main street, the Georgian mansion of **Bedale Hall** provides handsome premises for the tourist information centre with its fine plasterwork and 'flying' staircase. Just south of Bedale, **Thorp Perrow Arboretum** is a fine assembly of rare specimen trees, including national collections of ash, lime and walnut. It is especially attractive when the spring bulbs are out, or when the leaves turn in autumn. You can see birds of prey being put through their paces at its on-site falconry centre. Nearby Snape Castle dates from 1426. Katherine Parr, widow of one of the Neville family who owned it, lived here for ten years before becoming Henry VIII's sixth and final wife.

*Continue south along the*
*B6268 turning right on*
*the A6108 to the village*
**8** *of Masham.*

## 8 MASHAM

For the uninitiated, this place is pronounced 'Mazzam', but among real ale fans, it needs little introduction. Masham is the home of two famous breweries, **Theakstons** and its rival the **Black Sheep Brewery** (set up by an independent-minded family member when Theakstons was taken over by Scottish and Newcastle in 1989). Both produce excellent ales: Theakstons Old Peculier is a legendary brew but some claim Black Sheep is even better. Both also offer tours and tastings. Beer-drinking aside, Masham is a fine little town of dignified Georgian buildings around a typical Dales-style square, livelier than usual on market days (Wednesday and Saturday), and during its traditional September sheep fair. South west of Masham stands a startling Stonehenge lookalike known as the Druid's Temple. This scaled-down replica is no Neolithic antiquity but a folly commissioned by local landowner William Danby in the 1820s.

*Take the A6108 north west*
*from Masham, turning off*
*right for Jervaulx Abbey*
*after about 6 miles.*

→ • • • • • • • • • • • • **9**

*Clockwise from far left: Bedale church; castle ruins, Middleham; ruins of Jervaulx Abbey; beer barrels, Masham*

## 9 JERVAULX ABBEY

In a romantically untamed setting, the ruins of this monastery are entwined with clambering ivy and surrounded by wild flowers. Founded in 1156, Jervaulx was a Cistercian community like the grander abbeys of Rievaulx and Fountains to the south east. In its heyday, Jervaulx owned most of Wensleydale, and the monks here are believed to be the ones to have made the first Wensleydale cheese (*see p112*). Identifiable features include the Night Stairs, by which the monks reached the church from their dormitory to attend services in the small hours. The last abbot of Jervaulx was hanged at Tyburn for his vociferous opposition to the Dissolution.

## 10 MIDDLEHAM

Middleham has several claims to fame. Most obvious is its imposing Norman **castle** where Richard III spent a happy childhood and honeymoon days before his dubious accession to the throne. The castle contains a replica of the famous Middleham Jewel, a magnificent gold and sapphire pendant dating from the late 15th century, discovered here in 1985. The original is now kept in York. Local racehorse training stables give Middleham the soubriquet 'Newmarket of the North'. A castellated bridge crosses the River Ure here, and like most Dales towns, it has a large cobbled market place surrounded by Georgian buildings.

## 11 LEYBURN

Two major roads converge at this modest agricultural town on the edge of the national park, making it the principal gateway to Wensleydale from the east. Leyburn is a major auction centre for antiques, and has several unusual visitor attractions. One is the **Teapottery**, a self-explanatory craft workshop where a weird and wonderful range of tea-drinking equipment is on sale. Another is a violin-making studio, where visitors are welcome. Two interesting gardens can be viewed nearby. East of Leyburn, **Constable Burton Hall** gardens surround a handsome Georgian house, while at Coverham (near Middleham), **Forbidden Corner** is an intriguing walled garden with secret passages and joky statues. The neighbouring village of **Wensley**, after which the dale was originally named, was all but wiped out in an outbreak of the plague in 1563. Its 13th-century church of Holy Trinity is one of the most impressive anywhere in the Dales, the choir-stalls elaborately carved with poppies.

*Continue north along the A6108 as far as **Middleham**.* 10

*Drive another couple of miles north on the A6108 into **Leyburn**. Turn left here for the A684 and Wensley.* 11

*Just beyond Wensley, turn left off the A684 on local roads south into **Coverdale**.* 12

*Clockwise from above:*
*Kettlewell; Bainbridge;*
*Aysgarth Falls*

## 13 HUBBERHOLME

The delightful 13th-century **church** of Hubberholme
famously contains the ashes of author J B Priestley. It
has a Norman tower, a rare rood-loft dating from 1558,
and pews carved by 'Mouseman' Robert Thompson of
Kilburn. Look for the mouse carvings – his family firm's
trademark. Hubberholme is the meeting point of
Wharfedale and the much less well-known
Langstrothdale, an ancient hunting forest now
extensively planted with conifers.

## 14 AYSGARTH

After heavy rainfall, the **Aysgarth Falls**, just to the east
of town, make a memorable sight. Here the River Ure
tumbles over a series of low waterfalls at one of the
best-loved beauty spots of the Dales. Inevitably, it can
get very crowded in high summer. The peaty falls
(called Upper, Middle and Lower) are reached by a path
from the car park, and extend along about half a mile
of the river's course. Aysgarth itself has a fine church
with a 16th-century screen rescued from Jervaulx
Abbey. The **Yorkshire Museum of Carriages**, housed in
an old mill, displays a collection of Victorian vehicles,
including a hansom cab, a charabanc and an old milk-
float. A short detour northwards takes you to the
doughty fortress at **Castle Bolton**, an estate village
stretching along a single street. The 14th-century
fortifications were built by Sir Richard Scrope from
Masham. Mary Queen of Scots spent a six-month
stretch here. Huge towers and dungeons survive the
centuries, but have been empty since 1645. Fine views
and medieval gardens add to its appeal.

## 12 COVERDALE AND KETTLEWELL

This easterly tributary of Wensleydale is a quiet and
gentle valley enjoyably off the beaten tourist trail. The
upper reaches meander over a high pass alongside
lonely sheep farms and the grand fells of Whernside.
**Kettlewell**, at the southern end of the Coverdale road, is
back in Wharfedale again, here a U-shaped valley
liberally laced with dry stone walls. These days
Kettlewell makes a charming walking base, but its old
lead-miners' cottages and smelting mills indicate it
was not always such a rural retreat. During the late
18th and early 19th centuries it was something of an
industrial boomtown.

*Turn north on to the B6160*
*at Kettlewell and follow*
*the River Wharfe through*
*Starbotton and Buckden,*
*then detour briefly left*
13 *through **Hubberholme**.*

*Return to the B6160 and*
*head northwards,*
*following signs*
14 *to **Aysgarth**.*

*To avoid the busy A684,*
*take unclassified roads*
*along Wensleydale*
*to **Askrigg**.*

→ • • • • • • • • • 15

## 15   ASKRIGG

After Wensley's sudden decline from a plague outbreak in the 16th century, Askrigg became the main Dales trading centre for the clock-making, brewing and textile industries. However, the railway age transferred Askrigg's prosperity to Hawes, where Wensleydale's station was built. But Askrigg's largely unchanged historic buildings later became an unexpected source of revenue. During the 1980s this unspoilt little market town provided a location setting for the popular TV series *All Creatures Great and Small*, based on the stories of Thirsk vet James Herriot. 'Skeldale House' is still on the tourist trail, but many other elegant streamside houses and the 15th-century church are worth a look.

## 16   BAINBRIDGE

Here, as at Ripon, an ancient horn-blowing ceremony takes place each evening at 9pm during the winter months. It is said the tradition goes back to Norman times, and was intended to guide travellers to safety through the lonely forests that once surrounded this idyllic village. The broad, sloping green still has its stocks, and a restored corn mill now produces hand-made doll's houses. The low hill visible above the roofs is a glacial drumlin, once the site of a Roman fort. To the south, **Semer Water** is an Ice Age lake created when a retreating glacier dammed the River Bain.

*Take local roads south towards the A684 and Bainbridge.* 16

*Drive west along the A684 back to Hawes.*

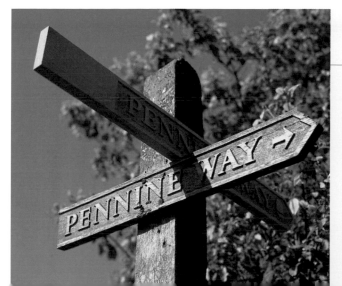

### WITH MORE TIME

Explore the upper reaches of **Swaledale**, and its tributary valley **Birkdale**, running towards the **Cumbrian** border. The fast-flowing Swale rises on moorland north of the village of **Keld**, where Britain's highest pub (the Tan Hill Inn at 528m, 1,732ft) stands on old drover's roads, actually the meeting point of three counties. Both the Pennine Way *(left)* and the Coast-to-Coast Path pass through Keld. **Arkengarthdale** is another picturesque side-valley off Swaledale, once known for lead-mining. Strange place-names like Whaw and Booze may arouse your curiosity.

# Whitby and the magic of the North York Moors National Park

Tucked within the folds of the wild moorland landscape of the North York Moors lie picturesque villages and the impressive ruins of abbeys and priories, such as Mount Grace, Rosedale and Rievaulx, glorious reminders of the heydays of the monasteries. But it is the ruins of Whitby's 7th-century abbey perched on the headland overlooking the harbour that perhaps enjoys the most dramatic setting of them all.

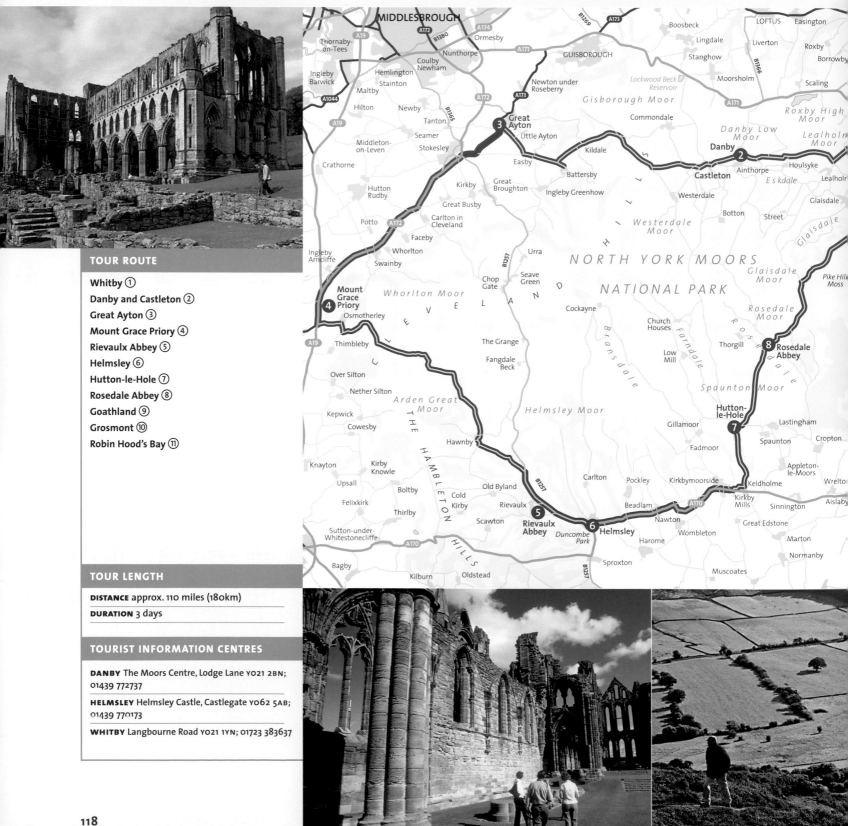

## TOUR ROUTE

Whitby ①

Danby and Castleton ②

Great Ayton ③

Mount Grace Priory ④

Rievaulx Abbey ⑤

Helmsley ⑥

Hutton-le-Hole ⑦

Rosedale Abbey ⑧

Goathland ⑨

Grosmont ⑩

Robin Hood's Bay ⑪

## TOUR LENGTH

**DISTANCE** approx. 110 miles (180km)

**DURATION** 3 days

## TOURIST INFORMATION CENTRES

**DANBY** The Moors Centre, Lodge Lane YO21 2BN; 01439 772737

**HELMSLEY** Helmsley Castle, Castlegate YO62 5AB; 01439 770173

**WHITBY** Langbourne Road YO21 1YN; 01723 383637

*Clockwise from far left:*
Rievaulx Abbey; Whitby;
North York Moors;
Whitby Abbey

# 1 WHITBY

The coastal town of Whitby has a unique, old-world charm with its skyline dominated by the ruins of the 7th-century **abbey** and its maze of alleyways and narrow streets that tumble down to the busy quayside below. From the old town at East Cliff, 199 steps lead up to Whitby's parish church, **St Mary's**, one of the finest examples of Anglo-Saxon architecture in the country, featuring 17th-century carved pews made by ship's carpenters and craftsmen. Its sinister-looking churchyard inspired Bram Stoker to write the Gothic novel *Dracula*. Whitby has provided a safe haven to fishing fleets for centuries, and it was once the main whaling port for northern England. A whalebone arch now commemorates this industry. This seafaring town became well known for its connections with the 18th-century explorer Captain James Cook and the father-and-son whaling masters of the Scoresby family. Today Whitby, with its higgledy-piggledy arrangement of red-roofed houses and attractive buildings on the steep slopes of the River Esk, is a delight to explore.

*Leave Whitby on the A171 west and then take local roads through Eskdale to Danby and on to Castleton.*

# 2 DANBY AND CASTLETON

**Danby** is best known for the national park's **Moors Centre**, an excellent place to find out about local walks and places of interest. The building was originally a shooting lodge for the Dawnay family, who ruled the roost hereabouts. It stands in terraced waterfront grounds, where an arched packhorse bridge called the Duck Bridge crosses the River Esk. The now ruined **Danby castle** dates from the 14th century, and was once the home of Katherine Parr, the sixth and luckiest wife of Henry VIII (who survived him). As its name suggests, **Castleton** once had a castle too, but all that remains is a grassy mound. Much of the stone is believed to have been pillaged for the castle at Danby. The Esk Valley Walk begins at Castleton, and follows the river all the way to the coast at Whitby. From Castleton Rigg, you can take a footpath route to Ralph Cross, the national park emblem at the head of Rosedale.

*From here continue on unclassified roads west cross country via Battersby and Little Ayton to Great Ayton.*

⊕ *Take the A173 south to its junction with the A172 at Stokesley and then follow this south to reach the A19. Take the A19, south looking for a signpost on your left*
④ *to **Mount Grace Priory**.*

*Cut across country on unclassified roads east via Osmotherley and Hawnby to the B1257. Continue south for a few miles and then turn right on local roads to **Rievaulx Abbey**.*

→ • • • • • • • • • • • ⑤

## 3 GREAT AYTON

The unassuming village of Great Ayton, overlooked by the conical hill Roseberry Topping, is in a conservation area. With a fine prospect of the Cleveland Hills escarpment to the south, it has two centres, High and Low Green, which are linked by the River Leven. The village once boasted a thriving textile and tanning industry but today it is popular stop on the Esk Valley Railway, which runs from Whitby to Middlesbrough. Great Ayton is best known for its most famous son, Captain James Cook, who spent the early part of his life here. The Cook family home on Bridge Street was built by James' father in 1755, though in 1934 it was dismantled and shipped to Australia, where it now stands in Melbourne's Fitzroy Gardens. A granite obelisk now marks the original site of Cook's cottage in Great Ayton.

### ROSEBERRY TOPPING

Blow the cobwebs away by taking a leisurely walk up this conical hill. The peculiar shape is due to a geological fault and a mine that collapsed early in the 20th century. From the summit there is a magnificent 360-degree view that allows you to see as far as Teeside in one direction and the Yorkshire Dales in another. Newton and Cliff Ridge Woods skirt the northern edge of the hill, and Cliff Rigg quarry still retains evidence of the extraction of whinstone, once used for road-building. The area is rich in wildlife, particularly moorland birds.

## 4 MOUNT GRACE PRIORY

Tucked neatly into the wooded western edge of the Cleveland Hills, the atmospheric ruin of Mount Grace Priory is one of the finest examples of a 14th-century Carthusian monastery. Typically, Mount Grace housed 15 or so hermit-monks living as solitaries in two-storey, 7m-sq cells (22sq-ft). The ground floor had a fireplace and a wooden staircase to the room above. Each also had a small garden, separated from the next by high walls, in which the monk worked alone. Meeting their fellows only for matins and vespers, and the occasional feast day when services were held in the church, the monks would spend ten hours each day in their cells, reading, praying, eating and meditating. Now in the guardianship of English Heritage, little remains of the priory, save for its gatehouse and church, a small herb garden, and a reconstructed and furnished cell, enabling you to experience the austere conditions in which the monks lived.

*Clockwise from above:*
*Rievaulx Abbey; Helmsley*
*town and castle; Roseberry*
*Topping outside Great*
*Ayton; Mount Grace Priory*

## 5 RIEVAULX ABBEY

In a deep valley by the River Rye, Rievaulx Abbey is celebrated for the beauty and tranquillity of its setting. It was founded in the 12th century as the first Cistercian outpost in the north, and intended to be a mission centre from which the 'white monks' could spread across the country. Indeed, by the 13th century the influence of Rievaulx had spread to no fewer than 19 other abbeys in the north of England, prospering largely thanks to sheep-farming as well as an active patronage of culture. Rievaulx's fortunes changed in the late 13th century, when the abbey suffered severe financial problems, war, famine and plague, and was later destroyed during the Dissolution of the monasteries. The austere and impressive ruins include extensive remains of the church, once one of the finest in the region, and cloistral buildings of which five arches survive.

Close by you will find the **Rievaulx Terrace and Temples**, a grassy terrace, bright in springtime and early summer with wild flowers, and an outstanding 18th-century landscape garden that also contains two mid-18th-century temples. Intended as a banqueting house, the Ionic temple has beautiful painted ceilings and fine furniture. From the garden's elevated position you get a fine view of the abbey ruins and over Ryedale below.

## 6 HELMSLEY

Helmsley's undulating red rooflines, honey-coloured buildings, market square, beautiful riverside walks, chintzy tea rooms and genteel country pubs have lost none of their fascination. Almost every view of this market town is dominated by the tall ruin of its **castle**, which dates from the 12th century and was once home to the Duke of Buckingham, court favourite of Charles I. It was severely damaged during the Civil War, but the nearby Tudor mansion survived largely intact.

Most people come to visit the fine baroque mansion of **Duncombe Park**, which has been, in turn, the Duncombe's family seat for nearly 300 years, a hospital, and a girls' school until it was re-occupied in 1985 by Lord Feversham. He restored the mansion and opened it to the public in 1990. The well-preserved, early 18th-century landscaped gardens are classically English and surrounded by parkland. You can wander at leisure across the great lawn and terraces, amid temples, yew trees and woodland walks, and the scented 'secret garden' surrounding the old conservatory. **Helmsley Walled Garden**, originally developed to supply produce to the Duncombe estate, lay abandoned until 1994, when a major restoration programme was initiated to bring the site back into life as a fully working kitchen garden, now open to the public.

*Continue past Rievaulx and rejoin the B1257 to* **Helmsley** *and locally signed roads to Duncombe Park* **6**

*Follow the A170 east for 7 miles, and then leave it for local roads north to* **Hutton-le-Hole**. **7**

↓ From Hutton-le-Hole
follow unclassified roads
⑧ north to **Rosedale Abbey**.

↓ Continue on local roads
north from Rosedale Abbey,
heading for Egton Bridge;
but before reaching the
village, turn right using
more unclassified roads
⑨ south to **Goathland**.

↓ Follow unclassified roads
north down to **Grosmont**
⑩ and Eskdale.

Take unclassified roads east
to reach the B1416. Turn
right for 3 miles to the
junction with A171. Then go
left for 1 mile before using
local roads east to descend
to **Robin Hood's Bay**.

→ • • • • • • • • • • • ⑪

## 7 HUTTON-LE-HOLE

Tucked neatly into the southern edge of the North York Moors National Park, the village of Hutton-le-Hole centres around a beautiful village green. Nearby, the open-air **Ryedale Folk Museum**, very much a 'hands-on' experience, depicts 4,000 years of North Yorkshire life in the form of reconstructed historic buildings including shops, thatched cruck cottages, an Elizabethan manor house, barns and workshops.

## 8 ROSEDALE ABBEY

Gloriously set on the heather-covered moors flanking the River Severn, the tiny, eponymous village of Rosedale Abbey retains just a hint of its industrial past, most noticeable in cottages built of bluish ironstone brick. In 1328, Edward III granted permission to the nuns of Rosedale Abbey to work the ore here, but 500 years later it was considered poor quality and worthless and production ceased. In the 19th century, however, Rosedale ore was discovered to be magnetic and of the highest quality. Five millions tons were extracted in 20 years, and in 1861 the Rosedale Ironstone Railway was constructed to carry the iron to the furnaces of Teeside. By the 1920s, the seams had worn thin and a depression was looming, presaging the final end of the mining operations here. Little remains of the original abbey except a stone pillar and a remnant staircase, though a good deal of the stonework went into building the village church. The ironstone railway tracks now serve to help walkers to enjoy the wider landscapes of the moors.

## 9 GOATHLAND

Despite its undoubtedly beautiful setting, few would visit the village of Goathland were it not for television. For it was here that many of the scenes of the series *Heartbeat*, set in the fictional village of Aidensfield, were filmed. Many of the series' landmarks are recognisable, including the village store, the offices of the garage/funeral director, the public house and, of course, the railway station, which is actually on the line of the North York Moors Railway. In a narrow wooded dell nearby is **Mallyan Spout**, a 21.5-m high waterfall (70ft) that is especially dramatic when the water is low and only a thin flow of water cascades down like at mystical veil.

## 10 GROSMONT

Grosmont (pronounced grow-mont) is set in a bucolic landscape of scattered fields and farms, and attracts hikers on the Coast-to-Coast Walk. But the village had a more gritty past as the hub of a thriving ironstone industry, and it is its railway and industrial heritage that attracts visitors today. In 1836, the building of one of the railway lines exposed a rich seam of ironstone of the highest quality, which was transported by rail to the coast at Whitby. The presence of the railway still features largely in the everyday life of the village, as it is the northern terminus of the North York Moors Railway (*see p123*). From Grosmont you can also enjoy easy walks across the adjacent moorland, in particular to the **Low Bridge Stones**, a small group of ancient stones on the edge of Goathland Moor.

*Clockwise from above:*
Robin Hood's Bay; North York
Moors Railway, view
from Goathland

## 11 ROBIN HOOD'S BAY

### COAST-TO-COAST WALK

Originally devised by Alfred Wainwright, the Coast-to-Coast Walk crosses northern England from St Bees Head in Cumbria to Robin Hood's Bay on the Yorkshire coast. A great swathe of the route runs from Richmond, across the Vale of Mowbray and onto the Cleveland Hills that form the northern escarpment of the North York Moors, before descending to tease a route through the villages of Eskdale as it heads for journey's end at Robin Hood's Bay.

Legend has it that Robin Hood found a quiet bay on the edge of the North York Moors and decided it would make an ideal retreat. Here, under the name of Simon Wise, he returned time and time again, keeping a small fleet of fishing boats, which he used to put to sea whenever danger threatened. The village that bears his name was once a fishing community, with a not insignificant sideline in smuggling: now it has caught the imagination of tourists, and is a popular holiday resort. Its red-roofed houses and shops are perched precariously at, or above, the water's edge, many so small and narrow that they have a 'coffin window' above the door to enable coffins, too large to be passed down the narrow staircases, to be removed from upstairs rooms. At high tide the sea runs into the village street, and at low tide the Scars, or rocks, run far out to sea and are full of rock pools.

*Leave Robin Hood's Bay
along the B1447 north to
rejoin the A171 and follow
this north back to* **Whitby**.

⊖ • • • • • • • • • • ➊

## WITH MORE TIME

The **North Yorkshire Moors Railway** was originally opened in 1836 as a horse-drawn tramway running from Whitby to Pickering. It was closed in 1965 but was resurrected by the North Yorkshire Moors Preservation Society, reopening in 1973. Operating throughout the year (though not every day) the railway line is run as a living museum. The trains travel through delightful scenery of wooded valleys and heather-clad moorland, and visit isolated villages where you can alight and walk or cycle across the moors.

# Stately homes in the Vale of York

The vales of York and Mowbray form a wide plain bordered by the Yorkshire Dales to the west, the hills of the North York Moors to the north and the Yorkshire Wolds to the east. This fertile region is dominated by rolling farmlands, but at its centre lies the vibrant city of York, known for its magnificent minster and its historic buildings. The Vale of York is also rich in stately homes, priories and abbeys, but the jewel in the crown is one of England's grandest houses, the striking Castle Howard.

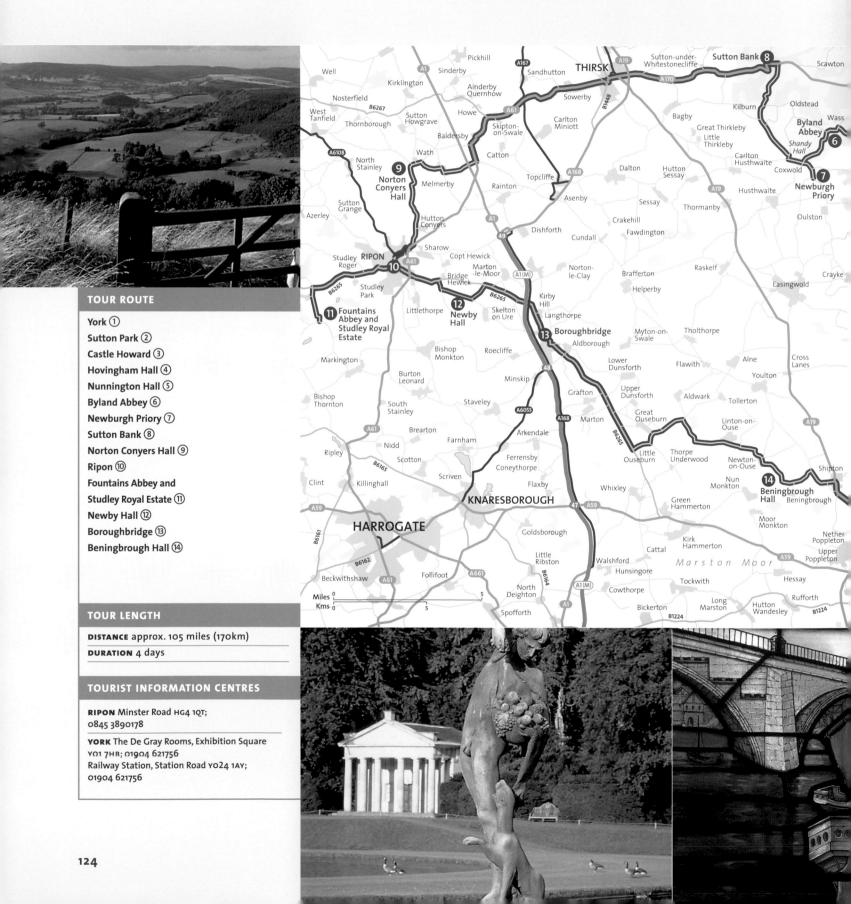

## TOUR ROUTE

York ①
Sutton Park ②
Castle Howard ③
Hovingham Hall ④
Nunnington Hall ⑤
Byland Abbey ⑥
Newburgh Priory ⑦
Sutton Bank ⑧
Norton Conyers Hall ⑨
Ripon ⑩
Fountains Abbey and
Studley Royal Estate ⑪
Newby Hall ⑫
Boroughbridge ⑬
Beningbrough Hall ⑭

## TOUR LENGTH

**DISTANCE** approx. 105 miles (170km)

**DURATION** 4 days

## TOURIST INFORMATION CENTRES

**RIPON** Minster Road HG4 1QT;
0845 3890178

**YORK** The De Gray Rooms, Exhibition Square
YO1 7HB; 01904 621756
Railway Station, Station Road YO24 1AY;
01904 621756

# 1 YORK

The fascination of York lies in the many layers of history that are reflected by the varied architecture and museums to see here. Almost 2,000 years ago the Roman Ninth Legion set up a small fort at Eboracum, strategically positioned on the River Ouse. This in turn became the Saxon stronghold of Eorforwick. And so it remained until 866 when the town was seized by the Vikings. Within 10 years Jorvik – as it was called – became the Viking capital and evolved into one of the most viable trading ports in Northern Europe. In the mid-11th century the last great king was killed. The Normans then fortified the city, and began work on the minster in 1220, on the site of the Roman headquarters. York flourished as the medieval wool trade expanded, under the direction of the monastic settlement. When this influence declined following the Dissolution, so, too, for a time, did the prominence of the city. During the 18th century, York became a fashionable social centre, and witnessed the building of many fine Georgian buildings. The railway, opened in 1839, and the city boomed. York's many highlights reflect the city's key periods of history.

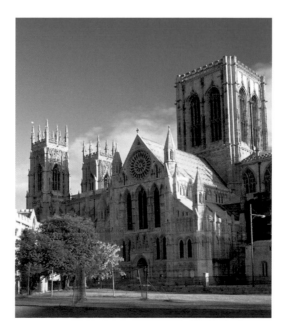

*Clockwise from far left:*
Sutton Bank; Castle Howard;
York Minster; stained glass,
Merchant Adventurers' Hall,
York; Studley Royal Estate

*Leave York north west to
the junction with the A19.
Turn right on the A1237 (the
ring road), and turn left
onto the B1363, continuing
to Sutton-on-the-Forest
and **Sutton Park**.*

→ • • • • • • • • • • • ❷

*Clockwise from above:*
view of city walls and York
Minster, York; gallery of
Roman sculpture, Castle
Howard; fountain, Castle
Howard; Merchant
Adventurers' Hall, York;
interior of York Minster

## YORK MINSTER

The largest Gothic cathedral in northern Europe, York's
magnificent **minster** is an amazing medieval
architectural achievement that took more than 250
years to build. Founded in AD627 by King Edwin of
Northumbria, it is dedicated to St Peter. The minster is
deservedly renowned for its glorious stained-glass
windows, 128 in all, justifying the claim that York
houses more than half of Britain's finest stained glass.
The huge Great East Window is a prime example, the
largest stained glass window in the world, created in
the early 15th century by John Thornton of Coventry.
Energetic visitors can climb the central tower's 275
steps to be rewarded with an incredible view of the
countryside around the city, and, in good weather, the
spire of Lincoln Cathedral, more than 60 miles away.

## YORK'S SIGHTS

The **Jorvik** centre leads visitors on a journey through
York in Viking times at the end of the first millennium,
and is one of the most popular attractions in Britain. It
was inspired by the finds from an archaeological dig in
the city between 1976 and 1981.

Built on Roman foundations, York has the best-
preserved medieval **city walls** in England, interspersed
with with gateways and towers. Most of the walls are
intact and can be followed on a rampart walk
extending over two miles. The network of lanes and
alleyways collectively known as **The Shambles** is
arguably Europe's best preserved medieval centre. The
streets are so narrow in some places, you can touch
both sides. The stunning, timber-framed **Merchant
Adventurers' Hall** on Fossgate reminds one what
craftsmanship went into medieval building. It is one of
the largest buildings of its kind and date, and yet was
built in 1357–61, before most of the craft or trade guild
halls in Britain were formed.

York's Georgian history is revealed in **Fairfax House**
on Castlegate, one of the finest mid-18th-century
townhouses in England. It typifies the best of rococo
decoration, with ornate stucco ceilings, and is home to
the fine Noel Terry collection of furniture. The **Treasurer's
House** is a stunningly beautiful, 18th-century
townhouse. Originally home to the treasurers of York
Minster and built on a Roman road (the ghosts of a
Roman legion reputedly march through the cellars), the
house was designed by John Carr and displays fine
period furniture, porcelain and clocks.

The **National Railway Museum**, the largest in the world,
houses an extensive collection of locomotives, rolling
stock, railway equipment and documents, and traces
the history of the railway from the Rocket to Eurostar.

## 2 SUTTON PARK

Located in the tranquil village of Sutton-on-the-Forest, Sutton Park is a private residence but opens its doors to the public. This elegant early Georgian house contains exquisite examples of hand-painted Chinese-influenced wallpaper and a wonderful collection of porcelain including Meissen and Sèvres. Here you can enjoy a stroll in the gardens overlooking spacious parkland thought to have been designed by Meikle, a follower of 'Capability' Brown.

## 3 CASTLE HOWARD

The breathtaking Castle Howard is still home to the family whose forebears conceived, designed, and built it more than 300 years ago. Set dramatically between two lakes, this palatial 18th-century stately home, designed by Sir John Vanbrugh, is one of England's most beautiful and grand historic houses. It has unrivalled collections of furniture, paintings, porcelain and statuary gathered by generations of the Howard family. All the rooms have knowledgeable guides on hand to relate the family history and stories about the building itself. You may even meet costumed guides posing as Sir John Vanburgh; Frederick, 5th Earl of Carlisle, an avid collector; Georgiana, the 6th Countess of Carlisle; or even housemaid Ann Tibbles. In the chapel three embroidered panels are from a set of eight by William Morris, representing Lucretia, Hippolyte and Helen of Troy (they were made into the oak-framed screen for the 9th Countess). However, at the heart of the house, the Great Hall is the most palatial room of all with its cupola rising an incredible 22m (70ft).

The grounds are every bit as spectacular as the house. Vanburgh's influence continues here, with many vistas dotted with pyramids, towers and obelisks, including the commanding Temple of the Four Winds originally constructed simply as a place to rest and eat. The Mausoleum, best viewed from Temple Hole Basin, is still the burial place of the Howard family and is virtually the size of a palace in its own right.

## 4 HOVINGHAM HALL

For more than 400 years Hovingham Hall has been the family seat of the Worsleys, an old Lancashire family. This gorgeous Palladian house was built between 1750 and 1770 by Thomas Worsley to his own design and is unique in being entered through The Riding School. Thomas Worsley was passionate about horses and architecture; the house remains the product of the extraordinary fusion of these two obsessions.

## 5 NUNNINGTON HALL

This mellow, honey-coloured manor house set on the banks of the River Rye was once home to the doctor of Henry VIII, Edward VI and Elizabeth I. From the magnificent oak-panelled hall, three staircases lead to the family rooms: the nursery, the haunted room and the attics with their fascinating Carlisle collection of miniature rooms, which are fully furnished to represent different periods. Outdoors, the totally organic walled-garden retains a lovely 17th-century character with delightful mixed borders, orchards of traditional fruit varieties, spring-flowering meadows and a collection of 50 different types of clematis.

Head north east using unclassified roads via Sheriff Hutton to **Castle Howard**. ③

Continue north on local roads to meet the B1257, and turn left for **Hovingham Hall**. ④

Head north on the B1257 and turn right along unclassified roads to **Nunnington Hall**. ⑤

Take local roads west to briefly return to the B1257, leaving it at Oswaldkirk to take unclassified roads west to **Byland Abbey**.

→ • • • • • • • • • • ⑥

⊥ From Byland Abbey take
  unclassified roads to the
⑦ nearby **Newburgh Priory**.

⊥ Return north on local roads
  to the A170, and cross the
⑧ main road for **Sutton Bank**.

⊥ Return to the A170 west
  towards Thirsk, and
  continue along the A61
  Then follow unclassified
  roads across the A1 west to
⑨ **Norton Conyers**.

⊥ Follow local roads south to
  briefly rejoin the A61 and
⑩ turn right for **Ripon**.

Take the B6265 west out
of Ripon and follow
unclassified roads to reach
**Fountains Abbey and
Studley Royal Estate**.

→ • • • • • • • • • • • • ⑪

## 6 BYLAND ABBEY

This beautiful ruin, set in the shadow of the Hambleton Hills, was once one of the great northern monasteries, rivalling Rievaulx (*see p121*) and Fountains (*see p129*) in importance. A truly outstanding example of early Gothic architecture, it originally had a wheel window on the west front that inspired the design for the Rose Window in York Minster (*see p126*). Its splendid collection of medieval tiles, remarkably still in situ, is the second largest in Europe.

## 7 NEWBURGH PRIORY

Lying in a fold in the hills near the ancient village of Coxwold, Newburgh Priory is an elegant stately home. Founded in 1145 and built on the site of an earlier Augustinian priory, it is a confusing mish-mash of medieval, Tudor, Jacobean and Georgian architecture. The entrance is probably medieval and leads to the former manorial court rooms, including the Black Gallery and Justice Room, brightly painted in contrast to the dark panelling of the entrance. Newburgh is the reputed burial place of Oliver Cromwell, whose remains – possibly minus his head – were said to have been brought here by his daughter Mary when she married the second Viscount Fauconberg. However, tradition dictates that the tomb is never to be opened. You can wander the extensive grounds or venture into the walled garden to admire the skilfully designed toparied yews.

.

## 8 SUTTON BANK

The steep escarpment of Sutton Bank is a splendid vantage point at the edge of the Hambleton Hills and the North York Moors, offering extensive views over the Vale of York and the Vale of Mowbray. Landmarks include Whitestone Cliff and Roulston Scar, the former overlooking the picturesque Lake Gormire. Close by are the peaceful villages of Sutton-under-Whitestonecliff, and Kilburn, famous for the White Horse designed by Thomas Taylor, a native of Kilburn, and cut in 1857.

## 9 NORTON CONYERS HALL

Norton Conyers is a mid-14th-century house with Tudor, Stuart and Georgian additions, and has been the home of the Graham family since 1624. Its elegant Dutch gables, which top each of the main façades, date from then. The interior contains some elegant 17th- and 18th-century furniture. The Great Hall is hung with splendid family portraits by Romney and Batoni, and paintings of hunting scenes, while the long table was almost certainly made in the late Middle Ages. However, Norton is best known for its association with Charlotte Brontë. She visited the house in 1839 and was told of the legend of a mad woman who had been incarcerated in one of the gable rooms. When Charlotte wrote *Jane Eyre* eight years later, she almost certainly had the mad woman in mind when she created Mrs Rochester, and Norton Conyers as the basis for Mr Rochester's house, Thornfield Hall.

## 10 RIPON

Ripon – the 'Cathedral City of the Dales' – is one of England's smallest cities. The huge market place is surrounded by an interesting mix of buildings of differerent, but mainly Georgian, architectural styles and eras. It is dominated by a 28m-high (90-ft) obelisk that has been used by the official red-coated horn blower to sound the 'setting of the watch' every day at 9pm for the last 1,000 years.

Today's **cathedral** is the fourth building to have stood on this site. Its great glory is the Saxon crypt – all that remains of an early stone church – less than 3m (10ft) high and 2m (7ft) wide. Architecturally, the cathedral is a mishmash of styles but the Early English west front, added in 1220, is one of the finest in England.

*Clockwise from above:*
*Studley Water Garden;*
*statuary, Ripon cathedral;*
*Byland Abbey*

## 11 FOUNTAINS ABBEY AND STUDLEY ROYAL ESTATE

Declared a World Heritage Site in 1987, Fountains Abbey is the National Trust's most visited site. The large estate contains the remains of a fine Cistercian abbey, ten historic buildings including a Victorian church, a medieval deer park and elegant ornamental lakes. The **abbey**, founded in 1132, was one of the nation's richest and most influential in the 13th century. It burned down in 1539 towards the end of the Dissolution of the monasteries; but all was not entirely lost for much of the masonry from the abbey went into building the nearby Elizabethan **Fountains Hall**. Today the abbey is Britain's largest monastic ruin.

John Aislabie inherited the Studley estate and devoted himself to the creation of the garden we see today. The **Water Garden** is arguably England's most important 18th-century example with its formal geometric design and wonderful vistas. It drew its inspiration from the great French landscape gardeners of that era but retained a remarkable individuality. The **Deer Park** is the oldest part of the estate, and is still home to 500 red, fallow and Sika deer as well as temples, follies and statues requisite of gardens of this period.

*Return to the B6265, follow*
*this east through Ripon and*
*then take unclassified roads*
*south to Newby Hall.*

Clockwise from above:
exterior, Newby Hall;
gardens, Beningbrough Hall;
tapestry room, Newby Hall;
aerial view, Newby Hall

## 12 NEWBY HALL

To the south east of Ripon, on the banks of the River Ure, red-brick Newby Hall was built in the style of Sir Christopher Wren in the 1690s. In the 1760s William Weddell, an ancestor of Richard Compton, the present owner, made the Grand Tour of Europe, returning with many works of art including a set of Gobelin tapestries and superb classical statuary that required a grand setting. Robert Adam, the foremost classical architect of the period, was commissioned by Weddell to adapt the hall to exhibit his collection: he designed the Entrance Hall, Library, domed Sculpture Gallery and Tapestry Room. The latter survives in its entirety and shows Adam's skill in creating harmony between the decoration of a room and its furnishings, which among other things feature a fine collection of Chippendale furniture. The gardens at Newby Hall – a series of close-knit rectangles – were influenced by Lawrence Johnston's famous garden at Hidcote, and have lovely double herbaceous borders, backed by yew hedges that sweep down to the River Ure. Each year Newby displays a different selection of contemporary sculpture throughout the woodland, orchard and gardens. Around 50 to 60 works in a variety of media including wood, bronze, stone, glass and steel are usually on show.

From Newby Hall return to
the B6265 south east to
**Boroughbridge**.

→ • • • • • • • • • • • ⑬

## 13 BOROUGHBRIDGE

This former coaching stop on the Great North Road is now bypassed by the A1 motorway, but it is worth visiting to investigate a curious trio of gritstone pillars just outside the town. The Devil's Arrows, as they are popularly known, measure as much as 7m (22ft) in height, and are believed to date back to the early Bronze Age. Just outside the exceptionally pretty Georgian village of Aldborough is an ancient Roman settlement at a fording point along the River Ure. Isurium Brigantium was the capital of the Brigantes, the largest tribe in Roman Britain and was where the Ninth Legion established camp. A stretch of wall and two well-preserved mosaic pavements can be seen.

## 14 BENINGBROUGH HALL

The symmetrical red-brick front of this stunning Georgian mansion is breathtaking. Built in 1716, the house possesses one of the finest Baroque interiors in England. The formality of early 18th century life at Beningbrough is reflected in the ground-floor setting of state bedrooms with intimate 'closets' in which visiting guests could receive friends in privacy. Throughout, there is elegant wood panelling and carving, most noticeable in the drawing room. More than 100 portraits on loan from the National Portrait Gallery decorate many of the walls, and on the first floor an unusual central corridor runs along the house from end to end.

Beningbrough also has a fully equipped Victorian laundry that gives a fascinating insight into the drudgery of servants' lives at that time. The walled garden is delightful and the surrounding parkland with its interesting wooden sculptures worth exploring.

*Head south on the B6265 and take unclassified roads east to **Beningborough Hall**.* ⑭

*Continue east, using local roads, to join the A19, and follow this south back to **York**.*
← • • • • • • • • • • • • ①

## WITH MORE TIME

**Eden Camp** *(left)* near Malton, created in an original World War II prisoner of war camp, offers a chance to experience life during those perilous years. Each of the 33 huts, built by Italian POWs, has a unique theme like woman at war, all designed, through sight, sound and smell, to portray the reality of wartime existence. By contrast **Wharram Percy** is the best-known of 3,000 medieval villages in Britain that were simply abandoned between the 11th and 18th centuries. You can still see the foundations of more than 30 simple houses, and the ruins of the church.

# Kingston upon Hull and East Yorkshire's vanishing coastline

Restored to its Viking boundaries after administrative meddling in the 1970s, Yorkshire's East Riding is steadily regaining its place on the map. Despite its relative isolation, this *terra incognita* can offer both the exceptional and the unexpected, from a breathtaking suspension bridge and Britain's biggest seabird colony to the world's only 'submarium' and the most rapidly eroding shoreline in Europe.

## TOUR ROUTE

Kingston upon Hull ①
The Humber Estuary ②
Spurn Head ③
Burton Constable Hall ④
The Holderness Coast ⑤
Burton Agnes Hall ⑥
Bridlington ⑦
Flamborough Head ⑧
Filey ⑨
Scarborough ⑩
Sledmere House and Gardens ⑪
Beverley ⑫

## TOUR LENGTH

**DISTANCE** approx. 200 miles (320km)

**DURATION** 3–4 days

## TOURIST INFORMATION CENTRES

**BEVERLEY** 34 Butcher Row HU17 OAB; 01482 867430

**HULL** 1 Paragon Street HU1 3NA; 01482 223559

**SCARBOROUGH** Brunswick Shopping Centre, Westborough YO11 1UE; 01723 383636

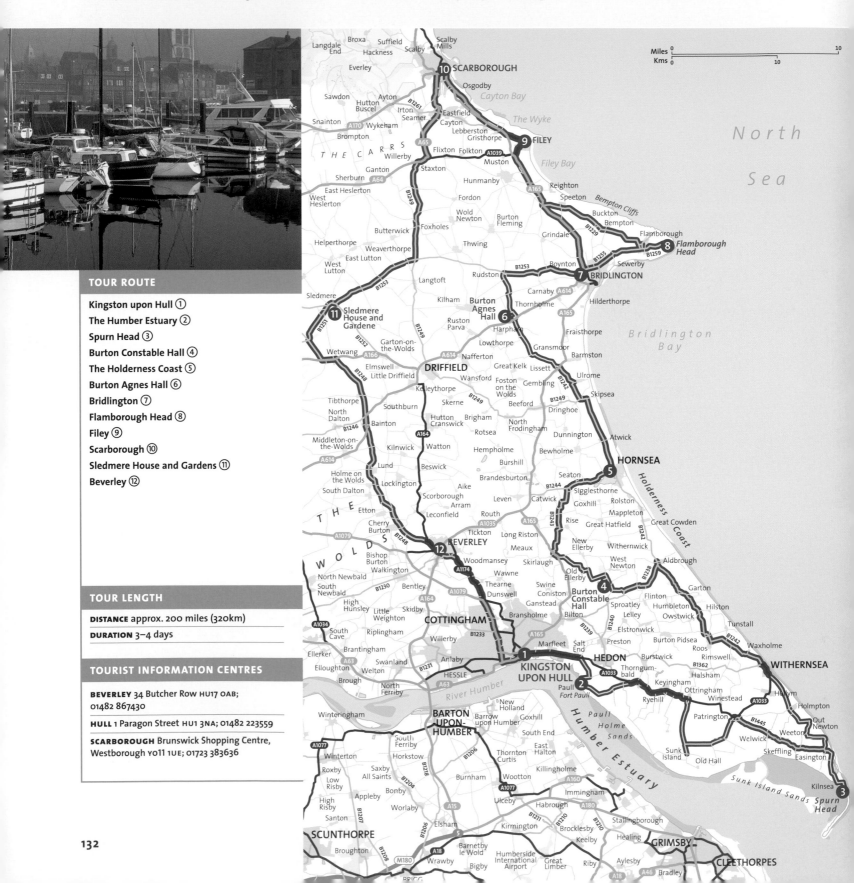

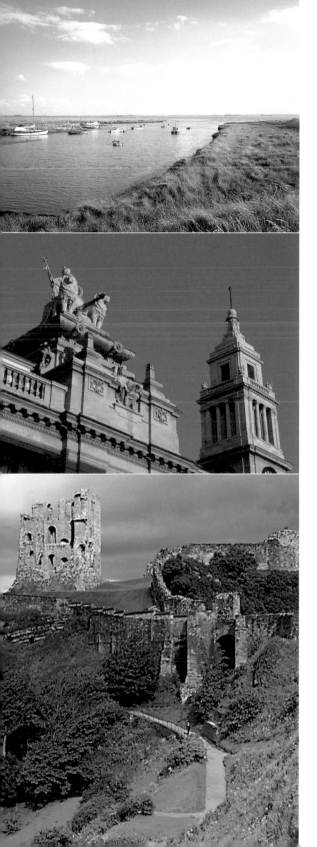

**Clockwise from far left:**
Hull docks and view of
Trinity Church; Humber
Bridge; Scarborough Castle;
Guildhall, Hull; Sunk Island

## 1 KINGSTON UPON HULL

Hardly anyone bothers with the sonorous title of
Kingston upon Hull these days, but this great seaport
at the confluence of the Hull and the Humber was
once a King's Town (Edward I being the founding
monarch). Wartime devastation and the decline of its
two main industries, shipbuilding and deep-sea fishing,
resulted in many problems, but recent regeneration has
brought vast improvement. Not many towns put the
gents on the tourist trail, but the beautifully maintained art-nouveau **public toilets** near the market
square deserve inspection. Pavement fish plaques
guide you through the old town, past a quaint cobbled
alley called the Land of Green Ginger, but many visit
the city for its excellent museums. The **Streetlife
Museum of Transport** displays an entertaining
collection of bicycles and tramcars in a convincingly
realistic period setting, while the **Hull and East Riding
Museum** traces the area's history from pre-Roman
times. The elegant **Ferens Art Gallery** is strong on
British 20th-century artists and seascapes. **Maister
House** is an impressive Palladian building belonging to
the National Trust, and **Wilberforce House**, birthplace of
the campaigner for the abolition of the slave trade,
contains a museum devoted to his life and achievements.

   Down on the waterfront, the revamped **marina**
welcomes pleasure craft, but you can still watch huge
cargo ships manoeuvring slowly up and down the
estuary. A **Maritime Museum** occupies the former Dock
Company offices, and contains exhibits on the old
whaling days. Two historic vessels, the *Spurn Lightship*
and the *Arctic Corsair*, give a flavour of Hull's harbour
scene in its heyday. A striking recent landmark is the
glittering geometric monolith jutting over the Humber
called **The Deep**. This is a blockbusting millennial
aquarium (or rather 'submarium') containing the
world's deepest viewing tunnel and an underwater lift.
To cap Hull's crescendo of sightseeing, head for the
riverside suburb of Hessle and the **Humber Bridge**.
When this engineering marvel first opened in 1981, it
broke records as the longest single-span suspension
bridge in the world (a couple of others have since
claimed its laurels). You can avoid the hefty road toll by
walking across the bridge, but allow time as it's over a
mile from end to end.

*Take the A1033 east out of
Hull, following the north
bank of the Humber. Turn
off for Fort Paull, then
rejoin the main road and
continue eastward, turning
right at signs for Sunk
Island and the
Humber Estuary.*

⬇ Return to the main road at
• Patrington, then take the
• B1445 to Easington and
③ **Spurn Head**.

⬇ Return to Easington and
• then follow minor coastal
• roads up to Withernsea.
• Then join the B1242 signed
• for Hornsea. At Aldbrough,
• take the B1238 inland and
• follow signs for **Burton**
④ **Constable Hall**.

⬇ Follow minor roads north
• to join the A165 briefly at
• Skirlaugh and head north
• east on the B1243 and
• B1244 towards Hornsea
⑤ and the **Holderness Coast**.

From Hornsea, take the
B1242 coast road
northwards as far as
Lissett, then head inland on
minor roads following
signs for **Burton Agnes Hall**
just over the A614.

→ • • • • • • • • • • • ⑥

## 2 THE HUMBER ESTUARY

The Humber Estuary is one of the largest in England, draining about a fifth of it's land area. At first sight, the views seem relentlessly flat, but it is a constantly shifting scene. Mudflats emerge with each ebbing tide, a happy hunting ground for wading birds. Tankers and freighters glide in and out of the docks and refineries on either bank. On the waterfront just beyond Hull's industrialized outskirts stands **Fort Paull**, a Victorian building containing a maze of underground passages and historical exhibits. **Hedon**, a mile or two inland, was once Hull's predecessor as the first port on the Humber. The tower of its splendid church soars above the coastal plains. Hedon church, and its similarly glorious, spired peer at **Patrington** (10 miles south east), are respectively dubbed the King and Queen of Holderness. Lanes lead from the main road to the eerily remote **Sunk Island**, an apron of reclaimed land that first emerged from the Humber Estuary in the 16th century. Protected by the natural tidal barrier of Spurn Head, the sandbanks gradually enlarged until they joined with the Holderness mainland in the 1830s. After a chequered history, this low-lying area is now successfully farmed.

## 3 SPURN HEAD

The hooked tentacle of Spurn Head curving into the mouth of the Humber is a geological phenomenon. Approached via the village of Easington, this three-mile sand-and-pebble promontory has a rough toll road running along its length; in places the spit is less than 10m (30ft) wide. Now maintained by Yorkshire Wildlife Trust as a nature reserve, it is a renowned birdwatching spot, especially during migration periods. The dunes and shingle banks are also a haunt of seals, butterflies and unusual plants like sea buckthorn. Wartime defences litter the area, and few would call it a beautiful scene, but it has a character and fascination all of its own.

## 4 BURTON CONSTABLE HALL

Well worth a detour, this Elizabethan house near the village of Sproatley contains magnificent interiors. It was substantially remodelled in the 18th century, and 'Capability' Brown was commissioned to landscape the grounds. About 30 rooms are open to the public, including a long gallery, a Chinese room and a display of scientific instruments. It has some fine Chippendale furniture and a formidable art collection.

## 5 THE HOLDERNESS COAST

The flat and forlorn coastline north of Spurn Head is eroding rapidly, at a rate of several metres a year – the most rapidly eroding shoreline in Europe. Inland, large fields of oats and barley wave beneath wide skies. Church towers are prominent landmarks; so too is **Withernsea's lighthouse** with its small museum on coastal rescue. **Hornsea** is the main resort along this stretch of coast, best known for its distinctive pottery now made into all manner of mugs and souvenirs and sold locally. The large freshwater lake of Hornsea Mere is an RSPB (Royal Society for the Protection of Birds) reserve – home to a great variety of waterfowl.

Clockwise from far left:
Burton Constable Hall;
Bridlington harbour; drawing
room, Burton Agnes Hall

## 6 BURTON AGNES HALL

The welcoming atmosphere of this splendid
Elizabethan country house is tangible, largely because
it is still a much-loved family home. Little has changed
since the turn of the 17th century. Enter via the ogee-
turreted red-brick gatehouse, and in the Great Hall you
will see a magnificent alabaster chimneypiece
decorated with domestic scenes. The oak staircase is
also beautifully carved. Some of the paintings on
display date from a later era (a jaw-dropping collection
of Impressionist and Post-Impressionist artists includes
Renoir, Cézanne and Gauguin). The Old Hall near the
church is even more venerable than the main house.

## 7 BRIDLINGTON

After the crumbling boulder clay of the Holderness
coast, the long golden sands of this archetypal seaside
resort present a more cheerful scene of buckets and
spades and donkey rides. Bridlington is a trippery, kiss-
me-quick sort of place, but the original town around
the bustling quay and the priory church still retains
some charming old houses. One 14th-century monastic
gatehouse – **Baylegate** – survived the Dissolution, and
contains a small history museum. Just north of the
town, **Sewerby Hall** is a fine example of an 18th-century
house. The interior contains various period rooms, an
art gallery and memorabilia connected with local
aviator Amy Johnson. In the grounds is a miniature
zoo and aviary. A train takes visitors to and from
Bridlington in summer.

*Follow signs north to
Rudston, then take the
B1253 east to **Bridlington**.* ⓭

*Follow the B1255/1259 coast
road to the promontory
of **Flamborough Head**,
then take the B1229
via  Bempton.*

⟶ • • • • • • • • • • • • ⓼

Clockwise from above: view of Scarborough; Scarborough Castle; Filey

## 8 FLAMBOROUGH HEAD

The chalk nose of Flamborough is an unforgettable sight, gnawed into a milky labyrinth of pillars and cavities by the waves. Blowy paths lead around the grass-carpeted headland, and a nature trail follows an Iron Age earthwork known as **Dane's Dyke**. Beneath two lighthouses, more than 30 species of seabirds congregate in huge numbers. North of Flamborough Head, **Bempton Cliffs** rise in sheer white walls to 122m (400ft). From the RSPB centre here you can rent binoculars and from safe vantage points watch an estimated 200,000 kittiwakes, guillemots, razorbills and fulmars scream and wheel to their precarious nesting ledges. This is England's only mainland gannetry, and one of the last haunts of the endangered puffin. Cruises sail round the headland in summer.

## 9 FILEY

Quieter and less glamorous than neighbouring Scarborough, Filey has an air of decorum and a perceptible touch of class. It is a largely Edwardian resort in an attractive setting enhanced by cliffs and hanging gardens. The wide, dark-sand crescent of Filey Bay is one of the best beaches anywhere on Yorkshire's coastline. **Filey Brigg**, a mile-long reef at its northern end, makes a popular beachcombing stroll past hundreds of rock pools, but check the tide tables first. Filey's little **museum** located in old fishing cottages is worth a visit. Two long-distance footpaths converge here – the Wolds Way and the Cleveland Way, so it's an ideal starting point for walks.

⬇ *Rejoin the A165 near*
· *Reighton and head*
· *northwards another*
⑨ *5 miles to Filey.*

*Return to the A165, the main coastal road, and continue another 7 miles to Scarborough.*

→ · · · · · · · · · · ⑩

## 10 SCARBOROUGH

Despite its popularity, Scarborough is a thoroughly civilized place of Regency elegance. It has a spectacular setting on high cliffs above two glorious sandy bays, guarded by a Norman **castle**. A medieval fishing village grew up around the old harbour, and from the 1620s onwards Scarborough gained a reputation as a superior watering place. Well-preserved Georgian, Victorian and Edwardian architecture line its streets. An enviable list of resort amenities and family attractions includes the famous Stephen Joseph Theatre, inspired by Sir Alan Ayckbourn, a long-standing resident. All his productions take their first bow in Scarborough. A couple of decent museums (the **Rotunda Museum** and **Wood End**, partially devoted to the Sitwell family) and a fine **Art Gallery** in an Italianate villa can be visited on a joint ticket. Miniature sea battles are staged in summer on the boating lake at Peasholm Park behind North Sands.

## 11 SLEDMERE HOUSE AND GARDENS

More than most, the influential Sykes family shaped the landscapes of the lonely northern Wolds. These prosperous Leeds merchants turned to agriculture in the 18th century, transforming the barren chalky downs into rich farmland. Sledmere Hall is the Sykes' family mansion, dating from 1751 in the grand neoclassical mode of the times. A fire broke out in 1911, but most of the hall's handsome contents were saved and the building was carefully restored. Besides fine Sheraton and Chippendale furniture, the tiled Turkish room and an Adam-style vaulted library are its main glories.

## 12 BEVERLEY

This dignified market town's attractions belie its modest size. All are dwarfed, literally and figuratively, by its grand **Minster**, which vies with any cathedral in the land for its superb Gothic stonework and woodcarving. The extensive collection of misericords and the ornate Percy tomb are its chief highlights. **St Mary's Church**, to the north of the centre, is another *tour de force* of medieval craftsmanship. Forty English kings are depicted on the painted ceiling, and brightly coloured musicians adorn the pillars. Beverley's partly pedestrianised centre lined with pleasing Georgian terraces and antique shops is worth a stroll. The **Guildhall** contains an 18th-century courtroom with splendid stucco plasterwork.

*Take the A65 southwards to Staxton, continuing south on the B1249 through Foxholes, then turn right on the B1253 to* **Sledmere Hall**. ⑪

*Continue south west on the B1251, join the B1248 and head south via Bainton across the Wolds to* **Beverley**. ⑫

*Follow the A1174 and A1079 south back to* **Hull**.
← • • • • • • • • • • ①

## WITH MORE TIME

Explore the **Yorkshire Wolds** *(left)* in more detail, pottering through charming estate villages and market towns. Pocklington, where Burnby Hall is famed for its waterlily fishponds, and Market Weighton deserve a glance. Howden near Goole has another fine minster. The well-signed Wolds Way gives fine views over the Humber Estuary at Welton. A monument in the churchyard of Market Weighton marks the grave of William Bradley, who was nearly 2.5m (8ft) tall. Bishop Burton is a typical Wolds village with a fine church and large pond.

# Gazetteer

## Castles and the Christian heritage of northern Northumberland

**Bamburgh Castle**
Bamburgh NE69 7DF
**Tel:** 01668 214515
www.bamburghcastle.com

**Chillingham Castle**
Chillingham, Alnwick NE66 5NJ
**Tel:** 01668 215359
www.chillingham-castle.com

**Grace Darling Museum**
Radcliffe Road, Bamburgh NE69 7AE
**Tel:** 01668 214465
www.northumberland.gov.uk
*Closed for refurbishment until July 2006*

**Lindisfarne Castle**
Holy Island, Berwick-upon-Tweed TD15 2SH
**Tel:** 01289 389244
www.nationaltrust.org.uk

**Lindisfarne Priory**
Holy Island, Berwick-upon-Tweed TD15 2RX
**Tel:** 01289 389200
www.english-heritage.org.uk

## The unspoilt coast of southern Northumberland

**Alnwick Castle**
Alnwick NE66 1NQ
**Tel:** 01665 510777
www.alnwickcastle.com

**The Alnwick Garden**
Denwick Lane, Alnwick NE66 1YU
**Tel:** 01665 511350
www.alnwickgarden.com

**Cragside House, Gardens and Estate**
Rothbury, Morpeth NE65 7PX
**Tel:** 01669 620333/620150
www.nationaltrust.org.uk

**Druridge Bay Country Park**
Red Row, Druridge Bay NE61 5BX
**Tel:** 01670 760968
www.northumberland.gov.uk

**Dunstanburgh Castle**
Craster, Alnwick NE66 3ET
**Tel:** 01665 576231
www.english-heritage.org.uk

**Seaton Delaval Hall**
Seaton Sluice, Whitley Bay NE26 4QR
**Tel:** 0191 2373040
www.seatondelaval.org.uk

**Warkworth Castle**
Warkworth, Alnwick NE65 0UJ
**Tel:** 01665 711423
www.english-heritage.org.uk

## Hadrian's Wall and the wilds of Northumberland National Park

**Chesters Roman Fort**
Chollerford, Humshaugh,
Hexham NE46 4EP
**Tel:** 01434 681379
www.english-heritage.org.uk

**Chesters Walled Garden**
Chollerford, Hexham NE46 4BQ
**Tel:** 01434 681483
www.chesterswalledgarden.fsnet.co.uk

**Chipchase Castle**
Wark, Hexham NE48 3NT
**Tel:** 01434 230203
www.northumberland.gov.uk

**Corbridge Roman Site**
Corbridge NE45 5NT
**Tel:** 01434 632349
www.english-heritage.org.uk

**George Stephenson's Birthplace**
Wylam NE41 8BP
**Tel:** 01661 853457
www.nationaltrust.org.uk

**Hexham Abbey**
Hexham NE46 3NB
**Tel:** 01434 602031
www.hexhamabbey.org.uk

**Hexham Old Gaol**
Hallgate, Hexham NE46 3NH
**Tel:** 01434 652349
www.hadrianswallcountry.org

**Housesteads Fort**
Bardon Mill, Hexham NE47 6NN
**Tel:** 01434 344363
www.nationaltrust.org.uk

**Kielder Castle Forest Park Centre**
Kielder Castle, Kielder,
Hexham NE48 1ER
**Tel:** 01434 250209
www.forestry.gov.uk

**Roman Vindolanda**
Chesterholm Museum, Bardon Mill,
Hexham NE47 7JN
**Tel:** 01434 344277
www.vindolanda.com

**Wallington**
Cambo, Morpeth NE61 4AR
**Tel:** 01670 773967
www.nationaltrust.org.uk

## Durham: Land of the Prince Bishops

**Auckland Castle**
Bishop Auckland DL14 7NR
**Tel:** 01388 601627
www.northumberland.gov.uk

**Barnard Castle**
Barnard Castle DL12 9AT
**Tel:** 01833 638212
www.english-heritage.org.uk

**Beamish, The North of England Open Air Museum**
Beamish DH9 0RG
**Tel:** 0191 370 4000
www.beamish.org.uk

**Bowes Museum**
Barnard Castle, Durham DL12 8NP
**Tel:** 01833 690606
www.bowesmuseum.org.uk

**Durham Castle**
Durham DH1 3RW
**Tel:** 0191 334 3800
www.durhamcastle.com

**Durham Cathedral**
Durham DH1 3EH
**Tel:** 0191 386 4266
www.durhamcathedral.co.uk

**Finchale Priory**
Brasside, Durham DH1 5SH
**Tel:** 0191 386 3828
www.english-heritage.org.uk

**Raby Castle**
Staindrop, Darlington DL2 3AH
**Tel:** 01833 660202/660888
www.rabycastle.com

**Rokeby Park**
Barnard Castle DL12 9RZ
**Tel:** 01833 637334
www.durham.gov.uk

**Washington Old Hall**
The Avenue, Washington Village
Washington NE38 7LE
**Tel:** 0191 416 6879
www.nationaltrust.org.uk

## The dramatic hills and dales of eastern Lakeland

**Acorn Bank Garden and Watermill**
Temple Sowerby, nr Penrith CA10 1SP
**Tel:** 017683 61893
www.nationaltrust.org.uk

**Appleby Castle**
Appleby-in-Westmoreland CA16 6XH
**Tel:** 017683 53823
www.cumbria-the-lake-district.co.uk

**Brough Castle**
Church Brough, Brough,
Kirkby Stephen CA17 4EJ
www.english-heritage.org.uk

**Carlisle Castle**
Carlisle CA3 8UR
**Tel:** 01228 591922
www.english-heritage.org.uk

**Carlisle Cathedral**
7 The Abbey, Carlisle CA3 8TZ
**Tel:** 01228 548151
www.carlislecathedral.org.uk

**Dalemain House and Gardens**
Dalemain, Penrith CA11 0HB
**Tel:** 017684 86450
www.dalemain.com

**Patterdale Hall**
Glenridding, nr Penrith CA11 0PT
**Tel:** 017684 82233
www.patterdalehall.org.uk

**Penrith Castle**
Castlegate, Penrith CA11 7HX
www.english-heritage.org.uk

**Rheged – The Village in the Hill**
Redhills, Penrith CA11 0DQ
**Tel:** 01768 868000
www.rheged.com

**Tullie House Museum and Art Gallery**
Castle Street, Carlisle CA3 8TP
**Tel:** 01228 534781
www.tulliehouse.co.uk

## The rugged fells of the western Lakeland

**Cockermouth Castle**
*Not open to the public*

**Cumberland Pencil Museum**
Southey Works, Greta Bridge,
Keswick CA12 5NG
**Tel:** 017687 73626
www.pencils.co.uk

**Honister Slate Mine**
Honister Pass, Borrowdale CA12 5XN
**Tel:** 017687 77230
www.honister-slate-mine.co.uk

**Howk Bobbin Mill**
Calderdale
www.visitcumbria.com

**Lakeland Sheep and Wool Centre**
Egremont Road, Cockermouth CA13 0QX
**Tel:** 01900 822673
www.sheep-woolcentre.co.uk

**Maryport Maritime Museum**
1 Senhouse Street, Maryport CA15 6AB
**Tel:** 01900 813738
www.thecumbriadirectory.com

**Maryport Steamship Museum**
South Quay, Maryport CA15 8AB
**Tel:** 01900 815954
www.thecumbriadirectory.com

**Mirehouse**
Keswick CA12 4QE
**Tel:** 017687 72287
www.mirehouse.com

**Senhouse Roman Museum**
The Battery, Sea Brows, Maryport CA15 6JD
**Tel:** 01900 816168
www.senhousemuseum.co.uk

**Wordsworth House**
Main Street, Cockermouth CA13 9RX
**Tel:** 01900 820884
www.nationaltrust.org.uk

## The charms of southern Lakeland

**Abbot Hall Art Gallery and Museum of Lakeland Life**
Abbot Hall, Kendal LA9 5AL
**Tel:** 01539 722464
www.abbothall.org.uk

**Beatrix Potter Gallery**
Main Street, Hawkshead LA22 0NS
**Tel:** 015394 36355
www.nationaltrust.org.uk

**Brantwood**
Coniston LA21 8AD
**Tel:** 015394 41396
www.brantwood.org.uk

**Cartmel Priory**
The Square, Cartmel,
Grange-over-Sands LA11 6QB
**Tel:** 015395 36874
www.nationaltrust.org.uk

**Dove Cottage and the Wordsworth Museum**
Grasmere LA22 9SH
**Tel:** 015394 35544
www.wordsworth.org.uk

**Furness Abbey**
Barrow-in-Furness LA13 0TJ
**Tel:** 01229 823420
www.english-heritage.org.uk

**Grizedale Forest Visitor Centre**
Grizedale Forest, Hawkshead LA22 0QJ
**Tel:** 01229 860010
www.forestry.gov.uk

**Hill Top**
Near Sawrey, Hawkshead,
Ambleside LA22 0LF
**Tel:** 015394 36269
www.nationaltrust.org.uk

**Holker Hall and Gardens and Lakeland Motor Museum**
Cark-in-Cartmel, nr Grange-over-Sands LA11 7PL
**Tel:** 015395 58328
www.holker-hall.co.uk

**Levens Hall**
Kendal LA8 0PD
**Tel:** 015395 60321
www.levenshall.co.uk

**Muncaster Castle**
Ravenglass CA18 1RQ
**Tel:** 01229 717614
www.muncaster.co.uk

**Rydal Mount and Gardens**
Rydal, nr Ambleside LA22 9LU
**Tel:** 015394 33002
www.rydalmount.co.uk

**Sizergh Castle**
Sizergh, nr Kendal LA8 8AE
**Tel:** 015395 60951
www.nationaltrust.org.uk

**Steamboat Museum**
Rayrigg Rd, Bowness, Windermere LA23 1BN
**Tel:** 015394 45565
www.visitcumbria.com

## Lancaster and the rural uplands of the Forest of Bowland

**Ashton Memorial and Williamson Park**
Lancaster LA1 1UX
**Tel:** 01524 33318
www.williamsonpark.com

**Carnforth Station Visitor Centre**
Warton Road, Carnforth LA5 9TR
**Tel:** 01524 735165
www.carnforth-station.co.uk

**Clitheroe Castle**
Castle Hill, Clitheroe BB7 1BA
**Tel:** 01200 424568
www.lancashire.gov.uk

**Ingleborough Cave**
Clapham LA2 8EE
**Tel:** 015242 51242
www.ingleboroughcave.co.uk

**Lancaster Castle**
Shire Hall, Castle Parade, Lancaster LA1 1YJ
**Tel:** 01524 64998
www.lancashire.gov.uk

**Leighton Hall**
Carnforth LA5 9ST
**Tel:** 01524 734474
www.leightonhall.co.uk

**Leighton Moss Nature Reserve**
Leighton Moss, Nr Carnforth
**Tel:** 01524 701601
www.rspb.org.uk

**White Scar Caves**
Ingleton LA6 3AW
**Tel:** 01524 242244
www.whitescarcave.co.uk

## The unexpected attractions of Lancashire's coastal plain

**Astley Hall Museum and Art Gallery**
Astley Park, Chorley PR7 1NP
**Tel.** 01257 515927
www.chorley.gov.uk

**Camelot Theme Park**
Charnock Richard, Chorley PR7 5LP
**Tel:** 01257 453044
www.camelotthemepark.co.uk

**Formby Point Squirrel Reserve**
Victoria Road, Freshfield L37 1LJ
**Tel:** 01704 878591
www.nationaltrust.org.uk

**Harris Museum and Art Gallery**
Market Square, Preston PR1 2PP
**Tel:** 01772 905410
www.visitpreston.com

**Marshside RSPB Nature Reserve**
Nr Southport
**Tel:** 01704 536378
www.rspb.org.uk

**Martin Mere Wildfowl and Wetlands Trust**
Between Ormskirk and Southport
**Tel:** 01704 895181
www.wwt.org.uk

**National Football Museum**
Sir Tom Finney Way, Deepdale
Preston PR1 6RU
**Tel:** 01772 908400
www.nationalfootballmuseum.com

**Pleasureland Southport**
Marine Drive, Southport PR8 1RX
**Tel:** 08702 200205
www.pleasureland.uk.com

**Rufford Old Hall**
Rufford, nr Ormskirk L40 1SG
**Tel:** 01704 821254
www.nationaltrust.org.uk

**Wigan Pier**
Wallgate, Wigan WN3 4EU
**Tel:** 01942 323666
www.wlct.org

## The ancient city of Chester and the Cheshire Plain

**Anderton Boat Lift**
Anderton, Northwich CW9 6FW
**Tel:** 01606 786771
www.andertonboatlift.co.uk

**Beeston Castle**
Chapel Lane, Beeston, Tarporley CW6 9TX
**Tel:** 01829 260464
www.english-heritage.org.uk

**Blue Planet Aquarium**
Cheshire Oaks, Ellesmere Port CH65 9LF
**Tel:** 0151 357 8800
www.blueplanetaquarium.com

**Boat Museum**
South Pier Road, Ellesmere Port CH65 4FW
**Tel:** 0151 355 5017
www.boatmuseum.org.uk

**Bridgmere Garden World**
Bridgemere, nr Nantwich CW5 7QB
**Tel:** 01270 521100
www.bridgemere.co.uk

**Chester Cathedral**
12 Abbey Square, Chester CH1 2HU
Tel: 01244 324756
www.chestercathedral.com

**Chester Zoo**
Upton-by-Chester, Chester CH2 1LH
**Tel:** 01244 380280
www.chesterzoo.org

**Cholmondeley Castle**
Malpas SY14 8AH
**Tel:** 01829 720383
www.shropshiretourism.info

**Dewa Roman Experience**
Pierpoint Lane, off Bridge Street,
Chester CH1 1NL
**Tel:** 01244 343407
www.dewaromanexperience.co.uk

**Dorothy Clive Garden**
Willoughbridge, Market Drayton TF9 4EU
**Tel:** 01630 647237
www.dorothyclivegarden.co.uk

**Grosvenor Museum**
27 Grosvenor Street, Chester CH1 2DD
**Tel:** 01244 402008
www.chestercc.gov.uk

**Hack Green Secret Nuclear Bunker**
Nantwich CW5 8AQ
**Tel:** 01270 629219
www.hackgreen.co.uk

**Historic Warships at Birkenhead**
(*HMS Plymouth and HMS Onyx*)
East Float, Dock Road, Birkenhead CH41 1DJ
**Tel:** 0151 6501573
www.historicwarships.org

**Lady Lever Art Gallery**
Port Sunlight Village, Wirral CH62 5EQ
**Tel:** 0151 478 4136
www.portsunlight.org.uk

**Nantwich Museum**
Pillory Street, Nantwich CW5 5BQ
**Tel:** 01270 627104
www.nantwichmuseum.org.uk

**Ness Botanic Gardens**
Ness, Neston CH64 4AY
**Tel:** 0151 353 0123
www.nessgardens.org.uk

**Salt Museum**
162 London Road, Northwich CW9 8AB
**Tel:** 01606 41331
www.saltmuseum.org.uk

**Speke Hall, Garden and Estate**
The Walk, Liverpool L24 1XD
**Tel:** 08457 585702
www.nationaltrust.org.uk

**Wirral Country Park Visitor Centre**
Station Road, Thurstaston, Wirral CH61 0HN
**Tel:** 0151 648 4371
www.wirral.gov.uk

## Cheshire's grand houses

**Biddulph Grange Garden**
Grange Road, Biddulph ST8 7SD
**Tel:** 01782 517999
www.nationaltrust.org.uk

**Bramall Hall**
Bramhall Park, Bramhall, Stockport SK7 1NX
**Tel:** 0845 8330974
www.bramallhall.co.uk

**Capesthorne Hall**
Siddington, Macclesfield SK11 9JY
**Tel:** 01625 861221
www.capesthorne.com

**Dunham Massey**
Altrincham WA14 4SJ
**Tel:** 0161 928 4351 (Infoline)
www.nationaltrust.org.uk

**Gawsworth Hall**
Church Lane, Macclesfield SK11 9RN
**Tel:** 01260 223456
www.gawsworthhall.com

**Hare Hill**
Over Alderley, Macclesfield SK10 4QB
**Tel:** 0161 928 0075
www.nationaltrust.org.uk

**Jodrell Bank Visitor Centre and Arboretum**
Macclesfield SK11 9DL
**Tel:** 01477 571330
www.jb.man.ac.uk

**Knutsford Heritage Centre**
90a King Street, Knutsford WA16 6ED
**Tel:** 01565 650506
www.macclesfield.gov.uk

**Little Moreton Hall**
Congleton CW12 4SD
**Tel:** 01260 272018
www.nationaltrust.org.uk

**Lyme Park**
Disley, Stockport SK12 2NX
**Tel:** 01663 766492 (Infoline)
www.nationaltrust.org.uk

**Millennium Walkway**
**Torrs Gorge**
Heritage Centre, Rock Mills Lane,
New Mills SK22 3BN
**Tel:** 01663 746904
www.newmillstowncouncil.com

**Nether Alderley Mill**
Congleton Road, Nether Alderley,
Macclesfield SK10 4TW
**Tel:** 01625 584412 (Countryside office)
www.nationaltrust.org.uk

**New Mills Heritage Centre**
New Mills, High Peak SK22 3BN
**Tel:** 01663 746904
www.newmillsheritage.com

**Paradise Mill**
Park Lane, Macclesfield SK11 6TJ
**Tel:** 01625 618228
www.silk-macclesfield.org

**Peover Hall and Gardens**
Over Peover, Knutsford WA16 6HW
**Tel:** 01565 830395
www.cheshire.gov.uk

**Quarry Bank Mill and the Styal Estate**
Styal, Wilmslow SK9 4LA
**Tel:** 01625 527468
www.nationaltrust.org.uk

**Silk Museum**
Park Lane, Macclesfield SK11 6TJ
**Tel:** 01625 612045
www.macclesfield.silk.museum

**Tatton Park**
Knutsford WA16 6QN
**Tel:** 01625 534435 (Infoline)
www.nationaltrust.org.uk

**Tegg's Nose Country Park**
Buxton Old Road, Macclesfield SK11 0AP
**Tel:** 01625 614279
www.cheshire.gov.uk

## Lichfield and the historic Potteries

**Alton Towers**
Alton ST10 4DB
**Tel:** 08705 204060
www.alton-towers.co.uk

**Ancient High House,**
Greengate Street, Stafford ST16 2JA.
**Tel:** 01785 619131
www.staffordbc.gov.uk

**Boscobel House**
Brewood, Bishops Wood ST19 9AR
**Tel:** 01902 850244
www.english-heritage.org.uk

**Brindley Mill**
Mill Street, Leek ST13 8HA
**Tel:** 01538 483741
www.brindleymill.net

**Cheddleton Flint Mill**
Leek Road, Cheddleton, nr Leek ST13 7HL
**Tel:** 01782 502907
www.staffsmoorlands.gov.uk

**Churnet Valley Railway**
Cheddleton Station, Station Road,
Cheddleton ST13 7EE
**Tel:**01538 360522
www.churnet-valley-railway.co.uk

**Coors Visitor Centre**
Horninglow Street, Burton-on-Trent DE14 1YQ
**Tel:** 0845 6000 598
www.bass-museum.com

**Erasmus Darwin Museum**
Darwin House, Beacon Street,
Lichfield WS13 7AD
**Tel:** 01543 306260
www.erasmusdarwin.org

**Gladstone Pottery Museum**
Uttoxeter Road, Longton,
Stoke on Trent ST3 1PQ
**Tel:** 01782 319232
www.2002.stoke.gov.uk

**Isaak Walton's Cottage**
Weston Lane, Shallowford, ST15 0PA
**Tel:** 01785 760278
www.staffordbc.gov.uk

**Lichfield Cathedral**
Lichfield WS13 7LD
**Tel:** 01543 306240
www.lichfield-cathedral.org

**Moseley Old Hall**
Moseley Old Hall Lane, Fordhouses,
Wolverhampton WV10 7HY
**Tel:** 01902 782808
www.nationaltrust.org.uk

**Museum of Cannock Chase**
Valley Heritage Centre, Valley Road,
Hednesford, Cannock WS12 5TD
**Tel:** 01543 877666
www.cannockchasedc.gov.uk

**Potteries Museum and Art Gallery**
Bethesda Street, Hanley,
Stoke-on-Trent ST1 3DW
**Tel:** 01782 232323
www2002.stoke.gov.uk

**Samuel Johnson Birthplace Museum**
Breadmarket Street, Lichfield WS13 6LG
**Tel:** 01543 264972
www.lichfield.gov.uk

**Shire Hall Gallery**
Market Square, Stafford ST16 2LD
**Tel:** 01785 278345
www.staffordshire.gov.uk

**Shugborough**
Milford, nr Stafford ST17 0XB
**Tel:** 01889 881388
www.shugborough.org.uk

**Stafford Castle**
Newport Road, Stafford ST16 1DJ
**Tel:** 01785 257698
www.staffordshire.gov.uk

**Sudbury Hall and Museum of Childhood**
Sudbury, Ashbourne DE6 5HT
**Tel:** 01283 585305
www.nationaltrust.org.uk

**Tutbury Castle**
Tutbury DE13 9JF
**Tel:** 01283 812129
www.tutburycastle.com

**Wedgwood Visitor Centre**
Barlaston, Stoke-on-Trent ST12 9ES
**Tel:** 01782 282986
www.thewedgwoodvisitorcentre.com

**Weston Park**
Weston-under-Lizard, Nr Shifnal TF11 8LE
**Tel:** 01952 852100
www.weston-park.com

**Wightwick Manor**
Wightwick Bank, Wolverhampton WV6 8EE
**Tel:** 01902 761400
www.nationaltrust.org.uk

## Chatsworth and the picturesque Derbyshire Dales

**Bakewell Old House Museum**
Old House, Cunningham Place,
Bakewell DE45 1AX
**Tel:** 01629 813 642
www.derbyshire-peakdistrict.co.uk

**Chatsworth**
Bakewell DE45 1PP
**Tel:** 01246 565300
www.chatsworth-house.co.uk

**Cromford Mill**
Mill Lane, Cromford, Matlock DE4 3RQ
**Tel:** 01629 823256
www.cromfordmill.co.uk

**Haddon Hall**
Bakewell DE45 1LA
**Tel:** 01629 812855
www.haddonhall.co.uk

**The Heights of Abraham**
Matlock Bath DE4 3PD
**Tel:** 01629 582365
www.heights-of-abraham.co.uk

**Ilam Park**
Ilam, Ashbourne DE6 2AZ
**Tel:** 01335 350245
www.nationaltrust.org.uk

**Matlock Bath Aquarium**
110 North Parade, Matlock Bath DE4 3NS
**Tel:** 01629 583624
www.matlockbathaquarium.co.uk

**Mining Museum and Temple Mine**
Temple Rd, Matlock Bath DE4 3NR
**Tel:** 01629 583834
www.derbyshire-peakdistrict.co.uk

**National Stone Centre**
Porter Lane, Middleton by Winksworth DE4 4L
**Tel:** 01629 824833
www.nationalstonecentre.org.uk

**Peak District Mining Museum**
The Pavilion, Matlock Bath DE4 3NR
**Tel:** 01629 583834
www.peakmines.co.uk

**Peak Rail**
Matlock Station, Matlock DE4 3NA
**Tel:** 01629 580381
www.peakrail.co.uk

**Winster Market House**
Main Street, Winster, nr Matlock
**Tel:** 01335 350503
www.nationaltrust.org.uk

**Wirksworth Heritage Centre**
Crown Yard, Market Place, Wirksworth DE4 4ET
**Tel:** 01629 825225
www.derbyshire-peakdistrict.co.uk

## The glorious High Peak

**Blue John Cavern**
Castleton S33 8WP
**Tel:** 01433 620642
www.bluejohn-cavern.co.uk

**Buxton Opera House**
Water Street, Buxton SK17 6XN
**Tel:** 0845 122190
www.buxton-opera.co.uk

**Chestnut Centre**
Chapel-en-le-Frith SK23 0QS
**Tel:** 01298 814099
www.peakdistrictonline.com

**Eyam Hall**
Hope Valley S32 5QW
**Tel:** 01433 631976
www.eyamhall.com

**Eyam Museum**
Hawkhill Road, Eyam S32 5QP
**Tel:** 01433 631371
www.eyam.org.uk

**Hardwick Hall**
Doe Lea, Chesterfield S44 5QJ
**Tel:** 01246 850430
www.nationaltrust.org.uk

**Hathersage Shop**
David Mellor Design Limited,
The Round Building, Hathersage S32 1BA
**Tel:** 01433 650220
www.davidmellordesign.com

**Old Pump Rooms**
The Crescent, Buxton SK17 6BQ
**Tel:** 01298 25106
www.derbyshire-peakdistrict.co.uk

**Peak Cavern**
Castleton S33 8WS
**Tel:** 01433 620285
www.peakcavern.co.uk

**Peveril Castle**
Market Place, Castleton, Hope Valley S33 8WQ
**Tel:** 01433 620613
www.english-heritage.org.uk

**Poole's Cavern**
Green Lane, Buxton SK17 9DH
**Tel:** 01298 26978
www.poolescavern.co.uk

**Speedwell Cavern**
Winnats Pass, Castleton S33 8WA
**Tel:** 01433 620512
www.speedwellcavern.co.uk

**Treak Cliff Cavern**
Castleton S33 8WH
**Tel:** 01433 620571
www.bluejohnstone.com

## West Yorkshire's Brontë country

**Betty's Cafe Tea Rooms**
1 Parliament Street, Harrogate HG1 2QU
**Tel:** 01423 877300
Crag Lane, Beckwithshaw, Harrogate HG3 1QB
**Tel:** 01423 505604
www.bettys.co.uk

**Bramham Park**
Bramham, Wetherby LS23 6ND
**Tel:** 01937 846000
www.bramhampark.co.uk

**The Brontë Parsonage Museum**
Church Street, Haworth BD22 8DR
**Tel:** 01535 642323
www.bronte.org.uk

**Chevin Forest Park**
Otley
www.leeds.gov.uk

**Cliffe Castle Museum**
Spring Gardens Lane, Keighley BD20 6LH
**Tel:** 01535 618231
www.bradfordmuseums.org

**East Riddlesden Hall**
Bradford Road, Keighley BD20 5EL
**Tel:** 01535 607075
www.nationaltrust.org.uk

**1853 Gallery**
Salts Mill, Shipley, Saltaire BD18 3LB
**Tel:** 01274 531185
www.saltsmill.org.uk

**Gibson Mill**
Hardcastle Crags Estate Office, Hollin Hall,
Crimsworth Dean, Hebden Bridge HX7 7AP
**Tel:** 01422 844518
www.nationaltrust.org.uk

**Harewood House**
Harewood, Leeds LS17 9LQ
**Tel:** 0113 218 1010
www.harewood.org

**Harry Ramsden's**
Otley Road, Guiseley, Leeds LS20 8LZ
**Tel:** 01943 874641
www.harryramsdens.co.uk

**Keighley and Worth Valley Railway**
The Railway Station, Haworth,
Keighley BD22 8NJ
**Tel:** 01535 645214
www.kwvr.co.uk

**Kirkstall Abbey**
Abbey Road, Kirkstall, Leeds LS5 3EH
**Tel:** 0113 230 5492
www.leeds.gov.uk

**Lotherton Hall and Gardens**
Aberford, Leeds LS25 3EB
**Tel:** 0113 281 3259
www.leeds.gov.uk

**Manor House Museum and Art Gallery**
Castle Yard, Church Street, Ilkley LS29 9DT
**Tel:** 01943 600066
www.bradfordmuseums.org

**Mercer Art Gallery**
Swan Road, Harrogate HG1 2SA
**Tel:** 01423 556130
www.harrogate.gov.uk

**National Museum of Photography,
Film and Television**
Bradford BD1 1NQ
**Tel:** 0870 7010200
www.nmpft.org.uk

**Ripley Castle and Gardens**
Harrogate HG3 3AY
**Tel:** 01423 770152
www.ripleycastle.co.uk

**Royal Pump Rooms Art Gallery and Museum**
Crown Place, Harrogate HG1 2RY
**Tel:** 01423 556188
www.harrogate.gov.uk

**Stockeld Park**
Wetherby LS22 4AW
**Tel:** 01937 586101

**Turkish Baths**
Royal Baths, Parliament Street,
Harrogate HG1 2WH
**Tel:** 01423 556746
www.harrogate.gov.uk

**Victorian Reed Organ and
Harmonium Museum**
Victoria Hall, Victoria Road,
Saltaire Village, Shipley BD18 4PS
**Tel:** 01274 585601
www.thisisbradford.co.uk

## The natural wonders of the southern Dales

**Bolton Priory**
Bolton Abbey, Skipton BD23 6EX
**Tel:** 01756 718009
www.boltonabbey.com

**Craven Museum**
Town Hall, High Street, Skipton BD23 1AH
**Tel:** 01756 706407
www.cravendc.gov.uk

**Kilnsey Park**
Kilnsey, nr Skipton BD23 5PS
**Tel:** 01756 752150
www.kilnseypark.co.uk

**Nidderdale Museum**
King Street, Pately Bridge HG3 5LE
**Tel:** 01756 752780
www.nidderdalemuseum.com

**Parcevall Hall Gardens**
Skyreholme, Skipton BD23 6DE
**Tel:** 01756 720311
www.parcevallhallgardens.co.uk

**Skipton Castle**
Skipton BD23 1AW
**Tel:** 01756 792422
www.skiptoncastle.co.uk

**Stump Cross Caverns**
Greenhow Hill, Pateley Bridge,
Harrogate HG3 5JL
**Tel:** 01756 752780
www.stumpcrosscaverns.co.uk

**Watershed Mill and Visitor Centre**
Langcliffe Road, Settle BD24 9LR
**Tel:** 01729 825539
www.watershedmill.co.uk

**Yorkshire Dales Falconry and
Conservation Centre**
Crows Nest, nr. Giggleswick, Settle LA2 8AS
**Tel :** 01729 822832
www.yorkshiredales.org

## Richmond and the picture-postcard northern Dales

**Bedale Hall**
North End, Bedale DL8 1AA
**Tel:** 01677 423797
www.hambleton.gov.uk

**Black Sheep Brewery**
Wellgarth, Masham, Ripon HG4 4EN
**Tel:** 01765 689227
www.blacksheepbrewery.com

**Constable Burton Hall**
Leyburn DL8 5LJ
**Tel:** 01677 450428
www.constableburtongardens.co.uk

**Dales Countryside Museum**
Station Yard, Hawes DL8 3NT
**Tel:** 01969 667450
www.yorkshiredales.org.uk

**Easby Abbey**
nr Richmond
www.english-heritage.org.uk

**Forbidden Corner**
The Tupgill Park Estate, Coverdale Middleham,
Leyburn DL8 4TJ
**Tel:** 01969 640638
www.yorkshiredales.org.uk

**Green Howards Regimental Museum**
Trinity Church Square, Richmond DL10 4QN
**Tel:** 01748 825 611
www.greenhowards.org.uk

**Jervaulx Abbey**
Jervaulx, Ripon HG4 4PH
**Tel:** 01677 460226
www.jervaulxabbey.com

**Kiplin Hall**
Nr Scorton, Richmond DL10 6AT
**Tel:** 01748 818178
www.kiplinhall.co.uk

**Middleham Castle**
Middleham DL8 4QR
**Tel:** 01969 623899
www.english-heritage.org.uk

**Richmond Castle**
Richmond DL10 4QW
**Tel:** 01748 822493
www.english-heritage.org.uk

**Richmondshire Museum**
Ryders Wynd, Richmond DL10 4JA
**Tel:** 01748 825 611
www.richmond.org.uk

**Swaledale Folk Museum**
Reeth Green, Reeth, nr Richmond DL11 6QT
**Tel:** 01748 884373
www.yorkshiredales.org.uk

**Thorp Perrow Arboretum**
Bedale DL8 2PR
**Tel:** 01677 425323
www.thorpperrow.com

**Yorkshire Museum of Carriages**
Yore Mill, by Aysgarth Falls,
Wensleydale DL8 3SR
**Tel:** 01748 823275

## Whitby and the magic of the North York Moors National Park

**Duncombe Park**
Helmsley, York YO62 5EB
**Tel:** 01439 772625
www.duncombepark.com

**Helmsley Castle**
Helmsley YO62 5OB
**Tel:** 01439 770442
www.english-heritage.org.uk

**Helmsley Walled Garden**
Cleveland Way, Helmsley YO62 5AH
**Tel:** 01439 771427
www.helmsleywalledgarden.org.uk

**Moors Centre**
Danby, Whitby YO21 2NB
**Tel:** 01439 772737
www.redcar-cleveland.gov.uk

**Mount Grace Priory**
Staddle Bridge, Northallerton DL6 3JG
**Tel:** 01609 883494
www.nationaltrust.org.uk

**North Yorkshire Moors Railway**
Pickering Station, Pickering YO18 7AJ
**Tel:** 01751 472508
www.nymr.demon.co.uk

**Rievaulx Abbey**
Rievaulx YO62 5LB
**Tel:** 01439 798228
www.english-heritage.org.uk

**Rievaulx Terrace and Temples**
Rievaulx, Helmsley YO62 5LJ
**Tel:** 01439 798340
www.nationaltrust.org.uk

**Ryedale Folk Museum**
Hutton-le-Hole, York YO62 6UA
**Tel:** 01751 417 367
www.ryedalefolkmuseum.co.uk

**Whitby Abbey**
Whitby YO22 4JT
**Tel:** 01947 603568
www.english-heritage.org.uk

## Stately homes in the Vale of York

**Beningbrough Hall**
Beningbrough, York YO30 1DD
**Tel:** 01904 470666
www.nationaltrust.org.uk

**Byland Abbey**
nr Coxwold, YO61 4BD
**Tel:** 01439 748283
www.english-heritage.org.uk

**Castle Howard**
York YO60 7DA
**Tel:** 01653 648444
www.castlehoward.co.uk

**Eden Camp**
Malton YO17 6RT
**Tel:** 01653 697777
www.edencamp.co.uk

**Fairfax House**
Castlegate, York YO1 9RN
**Tel:** 01904 655543
www.fairfaxhouse.co.uk

**Fountains Abbey and Studley Royal Estate**
Fountains, Ripon HG4 3DY
**Tel:** 01765 608888
www.nationaltrust.org.uk

**Hovingham Hall**
Hovingham, York YO62 4LU
**Tel:** 01653 628771
www.hovingham.co.uk

**Jorvik**
Coppergate, York YO1 9WT
**Tel:** 01904 643211
www.jorvik-viking-centre.co.uk

**Merchant Adventurers' Hall**
Fossgate, York YO1 9XD
**Tel:** 01904 654 818
www.theyorkcompany.co.uk

**National Railway Museum**
Leeman Road, York YO26 4XJ
**Tel:** 01904 686286
www.nrm.org.uk

**Newburgh Priory**
Coxwold, York YO61 4AS
**Tel:** 01347 868372
www.newburghpriory.co.uk

**Newby Hall**
Ripon HG4 5AE
**Tel:** 0845 4504068
www.newbyhall.co.uk

**Norton Conyers Hall**
Ripon HG4 5EQ
**Tel:** 01765 640333
www.historichouses.co.uk

**Nunnington Hall**
Nunnington, nr York YO62 5UY
**Tel:** 01439 748283
www.nationaltrust.org.uk

**Ripon Cathedral**
Ripon HG4 1QS
**Tel:** 01765 602072
www.riponcathedral.org.uk

**Sutton Park**
Sutton-on-the-Forest, York YO6 1DP
**Tel:** 01347 810249
www.statelyhome.co.uk

**Treasurer's House**
Minster Yard, York YO1 7JL
**Tel:** 01904 624247
www.nationaltrust.org.uk

**Wharram Percy Deserted Medieval Village**
Wharram le Street
www.english-heritage.org.uk

**York Minster**
York YO1 7JF
**Tel:** 01904 557216
www.yorkminster.org

## Kingston upon Hull and East Yorkshire's vanishing coastline

**Arctic Corsair**
River Hull, Kingston upon Hull
**Tel:** 01482 613902
www.hullcc.gov.uk

**Bayle Museum**
Baylegate, Old Town, Bridlington
**Tel: 01262 674353**
www. bridlington.net

**Beverley Minster**
Beverley HU17 0DP
**Tel:** 01482 868540
www.beverleyminster.co.uk

**Burton Agnes Hall**
Burton Agnes, Driffield YO25 0ND
**Tel:** 01262 490324
www.burton-agnes.co.uk

**Burton Constable Hall**
Skirlaugh HU11 4LN
**Tel:** 01964 562400
www.burtonconstable.com

**The Deep**
Hull HU1 4DP
**Tel:**01482 381000
www.thedeep.co.uk

**Ferens Art Gallery,**
Queen Victoria Square,
Kingston upon Hull HU1 3RA
**Tel:** 01482 613902
www.hullcc.gov.uk

**Filey Museum**
8–10 Queen Street, Filey YO14 9HB
**Tel:** 01723 515013
www.discoveryorkshirecoast.com

**Fort Paull Museum**
Battery Road, Paull,
nr Kingston Upon Hull HU12 8FP
**Tel:** 01482 882655
www.hullcc.gov.uk

**Hull and East Riding Museum**
36 High Street, Hull HU1 1PS
**Tel:** 01482 613902
www.hullcc.gov.uk

**Hull Maritime Museum**
Queen Victoria Square, Hull HU1 2AA
**Tel:** 01482 610610
www.hullcc.gov.uk

**Maister House**
160 High Street, Hull HU1 1NL
**Tel:** 01482 324114
www.nationaltrust.org.uk

**Rotunda Museum**
Vernon Road, Scarborough YO11 2PW
**Tel:** 01723 374839
www.rotundamuseum.co.uk

**Scarborough Art Gallery**
The Crescent, Scarborough YO11 2PW
**Tel:** 01723 374753
www.scarboroughmuseums.org.uk

**Scarborough Castle**
Castle Road, Scarborough YO11 1HY
**Tel:** 01723 372 451
www.english-heritage.org.uk

**Sewerby Hall**
Church Lane, Sewerby, Bridlington YO15 1EA
**Tel:** 01262 673769
www.eastriding.gov.uk

**Sledmere House and Gardens**
Driffield YO25 3XG
**Tel:** 01377 236637
www.sledmerehouse.com

**Spurn Lightship**
Hull Marina, Hull
**Tel:** 01482 613902
www.hullcc.gov.uk

**Streetlife Museum of Transport**
36 High Street, Hull HU1 1NQ
**Tel:** 01482 613 902
www.hullcc.gov.uk

**Wilberforce House**
36 High Street, Hull HU1 1NQ
**Tel:** 01482 613 902
ww.hullcc.gov.uk

**Withernsea Lighthouse Museum**
Hull Road, Withernsea HU19 2DY
**Tel:** 01964 614834
www.council.withernsea.com

**Wood End Museum**
The Crescent, Scarborough YO11 2PW
**Tel:** 01723 367326
www.scarboroughmuseums.org.uk

# Index